DATE DUE

ROCKET MAN

ROCKET MAN

The Encyclopedia of Elton John

CLAUDE BERNARDIN
and TOM STANTON

GREENWOOD PRESS
Westport, Connecticut • London

Library of Congress Cataloging-in-Publication Data

Bernardin, Claude.
    Rocket man : the encyclopedia of Elton John / Claude Bernardin and
Tom Stanton.
        p.   cm.
    Includes bibliography (p.   ) and index.
    Discography:
    ISBN 0–313–29700–2 (alk. paper)
    1. John, Elton.   2. John, Elton—Discography.   3. Rock musicians—
England—Biography.   I. Stanton, Tom.   II. Title.
ML410.J64B4   1995
782.42166′092—dc20   95–9938
    [B]

British Library Cataloguing in Publication Data is available.

Library of Congress Catalog Card Number: 95–9938
ISBN: 0–313–29700–2

First published in 1995

Greenwood Press, 88 Post Road West, Westport, CT 06881
An imprint of Greenwood Publishing Group, Inc.

Printed in the United States of America

The paper used in this book complies with the
Permanent Paper Standard issued by the National
Information Standards Organization (Z39.48–1984).

10 9 8 7 6 5 4 3 2 1

To

Kathleen M. Yentz Bernardin

and

Beth A. Bagley-Stanton

Contents

Photo essays follow "Elton: A-Z" and "Performances."

Acknowledgments

The authors jointly thank Elton John for the music and Bernie Taupin for the words. They also acknowledge the musicians, producers, management, and many others who through their contributions made the magic possible.

Tom Stanton thanks Jim Turano for his considerable efforts; John F. Higgins, Alan McCormick, and Joe Koslakiewicz for their knowledge; Nannette Bac (whose photo graces the cover), Sharon Kalinoski, Wayne (not Newton) Martin, Randy Alexander, John Lappen, Mary Anne Cassata, Stephan Heimbecher, and readers of *East End Lights* magazine for their contributions; Mike Varney, Frank Provenzano, Alicia Merritt, and Catherine Lyons for their encouragement; Jane Briggs-Bunting, Joe Falls, Neal Shine, Bob Talbert, Willie Morris and Clem Stone for spoken and unspoken inspiration; co-author Claude Bernardin for his expertise, commitment, and perspective; Zachary, William, Taylor, Betty, and Joe Stanton, Marge Bagley, and Dorothy and Joe Stabile for their faith and support; and Beth Bagley-Stanton, well, for everything.

Claude Bernardin thanks Schanda and Nigel Olsson for their help, Terry Hounsome for his special discography, *New Rock Record*, Giueseppe Bonaventura, Kevin Caples, Pete Dobbins, Sharon R. Fox, Leslie Fry, John F. Higgins, Sharon Kalinoski, John Koontz, Emmanuel L'Ardenois, Keith Levine, Jack Malloy, Alan McCormick, Domenico Mellone-Taranto, Tim Norris, Kathy Pilarcik, Frank Pozzouli, Susan Reid, David Sigler, Lily Stahley, Bob Trayers, Sam Vetovich, Donna Vela, Doug Wirth, Mike Zito, Tom Stanton for his effort, friendship, and tolerance, and all the other dedicated, fantastic fanatics who made this all possible. He also acknowledges the following individuals for their confidence and support: Mr. and Mrs. Charles Bernardin, Paul and Midi Bernardin, Robert Sharamatew, and Donna Martin. Mostly, he thanks Kathleen M. Yentz Bernardin for her love, support, patience, and friendship.

Introduction

Touring America in 1993 before the sellout crowds that have greeted him for more than two decades, Elton John ended his concerts alone, center stage. In the soft glow of the spotlight — his Versace outfit replaced by a casual jogging suit — the former Reg Dwight reflected on his often-troubled and unhappy life, a life buffeted by a painful childhood, suicide attempts, mood swings, weight problems, and alcohol and drug abuse. The star somberly thanked his fans. "You've been the one constant in my life," he said.

Indeed, while his career has experienced dips, Elton John has enjoyed an unfailing run on the charts that no one has topped. In every year since the 1970 release of "Your Song," he has landed at least one song in the Top 40. When he did it for the 24th straight year with "Simple Life," Elton surpassed Elvis Presley. Such consistency has packed concert halls, sold millions of albums, brought worldwide fame rivaled by few and secured him an undeniable place in U.S. culture. His performances are remarkable partly because of the varied audience he draws: moms and dads who bop to "Crocodile Rock" and teens who cry to "The Last Song." He has influenced a generation of such younger musicians as Axl Rose, George Michael and Bruce Hornsby, and broken records by Elvis, The Beatles and others who inspired him. The media attention bestowed upon Elton John has often focused on peripheral issues — his costumes and eyeglasses, his alcoholism and sobriety, his marriage and homosexuality, his hair weaves and transplants, his role in the battle against AIDS. Lost in such stories is the extraordinary body of work created by Elton John and his long-time collaborator, lyricist Bernie Taupin. While this book chronicles all aspects of the British performer's life, it emphasizes the music in its many colors: the familiar ballads that dominate the radio airwaves, the hard-rocking tunes of a piano maniac and the obscure epics that devoted fans treasure.

Rocket Man: The Encyclopedia of Elton John results from seven years of research, decades of listening and the authors' belief that the John-Taupin songwriting team is among the best of the 20th century. This book is divided into four sections:

"Elton: A-Z," offering a detailed look at the people, places and events that have framed his career; "Albums," exploring each of the artist's releases through 1995's *Made in England*; "Performances," a year-by-year look at his concerts; and "Songs," the most complete listing ever offered of songs recorded or written by Elton John. Two one-of-a-kind lists — the first noting artists who have recorded his songs and the second detailing songs he has played in concert — are included in the appendixes, which are followed by a bibliography of selected sources and an index.

ROCKET MAN

Elton: A-Z

A

A Cradle of Haloes: In this 1988 autobiography, Elton's longtime lyricist, Bernie Taupin, sketched his British childhood in Lincolnshire, a blue-collar farming community. He recalled coming of age, hanging with a youth gang, and facing prospects of a lifetime of menial labor. Though Taupin touched on his early musical influences (Bob Dylan, Jimi Hendrix, The Beatles), the book ended before he met Reg Dwight, the future Elton John. Aurum Press released *A Cradle of Haloes* in England, but Taupin found no market in America, where prospective publishers had hoped for a tell-all, rock-and-roll chronicle.

Ackles, David: The folk singer co-headlined with Elton at his American debut at the Troubadour in 1970. Elton and Taupin were fans of Ackles and felt badly that Elton over-shadowed the songwriter, whose songs never realized their potential in America. For years, Elton said his fondest recollection of the Troubadour show was sitting at a table after his incredible opening evening and sharing a bottle of whiskey that Ackles purchased to thank Elton. "Talking Old Soldiers" is Taupin's response to that evening. A year later, Taupin produced Ackles's *American Gothic* album.

Adams, Oleta: She contributed "Don't Let the Sun Go Down on Me" to the *Two Rooms* tribute album. Her interpretation brought a Grammy nomination.

Addictions: Since 1990, when he began treatment for addictions to alcohol, cocaine, food, and sex, Elton has enjoyed a spiritual and physical rebirth. By threatening to leave him, an ex-boyfriend forced the singer to confront his demons. Elton also found inspiration in the family of Ryan White and their dignified support for the Indiana teenager who died of an AIDS-related illness. Around 1974, Elton, a longtime drinker, expanded into drugs. His involvement grew more serious. He tried but failed to deal with his alcoholism. In interviews as early as 1971, he referred to his efforts to quit drinking. By the mid-1980s, his cocaine use had accelerated to the point that associates worried for his life. Chubby as a child, he continually struggled to keep from gaining weight, a battle that transformed itself into bulimia. Elton traced many of his problems to his strict upbringing, which he felt stifled his honesty and feelings. By the late 1980s, the star had grown heavy and, with his hair dyed platinum, looked old and in sad shape. His 1989 tour was characterized by bouts with alcoholism. "It really was Elvis Presley time again," the singer told the *Los Angeles Times* in 1992. "(Rock and roll) isn't a normal life. You get cut off from people ... isolated. ... It's easy to lose your values and your self-respect. I got to where I didn't know how to speak to someone unless I had a nose full of cocaine." He went for treatment at Parkside Lutheran Hospital in Chicago, Illinois, in July 1990 (room #3327) and then took a year off from recording and performing to get his life in order through counseling and 12-step programs. "I was emotionally dead," he told David Frost. "I was like a carcass shipped around from country to country, wheeled out on stage to play 'Your Song' again and again."

Adler, Larry: While recording on Sting's *Ten Summoner's Tales*, Adler, a famed harmonica player and close friend of George Gershwin, suggested Sting pay tribute to Gershwin. Sting lined up Elton. George Martin agreed to produce. *The Glory of Gershwin*, released in 1994, featured Sinead O'Connor, Robert Palmer, Cher, Elvis Costello, Carly Simon, Lisa Stansfield, Meat Loaf, Sting, and Elton, who sang "Someone to Watch over Me" and "Our Love Is Here to Stay." Adler, who moved to England after being branded a communist by Senator Joseph McCarthy, accompanied his guests, backed by a full orchestra. The release coincided with Adler's eightieth birthday.

AIDS: Elton, who is gay, became publicly involved in the fight against AIDS through Ryan White, a boy who contracted the disease after a blood transfusion. The two became friends in 1986, and Elton was at his bedside when the youth died in April 1990. The singer faced criticism in the gay community for taking the "safe" route of embracing a non-gay carrier of the disease. As Elton became more open about his own sexuality, he devoted greater efforts to the AIDS battle, admitting to being tested regularly for the disease. In the early 1990s, he began donating all proceeds from his singles to AIDS charities in England and America. After losing several dozen friends to the disease, he has become rock music's most public spokesman on AIDS, recording public service television ads and appearing at numerous charity events, including the Atlanta AIDS walk. His 1993 single, "The Last Song," focused on a gay man who, dying of AIDS, made peace with his estranged father. The release followed the launching of the Elton John AIDS Foundation (Box 52066, Atlanta, GA 30355). By auctioning off his art, jewelry, and record collections, he has raised millions for the fight. All proceeds from his American and British singles now go to the foundation.

Alien III: The movie's promoters borrowed a Taupin phrase, "the bitch is back."

Argosy: MCA signed Elton to a U.S. contract in 1970, but the label did so primarily to get the band Argosy, also represented by Dick James. MCA viewed Argosy as the hotter prospect, but the band never made it.

Armatrading, Joan: Elton and the black guitarist admire each other's work. "Elton John is my favorite live artist," she said in 1989. "He's the person I've seen the most in concert. He's never let me down." On a late 1980s British show paying tribute to her, Elton and Armatrading performed her "Stronger Love." Elton's producer, Gus Dudgeon, produced Armatrading's first album, and guitarist Davey Johnstone has recorded with her. Armatrading is well known in England.

Astley, Rick: Elton appeared on Astley's 1991 album, *Free*.

Atlanta, Georgia: Though he released a song called "Georgia" in 1978, Elton did not fall in love with the city until the late 1980s. In 1990, he moved his American residence there. His boyfriend at the time managed ice cream parlors in the trendy Buckhead area. Elton later became involved with real estate agent John Scott, who sold him a 6,000 square foot suite in an affluent condominium high-rise. Scott now directs the Elton John AIDS Foundation. Aside from a lavish condo, Elton owns a guest home in Atlanta. He lives a public life, jogging without bodyguards, shopping at local markets and record stores, visiting malls, attending ribbon-cutting ceremonies, participating in charity events, watching the Atlanta Braves, and eating at the Buckhead Diner, where his privacy is ensured by staff.

Auctions: When he decided to part with a few decades' worth of belongings from his mansion in England, Elton arranged an auction through the prestigious Sotheby's firm in London. In September 1988, he sold over 1,900 items, ranging from stage costumes and jewelry to artwork and furniture. Among the better-known bargains: a sequined Los Angeles Dodgers uniform for $12,400 and his Doc Marten Pinball Wizard boots for $22,000. The sale raised more than $8 million. (The four-volume auction catalogues are collector's items.) He must have enjoyed the cleansing feeling, for in 1993 he held two more auctions through Sotheby's, both helping AIDS charities. His private record collection of over 25,000 albums and 23,000 singles sold as a single lot for about $270,000, and his surplus jewelry topped $1.3 million.

Australia: On a per population basis, the land down under buys more Elton records than any other nation.

B

BBC: The British Broadcasting Corporation has long hosted many shows that allow entertainers to perform their songs live. Elton has been a regular guest. Most appearances, as well as the songs he performed, are noted here:

❖ December 1968, "Skyline Pigeon" and "All Across the Havens."

❖ July 20, 1969, backed by Hookfoot, "Lady Samantha" and "Sails."

❖ April 5, 1970, with Hookfoot, "My Father's Gun," "Your Song," "Ballad of a Well-Known Gun" and "Take Me to the Pilot."

❖ April 20, 1970, with Dee Murray and Nigel Olsson, "Border Song."

❖ October 22, 1970, "Burn Down the Mission" and others.

❖ January 14, 1971, "Your Song."

❖ December 27, 1971, sitting in with T. Rex on "Get It On."

❖ January 25, 1973, "Daniel."

❖ July 22, 1976, "Don't Go Breaking My Heart" with Kiki Dee.

❖ October 17, 1985, "Nikita."

❖ February 24, 1986, "Happy Birthday" on the anniversary of Terry Wogan's show.

❖ June 22, 1990, "Sacrifice."

Babbit, Bob: Played bass on *The Complete Thom Bell Sessions.*

Babylon, Guy: The Maryland-born keyboardist joined the band in 1988, performing on all world tours since then and playing on several albums, beginning with *Sleeping with the Past.* Music director Davey Johnstone brought Babylon into the group after discovering him at a Johnstone-produced session. They later joined forces as co-producers and members of Warpipes. Babylon also worked on the sound track for the movie *The Doors.* With a college degree in composition, Babylon moved to Los Angeles in 1980 to find session work. He backed many artists, from Tavares to Luis Cardenas, and made a living, he said, off failed projects. In 1986, Babylon joined future Elton bassist Bob Birch in a band called Ashton. Babylon owns a recording studio in North Hollywood. On 1995's *Made in England*, he and Elton co-arranged strings for the song "Man."

Backup singers: In all, over 100 artists have provided backing vocals for Elton John. This list focuses on singers who regularly backed him on concert tours:

❖ Alex Brown, 1988, a former member of Stevie Wonder's band, Wonder Love.

❖ Cindy Bullens, 1976, performed on Broadway in *La Strada*, wrote a minor hit for B.C. Generation, performed with Eleventh Hour, and dedicated her 1977 solo album to Elton.

❖ Alan Carvell, 1985-86, got a songwriting credit for developing the "oohs" and "ahhs" on "Angeline" from the *Leather Jackets* album.

❖ Ken Gold, 1976, writer and producer of songs by Aretha Franklin, Cliff Richard, and Frankie Valli.

❖ Natalie Jackson, 1988-93, a classically trained singer.

❖ Mortonette Jenkins, 1989-93, arranged vocals on several songs, including "A Woman's Needs." Lead singer on a Quincy Jones album, she appeared on Michael Jackson's *Off the Wall*.

❖ Marlena Jeter, 1988-93, has worked with Boz Scaggs and Nancy Wilson.

❖ Jon Joyce, 1976, TV appearances in 1970s. Session work with many stars, including Elvis Presley.

❖ Shirley Lewis, 1985-86, sister of Linda Lewis, who worked with Elton in the 1970s and had solo success.

❖ Gordon Neville, 1985-86, former lead singer of the Rick Wakeman Band.

Baldry, Long John: In the 1960s, Baldry built a career as a blues and folk musician in England. He played a part in the development of many future rock stars. In 1961, Baldry helped form Alexis Korner's Blues Incorporated, which included Mick Jagger. A few years later, he started the Hoochie Coochie Men, featuring Rod Stewart. In 1966, Baldry asked the band Bluesology to back him. The group included keyboardist Reg Dwight. Baldry's affiliation with Bluesology lasted two years. The B-side to his hit "Let the Heartaches Begin" featured Bluesology on songs written by Reg Dwight: In Britain, "Annabella"; in America, "Hey Lord, You Made the Night Too Long." When Baldry began playing night clubs, some Bluesology members, including Dwight, envisioned the job as a musical dead end. Dwight left the band, borrowing Baldry's first name and combining it with that of Bluesology saxophonist Elton Dean. Dwight began calling himself Elton John and later made the change legal. After breaking in big, Elton remained on good terms with the tall balladeer, even writing a song, "Rock Me When He's Gone," for Baldry's 1971 album, *It Ain't Easy*. Elton produced one side of the album; Rod Stewart, the other. The sound resembled the texture of Elton's *Tumbleweed Connection*. The album is considered a treasure by Elton collectors because of the remarkable piano work he contributed to "Flying." A year later, Elton lent Baldry his band and again produced his former employer, this time on *Everything Stops for Tea*. The album included a Ross Wilson song, "Come Back Again," which sounds strikingly similar to Elton's "Slave." Though he has recorded little in the decades since, Baldry lives in Canada and tours blues venues. He has also done voice work for TV cartoons (including "Bucky O'Hare"). Baldry has recently claimed to remember producing two unreleased Reg Dwight songs in 1967, with Stuart Brown on lead vocals for Bluesology. The titles are unknown.

Bands: Elton has never toured without accompaniment. Even on his "solo" tours in 1978-79 and 1993-94, percussionist Ray Cooper backed the star. For most of his career, he has played with a band. During his peak years in the 1970s, Elton recorded and toured with the same nucleus. With a few exceptions, later albums resulted from sessions with a variety of musicians, including, but not limited to, members of his touring band. What follows are the band rosters.

❖ 1970-71: Drummer Nigel Olsson and bassist Dee Murray.

❖ 1972-73: Olsson, Murray, and lead guitarist Davey Johnstone.

❖ 1974-75: Olsson, Murray, Johnstone, and percussionist Ray Cooper.

❖ 1975-76: Johnstone, Cooper, guitarist Caleb Quaye, drummer Roger Pope, keyboardist James Newton Howard, and bassist Kenny Passarelli.

❖ 1980: Olsson, Murray, Howard, and guitarists Ritchie Zito and Tim Renwick.

❖ 1982-83: Olsson, Murray, and Johnstone.

❖ 1984: Olsson, Murray, Johnstone, and keyboardist Fred Mandel.

❖ 1985-87: Johnstone, Mandel, drummer Charlie Morgan, bassist Dave Paton, percussionist Jody Linscott, and Onward International Horns.

❖ 1988-90: Johnstone, Mandel, drummer Jonathan Moffett, bassist Romeo Williams, and keyboardist Guy Babylon.

❖ 1992-93: Johnstone, Babylon, Morgan, bassist Bob Birch, and keyboardist Mark Taylor.

❖ 1994-95: Johnstone, Babylon, Morgan, Birch, and Cooper.

❖ 1995: Johnstone, Babylon, Morgan, Birch, Cooper, and guitarist John Jorgenson.

Firing his band: While touring the United States in 1974, Elton began pondering a major decision: whether to fire his original rhythm section. A year later, after *Captain Fantastic and the Brown Dirt Cowboy* entered the charts at number one, Elton stunned drummer Nigel Olsson and bassist Dee Murray by dismissing them. Coming at the pinnacle of Elton's commercial success, the move shocked fans and industry observers. The decision devastated both Olsson and Murray. "We'd been together for a long time," Elton said in a 1990 radio interview. "I knew that they were going to be extremely hurt, because they had been with me from the word go. ... I told them over the phone, which was an extremely awful way of doing it, and I regret that immensely." Olsson, however, said he learned by phone from one of Elton's underlings. The firing also hurt Olsson and Murray financially. At that time, Elton paid royalties to band members. In the 1980s, Olsson and Murray would reunite with Elton, though not permanently. Olsson continued to appear on Elton's albums as a backup singer. Murray died of cancer in 1992.

Barron Knights: This mid-1960s comedy group did parodies of British hits. In August 1968, Elton was doing session work for the Barron Knights at Abbey Road Studios in a room opposite where The Beatles were finishing "Hey Jude." There, he met Paul McCartney. Elton appeared on the Knights' "Here Come the Olympic Games."

Baseball: Living in Atlanta, home of baseball's Braves, Elton has become a fan of the sport, attending games and following the scores while touring. At a Boston concert in 1993, he donned a Red Sox uniform emblazoned with the words "Rocket Man." It was given to him by pitcher Roger Clemens, whom he described as one of his idols. Clemens is nicknamed "The Rocket." That evening, Elton dedicated "Rocket Man" to the pitcher and included a reference to him in the song.

Baxter, Jeff "Skunk": Best known for his work with Steely Dan and the Doobie Brothers, Baxter almost became part of Elton's group in 1975. He performed with the band at a Wembley Stadium show that year, but the association went no further.

Beach Boys: Few bands have had a greater influence on Elton than the Beach Boys. Their harmonies on songs like "God Only Knows" and "Good Vibrations" inspired classics like "Don't Let the Sun Go Down on Me," "Someone Saved My Life Tonight" and many others, including one that mentions Brian Wilson in the lyrics. In the mid-1970s, Elton wrote "Chameleon," a song he hoped the Beach Boys would record. But the group rejected it. On the *Two Rooms* tribute, the group performed "Crocodile Rock," though Elton wanted the band to remake "Harmony."

Good vibrations: Ten Elton John songs inspired by the Beach Boys.

❖ "Someone Saved My Life Tonight."
❖ "Don't Let the Sun Go Down on Me."
❖ "Your Sister Can't Twist."
❖ "Harmony."
❖ "Since God Invented Girls."
❖ "Goodbye Marlon Brando."
❖ "We All Fall in Love Sometimes/ Curtains."
❖ "Chameleon."
❖ "Pinky."
❖ "Dear God."

Beck, Jeff: The legendary guitarist nearly teamed up with Elton in 1970. The combination would have put Elton in a clearly secondary role financially to Beck, who had already built a reputation in America. Though Beck and Elton got along — and even rehearsed as a team — the arrangement fell apart when Beck's manager demanded 90 percent of the take for his client. To Elton's disappointment, manager Dick James rejected the deal, vowing that within six months Elton would be making more than Beck's $10,000-a-night. That year, at his American debut in Los Angeles, Elton made a couple hundred, but his success brought millions in the next two years.

Bell, Thom: Bell honed the 1970s Philadelphia sound, molding the soft soul ballads of the Stylistics and Spinners. In 1979 he produced a similar release featuring Elton, *The Thom Bell Sessions*. Bell's influence would be felt on many albums, because he convinced the British star to sing in a lower register (which would eventually prove inevitable). He also co-wrote a song, "Nice and Slow," with John and Taupin. The complete session was released on CD in 1989.

Bell, Tony: Played guitar on *The Complete Thom Bell Sessions*.

Bell Records: The American label had an exclusive contract for Dick James's acts, but passed on the chance to sign Elton John in 1970.

Bellotte, Pete: He wrote and produced *Victim of Love*, Elton's disastrous 1979 disco album. Bellotte, who knew Elton from the 1960s, wrote several Donna Summer hits with Giorgio Moroder, including "Last Dance," "Love to Love You Baby," and "I Feel Love." He also played with the band Trax.

Berline, Byron: Played fiddle on *21 at 33*.

Big Pig Music: Song collaborations by Elton and Taupin are copyrighted under Big Pig Music or Happenstance.

Birch, Bob: A St. Clair Shores, Michigan, native, Birch joined Elton's band in 1992 as the bass player. He had played in bands with keyboardist Guy Babylon since the mid-1980s, and in 1991 joined Warpipes, a group featuring Elton's music director, Davey Johnstone. That connection led to Birch touring with Elton during 1992-95 and recording with him in 1994 for the *Made in England* album. After earning a college degree in music, Birch taught school and worked in a bar band in the Detroit area before moving to Los Angeles in 1981. He has also toured with Jose Feliciano and played in several California groups.

Birthday: Elton was born Reginald Kenneth Dwight on March 25, 1947, in Pinner, Middlesex, a middle-class suburb of London, England.

Black album: Band members gave this nickname to the 1970 *Elton John* album. The moody cover features a stark, shadowy portrait of the young artist against a dark background. Given the release of The Beatles' "white album" in 1968, it's easy to see what inspired the nickname.

Blauel, Renate: After a brief romance, Elton married Blauel, a German sound engineer, on Valentine's Day, February 14, 1984, in St. Mark's Anglican Church near Sydney, Australia. They divorced in November 1988. Blauel had met Elton while working on an album. The wedding occurred five days after Elton proposed a second time and became a media event, partly because Elton had earlier admitted to being gay. Fans outside the church blared the star's "Kiss the Bride," nearly drowning out the ceremony, at which Bernie Taupin served as best man. The marriage proved to be rocky, though friends Prince Andrew and Sarah Ferguson successfully reunited them after an April 1987 separation. Elton said he hoped the marriage would settle his tumultuous life and perhaps produce children (it did not). Since their divorce, Blauel and Elton have had little contact. Still cordial to Elton's family, Blauel, who received a large cash settlement, has kept details of their relationship private. The parting has been described as amicable, though Elton has acknowledged that he deeply hurt Blauel.

Blue: With Clive Franks, Elton co-produced recordings by this Rocket Record act. The band charted in 1977 with a minor British hit, "Gonna Capture Your Heart" (co-written by Bernie Taupin), and quickly disappeared.

Bluesology: In 1960, 13-year-old Reg Dwight (the future Elton John) and Stuart Brown (a friend of Reg's cousin) started a neighborhood band, the Corvettes. Bass guitarist Geoff Dyson (later of the Mockingbirds) belonged briefly to the group, which took its name from a shaving lotion or the car, depending on whose version you believe. At best, the Corvettes earned two pounds a night playing a youth club at St. Edmund's Roman Catholic Church on Pinner Road. By late 1962, Reg, Brown, and company were playing local pubs under the name of Bluesology, borrowed from a record called "Djangology" by a three-fingered jazz guitarist, Django Rheinhardt. A year later, the band was playing weekly at the Establishment in the west end of London. Described as a "snobbish soul band," Bluesology played tunes by Jimmy Witherspoon, Arbee Stidham, Memphis Slim, and Muddy Waters. The group's original members were Reg Dwight on organ, Stuart Brown on vocals and guitar, Rex Bishop on bass, and Mick Inkpen on drums. A sax player was soon added. One Saturday morning in July 1965, Bluesology auditioned at the Kilburn State Cinema and went professional with the Roy Tempest Agency.

Bluesology on stage: British clubs played by Bluesology (1965-67): Bag O' Nails, The Bailey Organization, Barrowlands Ballroom, Batley Variety Club, Bluesville '67 Club, Casbah Club, Cavendish Club, The Cavern (a Liverpool haunt made famous by The Beatles), Chantinghall Ballroom in the Chantinghall Hotel, Club La Bamba, The Crawdaddy in the Clubhouse, Cromwellian Club, Cue Club, Domino Club, Douglas House, Ealing Jazz Club, Eel Pie Island (Rod Stewart was also on the bill), The Fiesta, Flamingo Jazz Club, Haverford West, Hilton Hotel, King MoJo Club, The Klooks Kleek, Last Chance Club, The Locarno (Jimi Hendrix was featured), Marquee Club (with Manfred Mann and the Spencer Davis Group), Maryland Ballroom, Northwood Hills Hotel, Nottingham Rowing Club, Olympia Ballroom, Phoenix Theatre, Plaza Ballroom, Princess Club, Ricky Tick Club, The Ritz, Rory Blackwell's Club, Scotch of St. James, Seville Theatre, The Shazz, South Harrow British Legion Hall, Southshields Latino, The Speakeasy, The State Cinema, Studio 51, Tito's, The Twisted Wheel, U.S. Servicemen's Club, Whiskey-A-GoGo, World's End Club, and 100 Club.

Songs performed by Bluesology: "Cry Like a Baby," "Hit the Road Jack," "Let the Good Times Roll," "Take These Chains from My Heart," "Frankie and Johnny," "Shake," "The Pain Gets a Little Deeper," "634-5789," "Big Bird," "Knock on Wood," "Raise Your Hand," "Things Get Better," "The Girl from Ipanema," "Back in Your Own Backyard," "The Gypsy," "If I Didn't Care," "Java Jive," "Melody of Love," "My Prayer," "We Three," "I Sold My Heart to the Junkman," "All or Nothing," "Danny Boy," "Over the Rainbow," "You'll Never Walk Alone," "Breathless," "Whole Lotta Shakin' Going On," "Ain't It a Shame," "Come See," "Gotta Get Away," "Hey Little Girl," "It Ain't No Use," "Rhythm," "Sometimes I Wonder," "Sweet Music," "The Matador," "The Monkey Time," "Um Um Um Um Um Um," "England Swings," "Kansas City Star," "King of the Road," "Dream Baby (How Long Must I Dream)," "Don't Fight It," "Down to My Last Heartbreak," "Everybody Needs Somebody to Love," "If You Need Me," "In the Midnight Hour," "It's Too Late," "Land of 1,000 Dances," "Loving You," "I Put a Spell on You," "Mr. Pitiful," "My Girl," "He'll Have to Go," "I Love You Because," "Bachelor Boy," "I'm the Lonely One," "It's All in the Game," "I Do Love You," "Sitting in the Park," "Summertime," "Unbelievable," "I've Got So Many Worries," "Tired of Wondering," "Hold What You've Got," "S.Y.S.L.J.F.M. (The Letter Song)," "She's Mine," "You Better Get It," "Just One Look," "What Ya Gonna Do About It," "River Deep/Mountain High," "Shotgun," "Got My Mojo Working," "Hoochie Coochie Man," "I Put a Tiger in Your Tank," "I'm Ready," "Mannish Boy," "Rolling Stone Blues," "It Ain't No Secret," "There's Good Rockin' Tonight," "Times Getting Tougher Than Tough," "Why, You're Next," and "Young Man's Blues."

Bluesology was hired as a backing band for touring American soul artists, sometimes playing four gigs a night during an 18-month tour of Europe. The band backed such stars as Major Lance, Billy Stewart, the Inkspots, the original Drifters (The Shadows), Doris Troy, and Patti LaBelle and the Blue Belles, which included future Supreme Cindy Birdsong. The group recorded a demo of "Times Getting Tougher Than Tough" and "Come Back Baby" at a small studio in Rickmansworth, Middlesex, England. The recording impressed Jack Baverstock, who signed the group to the Fontana label and re-recorded the songs. In July 1965 Bluesology released its first single, "Come Back Baby," written by Reg Dwight. In November a second single, "Mr. Frantic," also penned by Dwight, came out on the Fontana label. Neither charted. In the autumn of 1965, Bluesology performed on the rhythm-and-blues circuit in Germany. In December the group began its first official professional tour as a backing band for Major Lance's two-week tour of England. Former Corvettes member Geoff Dyson returned briefly as the group's booking agent. Arnold Tendler, a local jeweler, managed the band and helped out financially. Later, Bluesology reappeared on the British club

On the red organ: In the mid-1960s, Reg Dwight saw The Animals in concert. Alan Price, keyboardist for the group, inspired Reg to buy a bright red Vox Continental organ, which became part of his stage persona with the band Bluesology.

circuit and followed up with an extended tour of Europe featuring a new lineup: Dwight, Brown, Patt Higgs on trumpet, Dave Murphy on sax, Freddie Creasey on bass, and Paul Gale on drums. Higgs was later replaced by Chris Batesou. The lineup, with seasoned jazz veterans Higgs and Murphy, improved the band and expanded its musical range. In September 1966, at the Cromwellian Pub in England, Reg met Long John Baldry. An experienced and respected singer, Baldry asked Bluesology to join him after the band's tour of Sweden. In late December, Bluesology re-formed, with Long John Baldry on lead vocals. Only two members went along with the change. The new Bluesology consisted of Dwight, Brown, Fred Gandi on bass, Pete Gavin on drums, Neil Hubbard on guitar, Elton Dean on sax, Marc Charig on coronet and flugelhorn, and Alan Walker as a vocalist. Baldry charted in 1967 with "Let the Heartaches Begin," a number one hit and the year's fastest-selling single in England. But the recording did not feature Bluesology. The band digressed, becoming merely a backing group for Baldry's cabaret shows. Dwight grew disenchanted. But to keep a steady income, he remained with Bluesology as he forged a relationship with lyricist Bernie Taupin and began doing session work with The Hollies and others. In July 1967, Alan Walker

Bluesology recordings: Though the band released no albums, Bluesology recorded at least eleven songs between 1965 and 1968: "Come Back Baby," "Corinna, Corinna" (a remake of the 1961 hit), "Every Day I Get the Blues," "Heaven Help Us" (with Long John Baldry), "Hey Lord, You Made the Night Too Long," "Just a Little Bit," "Let the Heartaches Begin" (a re-recording of Baldry's earlier hit), "Mr. Frantic," "Since I Found You Baby," "Tell Me What I Say," and "Times Getting Tougher Than Tough." Elton sang lead vocals on "Come Back Baby" and "Mr. Frantic."

left Bluesology and was replaced by Marsha Hunt. Elton began concentrating on writing. He remained a member of Bluesology until the end of 1967. Marsha Hunt and Stuart Brown also became discontented and left the band. Brown moved to Greece, later attempting a solo career. He joined Cochise in 1969. Hunt performed in *Hair*. Reg Dwight left, as well, succeeded by Jimmy Horowitz, who married songwriter Lesley Duncan. Caleb Quaye replaced Neil Hubbard on guitar. Quaye was succeeded by Bernie Holland. Bluesology carried on for another six months before disbanding. In April 1968 Long John Baldry left to pursue a solo career. Bluesology alumnae went on to join Joe Cocker's band, Soft Machine, Juicy Lucy, Jody Grind, and others.

Blunstone, Colin: The ex-Zombies vocalist recorded for Elton's Rocket Record Company. A John-Taupin composition, "Planes," served as the title track for his 1976 album. In 1978, he released *Never Even Thought*, also on Rocket.

Bolognesi, Jacques: Played trombone on *Honky Chateau* and *Don't Shoot Me, I'm Only the Piano Player*.

Bon Jovi, Jon: Elton backed Bon Jovi on the *Blaze of Glory* movie sound track. Bon Jovi returned the favor, by singing "Levon" on the *Two Rooms* project. They have also jammed together onstage.

Bono: The lead singer of U2 counts Elton among his favorite songwriters. On the Amnesty International Tour of 1986, Bono wove "Candle in the Wind" into a medley of classic rock songs. Elton had hoped to sing with Bono on the *Duets* album.

Books: About two dozen books have been published about Elton John. Most were hastily produced in the mid-1970s to capitalize on the peak of his stardom. A few deserve mention:
❖ *Elton John: Five Years of Fun* (1975, Boutwell) by Robert Hilburn and Connie Pappas (later, Hillman). Printed for his fifth anniversary shows at the Troubadour Club, this limited edition hardcover has become a collector's item.
❖ *A Conversation with Elton John and Bernie Taupin* (1975, Flash) by Paul Gambaccini. The songwriters cooperated for this paperback.
❖ *Bernie Taupin: The One Who Writes the Words for Elton John* (1976, Knopf) by Bernie Taupin. His lyrics and poems were illustrated by numerous artists.
❖ *Elton John: It's a Little Bit Funny* (1977, Penguin) by David Nutter and Bernie Taupin. The photographer documented the 1976 tour.
❖ Sotheby auction catalogues (1988). Elton sold many of his belongings, and this set of four catalogues, filled with photos, offers outrageous insights into his lifestyle and interests.
❖ *Elton John* (1991, Harmony) by Philip Norman. Though devout fans recognize factual errors, the project is the most detailed biography to date. Norman enjoyed access to Bernie Taupin.
❖ *The Complete Lyrics: Elton John & Bernie Taupin* (1994, Hyperion). It is not complete, but does include nearly all songs that appeared on official albums, set to art.

Borowiecki, Teddy: Played accordion on *Made in England*.

Boston Tea Party: The Massachusetts venue hosted the opening of Elton's first American tour on October 29, 1970. Though Elton performed several shows at the venue, he was introduced nightly as "Elton Jones."

Bread and Beer Band: Tony King, a record producer and assistant at Apple Records and AIR Productions, assembled the studio group, which featured many of England's best session musicians. He hoped to rival the super session group at Motown. The band included King, Bernie Calvert of The Hollies, Roger Pope and Caleb Quaye of Hookfoot, Jamaican percussionists Lennox Jackson and Rolfo, and the future Elton John, Reg Dwight. The members knew each other. The band recorded an instrumental album during impromptu sessions in 1968 and 1969, when King and a young Chris Thomas were working closely with The Beatles at AIR Studios. In early August 1968, Beatles producer George Martin went on vacation, allowing Thomas more freedom in studio production, which he shared with King. The unreleased album featured psychedelic jazz interpretations of earlier hits. The instrumentals contained faint background vocals. The album had the same feel as "Hay Chewed," a track from Elton's 1969 *Empty Sky*. On nearly all tracks, the lead melody was disguised by an overpowering backbeat and instrumental jam. Elton played harpsichord on "If I Were a Carpenter" and electric and acoustic piano on the others. "The Dick Barton Theme," written for a popular 1968 BBC-TV program, was released as a single in 1969 and 1972. The B-side was "Breakdown Blues," co-written by Elton. The album was never officially released. King gave the masters to Elton as a 1976 birthday gift. "We used to go down to the pub in the afternoon, have a few beers and go back to the studio in the evening," recalled King in a 1976 interview. "Then we'd turn down all the lights at Abbey Road and get all moody. The Beatles had been using lots of colored lights while they were recording and we thought it was terribly avant-garde. So we used to steal them and use them during our sessions. When I played the acetate for Elton on his birthday, I thought it would be God-awful. We were surprised to find that it was half-decent." The unreleased album included these songs: "The Dick Barton Theme (The Devil's Gallop)," "Quick Joey Small (Run Joey Run)," "Needles and Pins," "God Knows (a Bit of Freedom)," "Billy's Bag," "Last Night," "Wooly Bully," "Mellow Yellow," "If I Were a Carpenter," "Zorba the Greek," "The Letter," and "Breakdown Blues" (written by Quaye, Dwight, Calvert, and Jackson).

Brecker Brothers: Jazz horn artists played on *Blue Moves*.

Brennan, Paul: Played pipes and flute on *Made in England*.

Brown, Steve: Working behind the scenes, Brown has been with Elton John almost since day one of his career. He joined Dick James Music a year after Elton and Taupin went on contract as songwriters. Brown encouraged the duo to write the music they liked, rather than the commercial, Tom Jones-type songs that James wanted. The early results, "Lady Samantha" and "Skyline Pigeon," brought encouragement. "Lady Samantha" became a semi-successful single in Britain, launching Elton as a solo act. After producing the first Elton album, *Empty Sky*, Brown recognized that Elton needed a more experienced producer for the follow-up. He tried to land George Martin of Beatles' fame, but got Gus Dudgeon instead. Brown has been involved through most of Elton's career, coordinating the *Two Rooms* tribute and serving as an executive producer on *Duets*. On musical matters and direction, Elton has put great faith in Brown's judgment. Through mid-1995, he remained a top member of Elton's management team. Ironically, before Brown worked with Elton, he served as a sound mixer at a 1968 session for Kiki Dee. He also belonged to a U.K. band, Emile Ford and the Checkmates.

Brown, Stuart: He was a friend of Reg Dwight's cousin and the musician with whom Reg started a neighborhood band, the Corvettes, in 1960. Brown co-founded Bluesology with Elton.

Browne, Jackson: Elton played piano on "My Redneck Friend," using the pseudonym Rockaday Johnnie.

Buck, Vance: Elton dedicated his 1992 album, *The One*, to Buck, a close friend and former employee who died of an AIDS-related illness shortly after the recording was released.

Buckhead Diner: The chic restaurant is one of Elton's hangouts in Atlanta.

Buckmaster, Paul: An orchestral arranger, Buckmaster helped create the radical sound of the first American album, *Elton John*. He had earlier worked with producer Gus Dudgeon on David Bowie's *Space Oddity*. Buckmaster met Elton at a Mile Davis concert in 1969. It was he who recommended Dudgeon produce the *Elton John* album. Buckmaster continued to work with Elton on *Tumbleweed Connection* and *Madman Across the Water*. Elton's sound grew less orchestral, and, by the mid-1970s, when an arranger was needed Elton usually called on James Newton Howard. Buckmaster later worked with a wide range of entertainers, including Paul McCartney and Dwight Yoakam, and wrote for television. He re-appeared on Elton's albums in 1978 and, more significantly, 1995, contributing arrangements for "Believe," "House," "Belfast" and "Cold" on *Made in England*.

Bunbury Tails: A host of stars have sung for this animated British television show. Produced by Barry Gibb of the Bee Gees, Elton recorded "Up the Revolution," a reggae-flavored number, which he did not write.

Burdon, Eric: Burdon and Elton have had a long-running feud. It revealed itself in January 1971 at a major industry event, the Midem Music Festival in Cannes, France. Performing with War, Burdon played beyond his allotted television time, refusing to yield the stage to Elton even after Elton, Nigel Olsson, and Dee Murray had been introduced. Elton walked off but was allowed to play a 30-minute set the next day. During this performance, the audience was rude and the curtain fell down. Elton vowed not to play in France again, and he kept the promise until 1978, after *Blue Moves* topped that nation's charts. Elton may have provoked the incident with Burdon. On January 2, 1971, two weeks before Midem, Elton was quoted in England's *Melody Maker* taking a slap at Burdon: "Have you got Eric Burdon's new one, Black Man's Burdon? There's one track I like, but he should have been born black and given us all a rest," said Elton. Years earlier, in the summer of 1965, Bluesology, including Elton, shared the bill with Burdon and The Animals at the Phoenix Theatre in England.

Bush, Kate: Aside from contributing her version of "Rocket Man" to the *Two Rooms* tribute, Bush, a major star in Britain, has released vocal and instrumental versions of "Candle in the Wind." Several members of Elton's bands, including drummer Charlie Morgan, have worked with Bush.

C

Cannata, Richie: The former Billy Joel saxophonist played on *21 at 33*.

Captain Fantastic: Nickname for Elton used in mid-1970s, particularly after the release of the album *Captain Fantastic and the Brown Dirt Cowboy*.

Caraeff, Ed: Photographer who worked with Elton on several albums.

Caribou: A studio ranch in Colorado owned by Jim Guercio, then the producer of Chicago. Elton recorded three albums at Caribou. The ranch was later destroyed by fire.

Carrack, Paul: A member of Squeeze, Ace, and Mike and The Mechanics, Carrack plays Hammond organ on "Man," from *Made in England*.

Cars: Automobiles are among the singer's passions. He has owned a fleet of more than twenty vehicles exceeding $10 million in value. Rare Bentleys, Jaguars, Porsches, and Rolls Royces have been part of the collection. A 12-cylinder Jaguar, featured in the "I'm Still Standing" video, sold for $90,000. He has been known to give more expensive cars to friends.

Cartier: Known for his lavishness, Elton often purchases gifts for friends, associates, and himself. Among his favorite shopping stops is Cartier, a jeweler about which Elton wrote a B-side ditty in the late 1970s. The song was used in a Cartier ad. In 1994, Elton performed an Edith Piaf classic, "La Vie en Rose," for a French Cartier TV commercial.

Castro, Lenny: Played percussion on *21 at 33*.

Cavendish, Sharon: Rod Stewart's feminine name for Elton John.

Central Park: On September 13, 1980, Elton and band performed for almost a half million fans at a free concert in the legendary New York park. Excluding televised events, Elton has never performed for a larger audience. The performance was released on video.

Chapin, Harry: The singer paid tribute to a few peers in 1973's "Songman." Chapin's song mentioned Elton and Bernie Taupin by name. The Chapin composition also included a few chords reminiscent of Elton's "Border Song."

Chautemps, Jean-Louis: Played sax on *Honky Chateau* and *Don't Shoot Me, I'm Only the Piano Player.*

Cher: Elton and the American singer-actress have been friends since he appeared on her TV show in the mid-1970s, duetting on "Bennie and the Jets." Several stories have erroneously reported that Cher and Renate Blauel, Elton's ex-wife, wrote the song "Don't Trust That Woman." In fact, Cher wrote it with Elton, who worked under the pseudonym of Lady Choc Ice. Proud of her lyrics, Cher reportedly sent the song to three writers (without telling the others). After crafting a melody, Elton sent a tape to Cher, for inclusion on her 1986 Geffen album. Elton liked the song and used it on his album, *Leather Jackets.* Cher wanted her name listed first in the credits, annoying Elton and prompting him to take an alias. Cher has said she wrote several songs with Elton, but just one has been released. Neither that incident, nor an earlier one, torpedoed their friendship. In 1976, Elton released "Snow Queen" as the B-side to "Don't Go Breaking My Heart." Fading with the words "I Got You Babe," the drug-related song offered a harsh view of Cher, compliments of Taupin. The singer later apologized. "Elton and I were going to a Paul McCartney concert together, and on the way home he was saying he wanted to apologize, that it wasn't his fault," Cher recalled in 1990. "And I said, 'It wasn't your fault for what?' Elton then explained that Bernie had written this terrible lyric about me. ... I've never heard it, but I know it's real nasty."

Childhood: As with most children, Elton's early years revolved around his parents: in his case, a caring mother, Sheila Dwight, who encouraged his love for pop music, and a stern father, Stanley Dwight, whom Elton feared. His parents had married in 1945, two years before their only child, Reginald Kenneth Dwight, was born on March 25, 1947, in post-war England in Pinner, Middlesex, a modest suburb of London. His father, a squadron leader in the Royal Air Force, rarely came home. After a lengthy absence, he returned one

---

Childhood homes
- ❖ 1947: Pinner home.
- ❖ 1950: 55 Pinner Hill, the home of Elton's grandmother.
- ❖ 1951-52: 111 Potter Street, Northwood Hills.
- ❖ 1967: 30A Frome Court, Northwood Hills. Elton and Taupin shared a room at Sheila and Fred Fairebrother's apartment.

Radio days: Reg Dwight was an impressionable seven-year-old, and the BBC radio airwaves were filled with piano instrumentalists. Many of Winifred Atwell's 1954-55 singles were piano medleys of such old standards as "Baby Face" and "Little Brown Jug." American pianist Charlie Kunz had a top U.K. hit in December 1954 with his "Piano Medley #114," yet another influence on Reg.

evening in 1949, having never seen his first child. Elton recalled in 1980, "My mother told me that when he walked in the door, she said, 'He's upstairs sleeping if you want to see him.' His reply was, 'It can wait until tomorrow.' " Coldness characterized their relationship. They shared a passion for two things: the Watford Football Club and music. Stanley Dwight played trumpet with Bert Weeden in a jazz dance band known as the Millermen. Regardless, the older Dwight preferred classical music and enjoyed George Shearing. He did not want his son exposed to pop music. But Reg's mother, Sheila, an avid music fan, bought the latest 78s by Guy Mitchell, Patti Page, Frank Sinatra, Frankie Laine, Johnnie Ray, and other favorites. They influenced Reg, an insecure only child who found great satisfaction in listening to music and then attempting to bang it out on an old King Brothers upright in the den of his grandmother's house. His father and Auntie Winn played piano at the house, and three-year-old Reg was quick to follow. One afternoon, Reg stunned them by playing "The Skater's Waltz" by ear. His parents were amazed, and soon Reggie would be running from the radio to the piano, teaching himself to play new tunes. He became the young star at evening dinner parties. He would be put to bed early on nights when guests were expected. Later, after dinner, he would be awakened and asked to perform. In 1954, at age seven, Reg began private classical piano lessons. His parents forced him to practice three hours a day. He didn't much care for the classics. Away from his parents and teacher, he secretly jumped into pop pieces. Winifred Atwell's honky tonk piano tunes influenced him tremendously. On a Friday afternoon in 1957, Sheila Dwight brought home two new pop singles that changed her ten-year-old's life. Bill Haley's "ABC Boogie" and Elvis Presley's "Heartbreak Hotel" sealed Reggie's dreams of a career in music. "I remember she brought the records home and said they were different from what we had been hearing," he said. "She thought I would like them. ... I was really starstruck. Pop music was my whole life." Soon, Sheila found Reg a new piano instructor who would allow him to play pop tunes. He won a part-time, junior exhibition scholarship to the Royal Academy of Music, where he studied classical music (Bach, Chopin, Bartok), sung in a choir and learned to sight-read (a talent he would lose out of neglect). His music instructor, Helen Piena, said his natural ear amazed her. He could play a musical piece after hearing it once. Over five years, Reg attended Saturday classes, sometimes skipping to play soccer or ride the train. With time, Reg grew tired of the regiment. He attended Pinner Grammar School weekly, spent evenings practicing piano and doing homework, and Saturdays he went to the academy. He found little time to hang out with friends. Stanley Dwight wanted his son to work toward a steady job as an Air Force pilot or bank teller. While on military duty, Dwight once wrote his wife, "Reggie must give up this idea of becoming a pop musician. He's turning into a wild boy." In March 1958, Buddy Holly toured Britain, and Reg, 11, attended one of his concerts. He began wearing glasses to emulate the singer. By age 12, he was miming Jerry Lee Lewis records in front of a mirror. Meanwhile, the relationship between Stanley and Sheila Dwight deteriorated. Divorce remained taboo, and family members encouraged the couple to stay together. They did, until the winter of 1962. Among other reasons, Stanley left because of Sheila's new relationship with Fred "Derf" Fairebrother, who later became Reg's stepfather. Stanley Dwight also had other relationships. The divorce pleased Reg because it freed him from his father. Reg picked up a job as a pub pianist at the Northwood Hills Hotel. A heavy child, he suffered from a terrible inferiority complex, despite his extraordinary talents. On March 5, 1964, Reg left Pinner Grammar School, three weeks before his final exams, to pursue a career in music. It was the American equivalent of dropping out of high school. With help from his soccer-star cousin, Roy Dwight, Reg (already playing in neighborhood bands) landed a gofer's job at Mills Music. Stanley Dwight married again and fathered four sons. He died in 1992 at age 66, but there was no happy reunion — a fact the British press publicized when Elton's father was near death. "In life sometimes that happens, when a parent and a child just don't connect," Elton said.

China: In 1977, Elton co-produced a self-titled album by the group China, which featured band members Davey Johnstone, James Newton Howard, and Roger Pope, along with Cooker Lo Presti. Elton sang backup on the album, which appeared on his label, Rocket Records. Johnstone has described the recording as "terribly self-indulgent." Taupin contributed two songs. The album included "On the Slide," "Meet Me Half Way," "Broken Woman," "Hametheme," "Savage," "Dear You," "One Way Ticket," "For a While," "Shameful Disgrace," and "This Time It's for You."

Chipmunks, The: The high-pitched, animated characters released a version of "Crocodile Rock."

Christie, Lou: Elton backed the singer on piano in a June 1969 appearance on BBC's "Disco Two" program.

Christmas albums: In 1993 and 1994, Elton gave specially made CD recordings to friends and business associates as Christmas gifts. Fifty friends received *Elton John Plays the Siran* in 1993. A year later, he pressed 100 copies of *The Fishing Trip*, a four-CD set. All songs were recorded live, presumably at a private performance. Both sets reportedly contained extended and reworked solo versions of such songs as "Song for Guy" and "Sixty Years On."

Cicada: Bernie Taupin and wife Stephanie Haymes, a former hostess at another elite eatery, own the Los Angeles restaurant. Located on Melrose Avenue, the trendy diner caters to a celebrity clientele.

Clapton, Eric: The legendary British guitarist has been friends with Elton since 1970. They have recorded and toured together. In December 1978 in England, Elton and George Harrison joined Clapton onstage for "Further on up the Road," the first of many times they would exchange visits. Clapton reciprocated in 1988 at the Hollywood Bowl and on "Rocket Man" in 1989 at Madison Square Garden, months after Elton and Dire Straits's Mark Knopfler had backed Clapton in Japan. All three were part of a super group performing June 30, 1990, at the Knebworth benefit in England. Clapton contributed a blues-injected version of "Border Song" to *Two Rooms*. It was befitting, perhaps, that Clapton should record this song because it was Elton's first hit in America. Clapton, then of Derek and the Dominos, appeared at the Fillmore East within days of Elton's 1970 appearance. They met in New York. In the early 1990s, while on an airplane, Clapton and Elton hatched the idea of a joint tour. It came together in 1992 with several concerts in Europe and four in America — two apiece at Shea Stadium and Dodger Stadium in June. Though their duet, "Runaway Train," was a single and appeared on Elton's *The One* album, the pair rarely performed it in concert, disappointing fans and reviewers.

Clark, Frank: Played guitar on *Elton John*.

Cleveland, Rev. James: The late gospel choir director contributed to *The Fox* and *Blue Moves* albums and appeared on stage with Elton in 1976.

Cocker, Joe: They met in 1968 at Dick James's offices. Cocker declined the chance to record "Border Song." It wasn't until the *Two Rooms* project in 1991 that he covered a John-Taupin composition, "Sorry Seems to Be the Hardest Word." On his 1992 *Night Calls* album, Cocker recorded "Don't Let the Sun Go Down on Me" — boasting that Taupin told him the song had never been sung better. Cocker's 1969 *Maddogs and Englishmen*, featuring Leon Russell on piano, was a major stylistic influence on the young Elton John.

Cohen, Leonard: The Canadian poet's late 1960s work influenced Elton and Taupin. A quarter of a century later, Cohen and Elton collaborated on a distinctive version of "Born to Lose." In 1994, Elton lent his name to a full-page ad hyping a Cohen release. "I implore anyone who has heard *The Future* album to desist from telling how exceptionally brilliant it is," he stated. "After all, we mere mortals have records to sell, too." Elton recorded a Cohen song for a 1995 tribute, *Tower of Songs*.

Colclough, Beauchamp: A counselor at London's Charter Nightingale Clinic, he helped Elton overcome his multiple addictions. His 1994 book, *Tomorrow I'll Be Different*, includes an introduction by Elton John. Elizabeth Taylor and Michael Jackson were among Colclough's other big-name clients.

Cole, B. J.: Played steel guitar on *Madman Across the Water* and *A Single Man*.

Collectables: With a solo career that has spanned a quarter of a century, Elton John has generated thousands of collectables, ranging from recordings to concert memorabilia. They cover a broad spectrum from the common tour books, shirts, pins, single picture sleeves, and posters to the more expensive gold and platinum presentation discs, Bally Captain Fantastic pinball machines, stage costumes, and designer eyeglasses. A comprehensive listing would fill a book. What follows is a purely subjective sample of 25 rare or interesting items that would make any Elton John collector smile:

❖ The first single by Bluesology, "Come Back Baby" (Fontana, 1965).

❖ A concert poster from the 1970 Halloween show at the Boston Tea Party, the opening date on his first U.S. tour.

❖ A promotional "Ego" watch.

❖ His 1968 "I've Been Loving You" single on the Philips label.

❖ A blue-and-silver, plane-shaped "Louder Than a Concorde" tie clip from the 1976 tour.

❖ A deck of cards promoting the *21 at 33* album.

❖ A copy of a limited-edition, brown-vinyl, autographed album of *Captain Fantastic and the Brown Dirt Cowboy.*

❖ A Dodger Stadium concert hat (1975).

❖ A Fillmore East program for the 1970 shows with Leon Russell.

❖ The 1977 single of "The Goaldigger Song," a soccer-charity release of just 500 copies, half autographed.

❖ A brass Elton John-palm tree belt buckle from the 1974 tour.

❖ A *Reg Strikes Back* coffee mug.

❖ *The Games* sound track album on Viking Records, 1970, including "From Denver to L.A." by Elton "Johns."

❖ A pink *Sleeping with the Past* guitar pick with Davey Johnstone's signature printed on one side and a silhouette of Elton in a top hat on the other side.

❖ A *Single Man* diary book.

❖ A *Blue Moves* jacket patch.

❖ "I Don't Wanna Go on with You Like That" single on blue vinyl.

❖ *Tommy* bath towels.

❖ A white, 10-inch ceramic figurine produced by Sisco and advertised in *Teen Magazine* in 1973. It features Elton sitting on a stool, one hand in the air, one on the keyboard, and the initials "EJ" on his vest.

❖ A commemorative mirror from the June 30, 1984, show at Wembley Stadium in England.

❖ A tan *Honky Chateau* watch, picturing a caricature of Elton in wing boots. His arms serve as the clock's hands.

❖ A *Captain Fantastic* jigsaw puzzle.

❖ A limited edition print of the *Blue Moves* cover painting, "The Guardian Readers" by Patrick Procktor.

❖ A sheet of Elton John stamps issued by the nation of Grenada in 1984.

❖ A wooden *Reg Strikes Back* ink pen shaped like a baseball bat.

Collee, Adrian: A longtime associate, he helps coordinate aspects of studio sessions and concert tours.

Collins, Charles: Played drums on *The Complete Thom Bell Sessions.*

Collins, Judy: Collins has performed two Elton songs, "Come Down in Time" and "Sweetheart on Parade," on separate albums, and "Skyline Pigeon" in concert.

Collins, Phil: He played "Burn Down the Mission" on *Two Rooms.*

Commercials: Elton gave Diet Coke a singing endorsement through two television commercials in the early 1990s. They were his best-known efforts, but there have been others. Elton has also appeared in TV ads for Sasson Jeans (1984) and Cadbury Chocolates (1985-86). In the early 1970s, he promoted several of his albums in television commercials. Among his radio recommendations: Greenwich Village's The Pink Pussycat Boutique, specializing in sex toys (1976). He has also recorded public service announcements for the American Cancer Society and his AIDS foundation. In print ads, Elton has supported Roland Pianos, Pioneer components, Ebony Menswear, and Chess King Men's Stores. Rimmel Cosmetics used the "your eyes" verse from "Your Song."

Commodore Orpington: Elton adopted this alias for the French release of "I'm Still Standing."

Congress: A few of Elton's early American releases appeared on the Congress label, the imprint used by UNI Records for foreign material.

Connolly, Billy: As part of the Humblebums (a group that included Gerry Rafferty), Connolly was on the bill when Elton performed May 7, 1970, at the Roundhouse Chalk Farm in London, England. Later, as a client of John Reid, Connolly (wearing huge banana shoes) opened for Elton on the 1976 tour, combining comedy and song. In the 1980s and 1990s, he starred in two American TV sitcoms.

Cook, Roger: Elton demoed some songs for Cook and partner Roger Greenaway, who also worked at Dick James Music in the late 1960s. Cook sang backup on *Elton John* and *Madman Across the Water* and covered "Skyline Pigeon."

Cooper, Alice: For a few years in the late 1970s, both Elton and Bernie Taupin wrote songs with other partners. Taupin and Cooper collaborated on 1978's *From the Inside*, an album focusing on their efforts to overcome alcoholism. It included the single "How You Gonna See Me Now?," in which Taupin referred to himself as "a hobo in the snow." Guitarists Davey Johnstone and Dee Murray played on the album and Kiki Dee contributed backing vocals. Around 1976, Elton and Cooper were friends and neighbors.

Cooper, Ray: Rock music's most dramatic — and probably best — tambourine player is Cooper. A percussionist, he joined the Elton John Band on *Caribou*, after playing on earlier albums. His most significant involvement with Elton relates to two tours. In 1979 the British musicians staged concerts that have become legendary among fans. Elton performed solo — "unplugged," before the term became vogue — at small, intimate venues. Midway through the concert, Cooper, dressed in black, with granny glasses and a short, bristly haircut and looking like an elderly mortician, joined the production, performing maniacally on timpani, bongos, cymbals, vibes, and gong. The tour grabbed headlines by taking in the former Soviet Union, Israel, and Northern Ireland. The USSR performances resulted in a television special and feature video, *To Russia with Elton*. In 1993 and 1994, Elton and Cooper resurrected the tour by visiting eight states, England, and Africa. Again, they played many obscure songs, such as "Idol," "The North," "Crazy Water," "Talking Old Soldiers," and "Indian Sunset." Cooper and John met in the 1960s, when Elton was still Reg Dwight and both were session players in England. Born in 1947 in Hertfordshire, England, Cooper played piano and drums as a child. After toying with a career onstage, he played the London jazz circuit with the likes of Cleo Laine and Maynard Ferguson. In 1969, he belonged to the folk-rock group Blue Mink, for which Gus Dudgeon produced a string of British hits. Cooper sat in on the 1971 *Madman Across the Water* sessions. He has worked with numerous musicians, including The Beatles, the Rolling Stones, and Eric Clapton. He also served as a co-producer for George Harrison's movie company, Handmade Films, and in management with John Reid Enterprises. He appeared in Robert Altman's *Popeye*. Cooper and Elton get along well, and the percussionist is often featured on his new releases.

Corvettes: Thirteen-year-old Reg Dwight formed the neighborhood band in 1959. It evolved into the group Bluesology, which began Reg Dwight's transformation to Elton John.

Costa, David: An artist and designer, Costa has been part of Elton's team since 1973's *Don't Shoot Me, I'm Only the Piano Player*. Studying art history in college, Costa was seduced by the music business and landed a job with the art department at Dick James Music. Costa, Mike Ross, and David Larkham designed the *Goodbye Yellow Brick Road* package. His role has grown. As head of Wherefore Art?, Costa remains in charge of most Elton design projects: album and single covers, tour programs, T-shirts, and other merchandise. He has worked with other stars as well, including George Harrison, Eric Clapton, and Phil Collins.

Costumes: Those who don't follow rock music know Elton best as the gaudy star of the mid-1970s who wore outrageous glasses and stage costumes. In the years since, he has become more conservative in his stage dress — though in red leather pants and matching sequined vest he would hardly qualify for Wall Street. When he opened in America in 1970, wearing silver boots and spandex clothes, Elton had already abandoned the moody, brooding image created by his self-titled album.

Combined with wild stage antics, his reputation for flamboyance grew. By 1974, four designers — Bob Mackie, Bill Whitten, Annie Reavie, and Tommy Nutter — were filling Elton's stage closet with feathered, sequined, and embroidered outfits. (The famed Mr. Blackwell has named Elton among the worst-dressed three times, in 1975, 1976, and 1985.) Elton attributed his stage persona to his rigid upbringing at the hands of his father, Stanley Dwight, who forbid his son to wear even Hush Puppies shoes. Around 1988, with the release of *Reg Strikes Back*, Elton pledged to never again return to his costumes of old. "You get to the point after 20 years where you become a parody of yourself," he said. Still, with the help of designer Gianni Versace, Elton has continued to dress colorfully — though no where near as garish as on the tours of 1973, 1974, and 1986.

Cover versions: Over 200 artists and bands have recorded John-Taupin songs, and they are listed in Appendix I. The following list offers a glimpse of the interesting variety of artists who have recorded their interpretations of John-Taupin classics: David Cassidy, "I'm Still Standing";

Electric boots and mohair suits: His six most memorable costumes.

❖ Statue of Liberty. Complete with crown and torch, he performed in July 1976 at Madison Square Garden at the height of America's bicentennial celebration.

❖ Donald Duck. He dressed as the beloved Disney character in an outdoor concert at Central Park in 1980.

❖ Los Angeles Dodger. In honor of his classic Dodger Stadium shows in 1975, he wore a sequined baseball uniform.

❖ Amadeus. Playing with the Melbourne Symphony Orchestra in Australia in 1986, he donned a bouffant wig and silver lame suit.

❖ Fluorescent balls. Day-Glo cork balls, attached to a Lurex suit with piano wire, appeared to float around the piano player in a 1974 concert.

❖ *Yellow Brick Road* suit. The sequined 1973 outfit featured the album cover.

And a few accessories...

❖ A 24-inch Eiffel Tower hat, 1984.

❖ *Tommy*'s 4-foot high Pinball Wizard boots, 1975.

❖ A parrot earring, 1982.

Richard Clayderman, "Sacrifice"; John Denver, "I Think I'm Gonna Kill Myself"; James Galway, "Blue Eyes"; Crystal Gayle, "Cage the Songbird"; Leslie Gore, "Daniel"; Lena Horne, "Your Song"; Juice Newton, "Country Comfort"; Kenny Rogers, "Border Song"; and Leo Sayer, "Someone Saved My Life Tonight."

Cox, Terry: Played drums on *Madman Across the Water* and *Elton John*.

Crehan, Dermont: Played violin on *Made in England*.

Crocker, John: Played clarinet and sax on *A Single Man*.

Cromwellian Club: Long John Baldry heard Bluesology, including keyboardist Reg Dwight, at this London club and convinced the group to be his backing band.

D

DJM: It stands for Dick James Music, the label on which Elton's earliest British albums appeared.

Daltrey, Roger: The Who's lead singer recorded "Don't Let the Sun Go Down on Me" for the vampire film *The Lost Boys*.

Dame Edna: British comedian Barry Humphries dresses as several characters, including sassy Dame Edna. In 1977 Edna released an English novelty song, "Every Mother Wants a Son Like Elton John." On a TV appearance, Elton sang it with Edna. For several years, Humphries and Elton had the same manager, John Reid.

Dean, Elton: Reg Dwight stole half of his new name, Elton John, from this saxophonist, a Bluesology band mate. "I was always uncomfortable with my name as a kid," said Dwight. Dean later played with Soft Machine.

Dedications: Many albums and songs have been dedicated by Elton (and Taupin) to friends and co-workers. Some are listed here:
- *A Single Man*, to Graham Taylor, coach of the Watford Football Club.
- *Sleeping with the Past*, to lyricist Bernie Taupin.
- *To be continued...*, to Hugh Williams, Elton's lover at the time.
- *The One*, to Vance Buck, a friend who died of AIDS.
- *Too Low for Zero*, to Toni Taupin, Bernie's second wife.
- *Rock of the Westies*, to recently fired Dee Murray and Nigel Olsson.
- *Duets*, to friend John Scott.
- *Made in England*, to a friend, "David."
- "Cage the Songbird" to Edith Piaf, the late French singer and actress.
- "Philadelphia Freedom," to tennis star and friend Billie Jean King.
- "Talking Old Soldiers," to singer David Ackles.

❖ "Tiny Dancer," to Maxine Taupin, Bernie's first wife.

❖ "Empty Garden" and "The Man Who Never Died," to John Lennon.

❖ "Song for Guy," to Guy Burchett, a Rocket Record errand boy who died on his motorcycle.

❖ "Princess," to Princess Diana of England.

❖ "Crystal," to a former boyfriend, according to the man's disputed tell-all book.

Dee, Brian: Played harmonium on "Levon" and organ on "Burn Down the Mission" and the *Elton John* album.

Dee, Kiki: The British singer's name became permanently attached to Elton John's in 1976 when their duet, "Don't Go Breaking My Heart," hit number one in both England and America. But their relationship began much earlier. Born Pauline Matthews in 1947 in Bradford, England, she began singing in bands at age 14. She worked at Newcastle TV Studio where Dusty Springfield's manager discovered her. At 16 she signed her first record contract. She placed second in the 1965 San Remo Festival in Italy, earning her recognition on the continent. Four years later, as Tamla Motown's first British act, Dee released *Great Expectations*. Recorded in Detroit, the album failed to draw attention. John Reid, as top Motown man in Britain, knew Kiki Dee. Later, he introduced her to Elton. In 1973, they signed her to the Rocket Record Company. Her first Rocket album, *Loving and Free*, was co-produced by Elton and Clive Franks, featured Elton's band, contained two John-Taupin songs, and included the English hit "Amoureuse." The Kiki Dee Band toured with the Guess Who, Steely Dan and the Beach Boys. The title track of her follow-up album, *I've Got the Music in Me*, hit number twelve in America. She opened for Elton on his world tour. Following the success of her 1976 duet with Elton, Dee released a self-named album, produced by Elton and Franks. Her single "First Thing in the Morning" featured a John-Taupin B-side, "The Man Who Loved to Dance." Through the late 1970s, Dee lived in California but remained active with Rocket, recording two more albums and releasing a greatest hits collection. She also sang backup for other artists, including Alice Cooper. The 1980s began with Dee recording "Nothing's Gonna Stop Us Now" for the Gene Wilder film *Stir Crazy*. When Rocket began carrying only Elton, Dee released a new album, *Perfect Timing*, on RCA. Producer Pip Williams convinced Dee and Elton to reunite for "Loving You Is Sweeter Than Ever," a minor U.K. hit. Dee and Elton have stayed friends, appearing together at concerts, in videos and on recordings. In the mid-1980s, Dee found success in the theater, performing lead roles in the British productions of *Pump Boys in Dinettes* and *Blood Broth-*

Kiki Dee albums
❖ *Patterns*, 1968.
❖ *Great Expectations*, 1970.
❖ *Loving and Free*, 1973.
❖ *I've Got the Music in Me*, 1974.
❖ *Kiki Dee*, 1977.
❖ *Stay with Me*, 1978.
❖ *Greatest Hits*, 1980.
❖ *Perfect Timing*, 1981.
❖ *Angel Eyes*, 1989.
❖ *The Very Best of Kiki Dee*, 1994.

ers (the U.K. sound track featured her work). A 1989 album, *Angel Eyes*, produced by the Eurythmics's Dave Stewart, drew little attention. But in 1993, with another Elton duet, "True Love," peaking at number two on the British charts, Dee, who had survived a bout with cancer, was poised to reignite her singing career. Her 1994 album, *The Very Best of Kiki Dee*, included new releases.

> **Songs for a friend**: Elton has supplied his early protege, Kiki Dee, with several songs. She has released "Lonnie and Josie," "Supercool," "The Last Good Man in My Life," "Hard Luck Story," "The Man Who Loved to Dance," and "Snow Queen."

Denham, Vince: Played sax on *Sleeping with the Past*.

Diamond, Neil: Elton met Diamond in 1970, before performing at the Troubadour in Los Angeles. Diamond's friend, David Rosner, who handled some of Elton's management duties, brought the two together. After hosting a small party for Elton at his home, Diamond introduced him on opening night at the Troubadour.

Dickson, Graham: A sound engineer, he played electronic percussion on *Leather Jackets*.

Diet Coke: In the early 1990s, Elton, who has had a lifelong weight problem, became a spokesman for Diet Coke. The pop company is headquartered in Atlanta, Georgia, his adopted home. Elton has appeared in two TV commercials for the drink. In one, he duetted with Paula Abdul. In the other, through film and computer technology, he interacted with deceased legends Humphrey Bogart, James Cagney, and Louis Armstrong. The soft drink company has sponsored his tours, and the singer has proven to be a loyal supporter, sipping Diet Coke onstage and asking for it in restaurants.

Dietrich, Marlene: Dressed as the sultry actress, Elton duetted with Dietrich on "Falling in Love Again" at one of her 1972 farewell concerts at New London Theatre.

Difford, Chris: A member of Squeeze, he co-wrote "Duets for One" with Elton.

Discography: Two books have attempted to catalog all of Elton's British and American releases. The first, by Alan Finch, was published in England by Omnibus in 1981; the second, by John DiStefano, was published in America by *East End Lights* in 1993. What follows is a brief discography listing American album releases and singles. Numerous promos, demos, obscurities, special projects, and foreign recordings are not included. A complete British-American listing of all variations would include more than 2,000 entries.

Albums
1969   *Empty Sky* (released in America in 1975)

1970	*Elton John*
1970	*Tumbleweed Connection*
1971	*Friends* (movie sound track)
1971	*11-17-70* (live radio show)
1971	*Madman Across the Water*
1972	*Honky Chateau*
1973	*Don't Shoot Me, I'm Only the Piano Player*
1973	*Goodbye Yellow Brick Road*
1974	*Caribou*
1974	*Greatest Hits*
1975	*Captain Fantastic and the Brown Dirt Cowboy*
1975	*Rock of the Westies*
1976	*Here and There* (live album)
1976	*Blue Moves*
1977	*Greatest Hits Vol. 2*
1978	*A Single Man*
1979	*Victim of Love*
1980	*21 at 33*
1980	*Milestones* (a K-Tel collection)
1981	*The Fox*
1982	*Jump Up!*
1983	*Too Low for Zero*
1984	*Breaking Hearts*
1985	*Ice on Fire*
1986	*Leather Jackets*
1986	*Your Songs* (an MCA collection)
1987	*Live in Australia with the Melbourne Symphony Orchestra*
1987	*Greatest Hits Vol. 3*
1988	*Reg Strikes Back*
1989	*The Complete Thom Bell Sessions*
1989	*Sleeping with the Past*
1990	*To be continued...* (box set)
1991	*Two Rooms* (a tribute to Elton and Taupin by other artists)
1992	*The One*
1992	*Rare Masters*
1992	*Greatest Hits 1976-1986*
1993	*Duets*
1994	*The Lion King*
1995	*Made in England*

The European market saw major (and minor) releases that did not surface in great numbers in America. Among these collections were *The Box Set* (five LPs put out by Dick James Music) in 1979, *Lady Samantha* in 1980, *The Superior Sound of Elton John* in 1984, and *The Very Best of Elton John* in 1990.

Singles

1965	"Come Back Baby" by Bluesology in Britain
1966	"Mr. Frantic" by Bluesology in Britain
1968	"I've Been Loving You" in Britain
1969	"Lady Samantha"
1969	"It's Me That You Need" in Britain
1970	"From Denver to L.A."
1970	"Border Song"
1970	"Rock and Roll Madonna" in Britain
1970	"Your Song"
1971	"Friends"
1971	"Levon"
1972	"Tiny Dancer"
1972	"Rocket Man"
1972	"Honky Cat"
1972	"Crocodile Rock"
1973	"Daniel"
1973	"Saturday Night's Alright (for Fighting)"
1973	"Goodbye Yellow Brick Road"
1973	"Step into Christmas"
1974	"Bennie and the Jets"
1974	"Don't Let the Sun Go Down on Me"
1974	"The Bitch Is Back"
1974	"Lucy in the Sky with Diamonds"
1975	"Philadelphia Freedom"
1975	"Someone Saved My Life Tonight"
1975	"Island Girl"
1976	"Grow Some Funk of Your Own"/"I Feel Like a Bullet"
1976	"Don't Go Breaking My Heart" (duet)
1976	"Sorry Seems to Be the Hardest Word"
1977	"Bite Your Lip (Get up and Dance)"
1978	"Ego"
1978	"Part-Time Love"
1979	"Song for Guy"
1979	"Mama Can't Buy You Love"
1979	"Victim of Love"
1979	"Johnny B. Goode"
1980	"Little Jeannie"
1980	"Don't You Wanna Play This Game No More"
1981	"Nobody Wins"
1981	"Chloe"
1982	"Empty Garden"
1982	"Blue Eyes"

1982	"Ball & Chain"
1983	"I'm Still Standing"
1983	"Kiss the Bride"
1983	"I Guess That's Why They Call It the Blues"
1984	"Sad Songs (Say So Much)"
1984	"Who Wears These Shoes?"
1984	"In Neon"
1985	"That's What Friends Are For" (group recording)
1985	"Act of War"
1985	"Wrap Her Up"
1986	"Nikita"
1986	"Heartache All Over the World"
1987	"Flames of Paradise" (duet)
1987	"Candle in the Wind" (live)
1988	"Take Me to the Pilot" (live)
1988	"I Don't Wanna Go on with You Like That"
1988	"A Word in Spanish"
1989	"Through the Storm" (duet)
1989	"Healing Hands"
1989	"Sacrifice"
1990	"Club at the End of the Street"
1990	"You Gotta Love Someone"
1991	"Don't Let the Sun Go Down on Me" (live duet)
1992	"The One"
1992	"Runaway Train" (duet)
1992	"The Last Song"
1993	"Simple Life"
1993	"True Love" (duet)
1994	"Don't Go Breaking My Heart" (duet)
1994	"Can You Feel the Love Tonight?"
1994	"Circle of Life"
1995	"Believe"
1995	"Made in England"

Dodger Stadium: On October 25-26, 1975, Elton became the first rock star to play the Los Angeles venue since The Beatles in 1966. Writer Robert Hilburn described it as "Elton's finest hour." Elton returned to the stadium for a concert stand with Eric Clapton in 1992.

Dogs: Elton is a dog man, not a cat man. He has had many as pets, including Thomas, whom he purchased from the Battersea Dogs Home in London. During his recovery in the 1990s, Elton took Thomas for long walks in Holland Park.

Dogs in the Kitchen: A topic of Elton legend, the poetic lyric appears in a scrapbook that accompanies *Captain Fantastic and the Brown Dirt Cowboy.* Not set to music, the poem has been the focus of fan curiosity.

Drake, Nick: Elton made demo recordings of Drake's work in the late 1960s on what is known as the *Saturday Sun* sessions.

Duck, Ian: A member of Hookfoot, which backed Elton early in his career, Duck played harmonica on "Son of Your Father."

Dudgeon, Gus: An Englishman, Dudgeon was to Elton John what George Martin was to The Beatles: a producer who developed a trademark sound, helped bring his artist to a huge audience, and established a musical yardstick against which later albums would be measured. Dudgeon produced Elton's most successful work, including all but one chart-topping album and single in America. He started in music in the early 1960s as a tape operator at London's popular Olympic Studios. Dudgeon worked with such prominent groups as the Rolling Stones and the Zombies. Stones producer Andrew Oldham served as his mentor. By 1966 Dudgeon was a studio engineer at Decca Records, where he played a hand in the hit "Sha La La La Lee" by Small Faces. Two years later, he left Decca to pursue a career as a producer, hitching up with The Bonzo Dog Doo-Dah Band for the *Doughnut in Granny's Greenhouse* album. He also produced The Strawbs and Magna Carta (both included Rick Wakeman), Michael Chapman, Locomotive, and Sounds Nice. But it was his association with David Bowie that led him to Elton. In 1969 Steve Brown and Elton launched a search for a producer and arranger to handle his second album. They had chosen arranger Paul Buckmaster for his work on Bowie's *Space Oddity.* Buckmaster suggested Dudgeon. Through his celebrated association with Elton, Dudgeon inspired a generation of younger producers (among them, Don Was and Greg Penny). He introduced guitarist Davey Johnstone into Elton's band and cultivated the signature sound of Nigel Olsson's drums and the backing vocals. After *Blue Moves* in 1976, Elton changed musical directions and Dudgeon decided to leave the artist. They worked together again in the mid-1980s. During his career, Dudgeon has produced a varied group of musicians: Roy Orbison, Joan Armatrading, John Mayall, Chris Rea, John Miles, Kiki Dee, Marianne Faithful, the Chanter Sisters, and many others. Dudgeon admires the work of Van Morrison, the Beach Boys and John Lennon, the latter with whom he became friends in the 1970s.

Duets: With the success of 1976's "Don't Go Breaking My Heart," Kiki Dee and Elton John helped resurrect a pop-musical form that had nearly disappeared in the 1970s. Though their union ranks as his best-known duet, it is merely one of many he has recorded — even before his 1993 *Duets* album. Several have been hits. Here is a list of his musical marriages:
❖ Eric Clapton, "Runaway Train."
❖ Leonard Cohen, "Born to Lose."
❖ Kiki Dee, "Don't Go Breaking My Heart," "Loving You Is Sweeter Than Ever"

and "True Love."

❖ Marcella Detroit, "Ain't Nothing Like the Real Thing."

❖ Aretha Franklin, "Through the Storm."

❖ France Gall, "Les Aveux" and "Donner Pour Donner."

❖ Don Henley, "Shakey Ground."

❖ Millie Jackson, "Act of War."

❖ Nik Kershaw, "Old Friend."

❖ Gladys Knight, "Go On and On."

❖ k. d. lang, "Teardrops."

❖ George Michael, "Don't Let the Sun Go Down on Me."

❖ P.M. Dawn, "When I Think About Love (I Think About You)."

Maybe someday: Strong candidates — real and imagined — for future duets: Sting, Kiki Dee, Patti LaBelle, Billy Joel, James Taylor, Barbra Streisand, Freddie Mercury (via tape, a la Natalie and Nat King Cole on "Unforgettable"), Michael Stipe of R.E.M., Kiki Dee, Leon Russell, Bono, Neil Young, and Kiki Dee, his most frequent partner.

No duets: Elton has not recorded duets with these artists — and he very likely never will.

❖ David Bowie: The two glam rockers were scheduled for a joint concert in 1983. But it was cancelled because of their incompatibility.

❖ Barry Manilow: They are polite acquaintances, but not mutual fans. In a 1990 interview, Manilow described Elton as a good songwriter and a sad person who brings on his own misery.

❖ Prince: He once snubbed Elton, who had sought him out to deliver a compliment in person. "He just looked at me and walked away," said John in 1991. "I've hated the little bastard ever since."

❖ Bonnie Raitt, "Love Letters."

❖ Chris Rea, "If You Were Me."

❖ Cliff Richard, "Slow Rivers."

❖ Little Richard, "The Power."

❖ RuPaul, "Don't Go Breaking My Heart."

❖ Jennifer Rush, "Flames of Paradise."

❖ Cat Stevens, "Honeyman" (unreleased).

❖ Tammy Wynette, "A Woman's Needs."

❖ Paul Young, "I'm Your Puppet."

Three other songs that reached number one qualify as near-duets. Elton figured prominently in the sound of "Bad Blood" by Neil Sedaka, "Whatever Gets You Thru the Night" by John Lennon, and "That's What Friends Are For" by Dionne Warwick and Friends.

Duncan, Kirk: Before Elton worked with Taupin, he co-wrote songs with Duncan and Nicky James. They were affiliated with The Hollies's publishing arm, GRALTO, and, like Elton, hung out at Dick James Music. Duncan and John (then Reg Dwight) co-wrote "Who's Gonna Love You?" and others.

Duncan, Lesley: An early supporter and friend, she wrote "Love Song" (on *Tumbleweed Connection*) and sung backup at early concerts and on several albums. Elton has appeared on her releases as well.

Dwight, Reginald Kenneth: Elton's birth name, changed when he began his solo career. He was named for his mother's brother.

Dylan, Bob: Taupin idolized his work, calling him "my messiah" in his autobiography, *A Cradle of Haloes*. Early in his career, Elton also credited Dylan as an influence. Taupin expressed awe in 1970, their first year in America, when Elton arranged for Dylan to come backstage at a Fillmore East show. Twenty years later, producer Don Was persuaded Elton to appear on Dylan's *Under the Red Sky* album. He plays piano on "2 x 2."

E

East End Lights: The American fan magazine about Elton John has been publishing since 1990. For information, write *EEL*, Box 760B, New Baltimore, MI 48047.

Egan, Brian: Played acoustic guitar on "Burn Down the Mission."

Eli, Bobby: Played guitar on *The Complete Thom Bell Sessions*.

Emblow, Jack: Played accordian on "Razor Face."

Enuff z' Nuff: The group has often cited Elton as a major influence.

Estefan, Gloria: She covered "Don't Let the Sun Go Down on Me."

Estus, Deon: Played bass on *Ice on Fire*.

F

Family Dogg: Elton played piano on the group's 1969 hit, "Way of Life."

Farm Aid IV: In 1990, with friend Ryan White hours from death, a subdued Elton took the stage at the benefit organized by country star Willie Nelson. He broke down during "I'm Still Standing" and then dedicated "Candle in the Wind" to Ryan White.

Fay, Don: Played sax and flute on *Empty Sky*.

Feibelman, Maxine: Bernie Taupin's first wife. They married in 1971 and divorced in 1975. Taupin reflected on their breakup on the melancholy *Blue Moves* album.

Feldman, Victor: Played bass on *21 at 33* and *The Fox*.

Feliciano, Jose: While introducing Elton to American audiences in 1970, rock critics continually described his voice as similar to Jose Feliciano's — minus the accent. Feliciano later covered two John-Taupin works, "Take Me to the Pilot" and "Border Song."

Findley, Chuck: Played trumpet and trombone on *21 at 33*.

Fontana: Singles by the group Bluesology, with Elton, appeared on the label.

For Our Children: The Disney album benefited the Pediatric AIDS Foundation. Elton contributed "The Pacifier," for which Taupin had written lyrics. However, the song appeared as an instrumental.

Forbes, Bryan: He produced the 1973 television documentary *Elton John and Bernie Taupin Say Goodbye Norma Jean and Other Things*. A year earlier, Forbes, well known in the British movie industry, and wife Nanette became friends with Elton, who lived nearby. He doted on their daughters, and they introduced him to famous stars, like Groucho Marx and Mae West.

Fortina, Carl: Played accordian on "Sorry Seems to Be the Hardest Word."

Franklin, Aretha: She was among the first artists to cover a John-Taupin composition, "Border Song." Nearly two decades later, in 1989, she and Elton charted with a duet, "Through the Storm." An admirer of her work, he appeared on her 1993 TV special, where she and Elton sang "Border Song" and others.

Franks, Clive: He has been involved in Elton's career since the first album, *Empty Sky*, on which he served as tape operator. Franks's role has grown more important. On tour, he serves as sound engineer. He has co-produced three Elton John albums: *A Single Man*, *21 at 33*, and *The Fox*, playing bass on the first. Elton and Franks also co-produced several Rocket Record acts, working as Frank N. Stein Productions (Frank for Clive Franks and Stein for Steinway piano). As a footnote, Franks is heard whistling at the end of "Hymn 2000" on 1969's *Empty Sky*. Around that time, Franks was a member of two struggling U.K. groups, the Fables and the Claggers. Elton served as best man at his wedding.

Frome Court: During the late 1960s, Elton lived with his mother in this Pinner Road flat in Northwood Hills, England. He and lyricist Bernie Taupin bunked in one room, while writing their first songs.

Frost, David: Like newspaper critic Robert Hilburn, Frost rates as one of the media celebrities to whom Elton frequently turns. Since 1970, Frost has been Elton's chosen television interviewer. Over the years and on screen with Frost, Elton has admitted to being a bisexual and confessed to multiple drug addictions.

G

Gall, France: The French star recorded two duets with Elton in 1980, "Les Aveux" and "Donner Pour Donner," the former hitting number one in France. Her late husband was songwriter Michel Berger.

Galway, James: The flutist performed an Elton composition, "Basque," on his album *The Wind Beneath My Wings*. The song won Elton a 1992 Grammy for best instrumental composition, though written a decade earlier and never released by him.

Gambaccini, Paul: A friend and journalist who has interviewed Elton for radio and *Rolling Stone*, he is expected to co-author Elton's autobiography, when that time comes. In a 1980 British TV interview, Gambaccini tested Elton's reputation as a quick songwriter. Elton met the challenge, quickly setting to music the poem "No Man Is an Island." In the same chat, he played bits from three unreleased songs: "Free the People," "Basque," and Reach Out to Me."

Gaynor, Mel: The Simple Minds drummer played on *Ice on Fire*.

Geffen: After founding his own record label, David Geffen signed Elton on September 21, 1980, luring him away from MCA. "It was six years of pure hell," Elton told the *Boston Globe* in 1988, "and I hope I never see that bearded (bleep) again." Elton released six albums and one greatest hits collection on Geffen. But the experience left him frustrated. The albums rated among his worst selling, due partly to poor promotion. Geffen became heavily involved in the recordings, removing songs from albums and directing Elton to reunite his old band. Lyricist Gary Osborne blamed Geffen for ending his working relationship with Elton. In 1983, Geffen insisted on changes. "It became a big plan," said Osborne. "Geffen seriously got worried." According to Osborne, Geffen felt that the way to boost Elton's sales was to bring back the old team: lyricist Bernie Taupin and band members Davey

Johnstone, Nigel Olsson, and Dee Murray. The result was *Too Low for Zero*.

Gielgud, Sir John: The knighted actor duetted with Elton on "Me and My Shadow" in December 1984 onstage at Drury Lane Theatre in London. The occasion was a performance of *The Mother Goose Play* to benefit a children's theater organization in which Elton has been active since 1972.

Glasses: By the time he was 13, Reg was wearing fashionable glasses to emulate Buddy Holly and Hank B. Marvin of Cliff Richard's Drifters. Reg grew increasingly nearsighted, and the eyeglasses became a necessity. The spectacles, of course, became part of Elton's persona as the gaudy prince of pop. Press reports put his collection in the hundreds. He certainly has demonstrated an appetite for unusual eyewear. When he cleared out his house in a 1988 auction and sold his stage wear and other items, seventy-five pairs of eyeglasses went to high bidders. The most unusual of the batch were created by LA Eyeworks in California. Elton continues to wear colorful specs, but the frames are less elaborate now.

> **Ostentatious eyewear**: Five pairs of glasses worth remembering.
> ❖ E-L-T-O-N lighted frames.
> ❖ Black grand pianos with pink and blue lenses.
> ❖ Palm trees.
> ❖ White feather glasses.
> ❖ Clouds with blue, yellow, and pink lenses.

Glover, Dave: A member of Hookfoot, he played bass on *Madman Across the Water* and *Tumbleweed Connection*.

Goldberg, Whoopi: They traded favors in 1992. He appeared on her short-lived TV talk show, and she performed at an AIDS benefit in New York (singing "Jumpin' Jack Flash" with him).

Gomez, Leroy: Played sax on "Social Disease."

Goon Show: A big fan of the classic British TV show, Elton bought the old scripts for the comedy in April 1981. In earlier days, he often mimicked the characters. Peter Sellers, an idol, starred in the show.

GRALTO: The Hollies publishing company of Graham Nash, Allan Clarke, and Tony Hicks thought it had a deal to handle Reg Dwight's songwriting. But the firm lost out when Dwight and Bernie Taupin signed with Dick James in the late 1960s.

Grammys: Elton has won four Grammys, one in 1986 for singing on Dionne Warwick's "That's What Friends Are For," another for his role in the Prince's Trust recording, another in 1992 for writing an instrumental, "Basque," performed by James Galway, and in 1995 for best male pop performance for "Can You Feel the

Love Tonight?" Elton has been critical of the awards ceremony for two decades, calling it a farce. His work has collected nominations in major categories. *Elton John* (1970), *Goodbye Yellow Brick Road* (1973), *Caribou* (1974), and *Captain Fantastic and the Brown Dirt Cowboy* (1975) contended for album of the year honors. "Daniel," "Don't Go Breaking My Heart," "Blue Eyes," "Restless," "Candle in the Wind," "The One," "Mama Can't Buy You Love," and "Don't Let the Sun Go Down on Me" (as a live duet) received nominations for vocal performance.

Green, Colin: Played guitar on *Elton John*.

Greenaway, Roger: He and songwriting partner Roger Cook served as mentors to Reg Dwight when they worked for Dick James Music. He recorded demos of their songs.

Grenada: The small nation issued a $1 Elton John stamp in the mid-1980s. His was one of a series on rock stars.

Guest appearances: Aside from his own songs and albums, Elton has lent his musical talents to other artists. This list includes songs he contributed to as a session player in the 1960s and, later, as a superstar.

❖ Rick Astley, *Free*, 1991. Plays on "Behind the Smile" and "Wonderful You."

❖ Kevin Ayers, *Sweet Deceiver*, 1973. Plays piano on "Guru Banana" and "Circular Letter."

❖ Long John Baldry, *It Ain't Easy*, 1971. Plays piano on side two. *Everything Stops for Tea*, 1972. Sings backup on "Come Back Again," "Wild Mountain Thyme," "Iko, Iko," and "Seventh Son."

❖ Barron Knights, "Here Come the Olympic Games," 1968. Plays piano.

❖ Blue, *Another Night Time Flight*, 1977. Plays piano, using an alias, Redget Buntovan.

❖ Jon Bon Jovi, *Blaze of Glory*, 1990. Plays on "Billy Get Your Guns" and "Dyin' Ain't Much of a Livin'," singing backup on the latter.

❖ Jackson Browne, *For Everyman*, 1973. Plays piano on "Redneck Friend."

❖ The Chanter Sisters, *Birds of a Feather*, 1970. Plays piano. The album contains three John-Taupin songs, including "Take Me to the Pilot."

❖ China, *China*, 1977. Sings on "Shameful Disgrace."

❖ Kiki Dee, *Loving and Free*, 1973. Plays piano and sings on several tracks, including a non-album B-side, "The Last Good Man in My Life." *Perfect Timing*, 1981. Duets on "Loving You Is Sweeter Than Ever."

❖ Lonnie Donegan, *Puttin' on the Style*, 1976. Plays on the title track and "Diggin' My Potatoes."

❖ Lesley Duncan, *Sing Children Sing*, 1971, and *Moon Bathing*, 1975.

❖ Bob Dylan, *Under the Red Sky*, 1990. Plays piano on "2 x 2."

❖ Family Dogg, "Way of Life," 1969. Plays piano.

❖ Aretha Franklin, *Through the Storm*, 1989. Duets on title track.

❖ George Harrison, *Cloud Nine*, 1987. Plays on title track, "When We Was Fab," "Devil's Radio," "This Is Love" and "Wreck of Hesperus."

❖ The Hollies, "He Ain't Heavy, He's My Brother," 1969. Backing vocals and piano. "Perfect Lady Housewife," 1970. Backing vocals and organ. "I Can't Tell the Bottom from the Top," 1970. Plays piano.

❖ Davey Johnstone, *Smiling Face*, 1973. Plays piano on "Keep Right On."

❖ Tom Jones, "Delilah," 1968, and "Daughter of Darkness," 1970. Backing vocals on both.

❖ John Lennon, *Walls and Bridges*, 1974. Plays and sings on "Whatever Gets You Thru the Night" and "Surprise, Surprise."

❖ Eddie Murphy, *Love's Alright*, 1992. One of many guests to sing on "Yeah."

❖ Gary Neuman, *Radio Heart*, 1987. Plays on "Strange Thing" and "The Victim."

❖ Olivia Newton-John, *The Rumour*, 1988. Plays and sings on the title track.

❖ Nigel Olsson, *Nigel Olsson*, 1975. Plays on "Only One Woman" and sings on the song's B-side, "In Good Time," written by Davey Johnstone. *Changing Tides*, 1980. Plays on "Saturday Night."

❖ Jennifer Rush, *Heart over Mind*, 1987. Duets on "Flames of Paradise."

❖ Brian and Brenda Russell, *Word Called Love*, 1976. Plays and sings on "Tell Me When the Whistle Blows."

❖ Saxon, *Rock the Nation*, 1986. He plays on "Party 'Til You Puke" and "Northern Lady."

❖ Scaffold, "Gin Gan Goolie," 1969. Plays piano.

❖ Neil Sedaka, *The Hungry Years*, 1975. Sings on "Bad Blood." *Steppin' Out*, 1976. Sings on title track.

❖ Ringo Starr, *Goodnight Vienna*, 1974. Plays piano on "Snookeroo."

❖ Rod Stewart, *Smiler*, 1974. Plays piano and sings on "Let Me Be Your Car."

❖ Bernie Taupin, *He Who Rides the Tiger*, 1980. Sings on "Love (The Barren Desert)." *Tribe*, 1987. Sings on "Citizen Jane" and "Billy Fury."

❖ Dionne Warwick, *Friends*, 1985. Sings on "That's What Friends Are For."

❖ Wham!, *Music from the Edge of Heaven*, 1986. Plays on "The Edge of Heaven." Few details are available, but Elton also participated in sessions by the Mike Sammes Singers, Rita Bateman, Bobby Bruce, Roger Cook and Roger Greenaway, Simon Dupree, the Ladybirds, and Picketty Witch.

Guest artists: Elton has often asked other artists to appear on his recordings. These musicians and singers accepted the offer. Also noted are the albums on which they appeared. We excluded the *Duets* album:

❖ Beach Boys members on *Caribou*, *Blue Moves*, *21 at 33*, and *Reg Strikes Back*.

❖ The Brecker Brothers on *Blue Moves*.

❖ Paul Carrack of Squeeze and Mike and The Mechanics on *Made in England*.

❖ Rev. James Cleveland and choir on *The Fox* and *Blue Moves*.

❖ David Crosby and Graham Nash on *Blue Moves*.

❖ Daryl Dragon of The Captain and Tennille on *Blue Moves*.

❖ David Gilmour of Pink Floyd on *The One*.

❖ Eagles Don Henley, Glen Frey and Timothy B. Schmit on *21 at 33*.

❖ Herbie Flowers, known for his work with David Bowie, T. Rex, and Sly and the Family Stone, on bass on *Tumbleweed Connection*, *A Single Man*, and *Madman Across the Water*.

❖ Freddie Hubbard, jazz saxophonist, on *Reg Strikes Back*.

❖ Nik Kershaw on *Ice on Fire*.

❖ LaBelle, a female group headed by Patti LaBelle, on *Rock of the Westies*.

❖ John Lennon (alias Dr. Winston O'Boogie) on "Lucy in the Sky with Diamonds."

❖ George Michael on *Ice on Fire*.

❖ Peter Noone of Herman's Hermits on *21 at 33*.

❖ Jean-Luc Ponty, who plays electric violin, on *Honky Chateau*.

❖ Queen members Roger Taylor and John Deacon on *Ice on Fire* and *Leather Jackets*.

❖ Mick Ronson of David Bowie's Spiders on an alternate version of "Madman Across the Water."

❖ David Sanborn on *Blue Moves*.

❖ Sister Sledge on *Ice on Fire*.

❖ The Spinners on *The Complete Thom Bell Sessions*.

❖ Dusty Springfield on *Tumbleweed Connection* and *Caribou*.

❖ Toni Tennille on *Caribou*, *Blue Moves*, and *21 at 33*.

❖ Toto members on *A Single Man*, *21 at 33*, and *Jump Up!*

❖ Pete Townshend on *Jump Up!* and *Reg Strikes Back*.

❖ Rick Wakeman on *Madman Across the Water*.

❖ Stevie Wonder on *Too Low for Zero*.

Hair: Elton's premature balding became evident in the early 1970s, around age 25. For several years, as concert photos testify, he did not try to hide it. That changed. By age 30, he was nearly bald and finding increasing comfort in hats. That lasted through the 1980s, despite a couple of painful hair transplants, which left plugs of hair atop his head, for a while, anyway. His hair has never been much of a fashion statement. Through most of the 1970s, it was nondescript, mainly shaggy. Later, he went through a series of styles: closely cropped in the early 1980s, shoulder length in the mid-1980s and died platinum by the end of the decade. After confronting his drug and alcohol abuse, Elton launched the 1990s with a $27,000 hair weave. At a public appearance in Boston in 1993, he made note of his new hair. "No more fucking hats," he said.

Mad Hatters: Throughout his career, Elton has worn hats. As a connoisseur, he went through stages and styles:
❖ Scottish tams, late 1970s, as seen on the cover of *The Complete Thom Bell Sessions*.
❖ Boaters, mid 1980s. He owned dozens and wore one to his wedding.
❖ Baseball caps. Favorites have included those of the Los Angeles Dodgers, Atlanta Braves, and Boy of London.
❖ Jeweled Nehru hats. His last pre-weave studio photos featured gem-encrusted creations.

Halcox, Pat: Played trumpet on *A Single Man*.

Hall and Oates: The pop duo gave a soulful flavor to "Philadelphia Freedom" on the *Two Rooms* album. Initially, Elton disliked the rendition. But in later concerts, he often reinterpreted the song in similar fashion.

Hall, Larry: Played flugelhorn and trumpet on *21 at 33*.

Halley, Bob: Halley's role has evolved from chauffeur in 1974 to live-in companion to personal assistant and confidant. He travels with the entertainer and handles a myriad of personal duties.

Harker, Roland: Played guitar on *Elton John*.

Harrison, George: The 1988 video for "When We Was Fab" included a walk-on appearance by Elton. He was part of the all-star band that played on the ex-Beatle's *Cloud Nine* album.

Hatot, Alain: Played sax on *Honky Chateau* and *Don't Shoot Me, I'm Only the Piano Player*.

Haymes, Stephanie: Bernie Taupin's third and current wife. They married in 1993, with Elton performing a ballad that he and Taupin wrote for the occasion.

He Who Rides the Tiger: Taupin's 1980 solo album, on which Elton appeared.

Hentschel, David: The studio engineer helped develop the beginning of "Funeral for a Friend" and played synthesizers on *Honky Chateau*, *Captain Fantastic and the Brown Dirt Cowboy*, *Caribou*, and *Goodbye Yellow Brick Road*. He has also produced the band Genesis, as well as others

Hercules: Elton's middle name and the title of a 1972 song.

Heron, Mike: In 1970 Elton recorded demos of Heron's songs as part of the *Saturday Sun* session. Earlier, Heron belonged to the Incredible String Band.

Hey, Jerry: Played flugelhorn on *21 at 33*.

Hicks, Clive: Played guitar on *Elton John*.

Hilburn, Robert: The *Los Angeles Times* music critic helped launch Elton John in America, based on his strong review of the Troubadour shows in 1970. In return, Elton has granted him access enjoyed by few other journalists.

Hillman, Connie Pappas: She heads the star's American management team and has played a key role since the early 1970s, often carrying the title of U.S. tour producer. Her duties are much more varied, though. Married to Chris Hillman, formerly of The Byrds, Hillman avoids the limelight.

Hodes, Lenny: The Los Angeles publisher loved Elton's early work and introduced it to Russ Regan of UNI Records, who also supported the young songwriter.

Hollies, The: Elton contributed piano work to the group's recording sessions in 1969 and 1970. Members of the band founded GRALTO Music, which had an early financial interest in Elton's songwriting.

Holly, Steve: Played drums on *A Single Man* and percussion on *Jump Up!*

Hollywood star: On November 21, 1975, Elton received his star on Hollywood's Walk of Fame. His star is near the front of the famed Mann's Chinese Theater.

Honors: Should you find yourself embroiled in an argument over rock-star achievements in America, this pro-Elton ammunition might prove helpful. Elton...

❖ was the top-selling artist of the 1970s (seventh in the 1980s);

❖ is second only to Elvis for number of Top 40 hits and most gold albums;

❖ was the first artist to have two consecutive albums enter the charts at number one;

❖ was the first star to hit number one with a greatest hits package;

❖ is second to The Beatles for most consecutive number one albums;

❖ and accounted for 2 percent of all global record sales in 1975.

> **Beam him up, Scotty**: Perhaps the weirdest honor of all came in the fall of 1977. "Rocket Man" was voted best science fiction song at the National Science Fiction Awards. Taupin accepted the award. And — brace yourself — William Shatner performed the song.

Hookfoot: The band was comprised of friends of Elton who played on his early albums: Caleb Quaye, Roger Pope, Ian Duck, and Dave Glover. In October 1969 the group signed with Dick James Music and cut several critically acclaimed albums and singles. The band's nucleus also worked under the name Mr. Bloe, a group that scored a major British hit in July 1970. In the liner notes to Hookfoot's 1971 album, Elton proclaimed the group as "potentially the best new English band." Hookfoot toured briefly with Elton and, at his request, backed up Long John Baldry on an album co-produced by Elton. The group's name came from Pope's habit of hooking his left foot around his high hat to keep it from sliding. Hookfoot recorded several albums before splitting up in January 1974. A year later, Quaye and Pope joined Elton's band.

Horn, Jim: Played sax on *The Fox* and sax and piccolo on *21 at 33*.

Hornsby, Bruce: The rock pianist cites Elton and Leon Russell as musical inspirations. As a lounge act in the mid-1970s, Hornsby did an Elton take-off, complete with gaudy costumes. They met each other backstage at a London media appearance. In October 1988 he joined Elton onstage in New York to play "Saturday Night's Alright (for Fighting)" and performed with Elton at a 1992 AIDS benefit. "Elton's music has always meant a lot to me," he said. He also appeared on *Two*

Rooms, offering a jazzy take on "Madman Across the Water."

Howard, James Newton: Of all the musicians once affiliated with Elton, James Newton Howard may enjoy the greatest success in his own right. Born in California in 1948, Howard grew up in Los Angeles and started studying classical piano at age four. His grandmother played violin for the Pittsburgh Philharmonic. After high school, before finishing his studies at the University of Southern California, he joined Mama Lion, an L.A.-based rock band. As his reputation grew, Howard picked up work as a top session man, becoming aligned with many of the musicians who would later become the group Toto.

> **Music for the movies**: Films scored by James Newton Howard: *Alive, American Heart, Dave, Dying Young, Everybody's All American, Falling Down, Five Corners, Flatliners, French Kiss, Glengarry Glenross, Grand Canyon, Guilty by Suspicion, Head Office, Intersection, Junior, Just Cause, King Ralph, Major League, Nobody's Fool, Outbreak, Pretty Woman, Promised Land, Some Girls, Tap, The Fugitive, The Prince of Tides, Three Men and a Little Lady, Tough Guys, Waterworld,* and *Wild Cats.*

In 1974, Howard released a self-titled instrumental album that showcased his keyboard wizardry. Session work with Carly Simon, Diana Ross, and Harry Nilsson landed him a spot in Melissa Manchester's band in 1974 and 1975. But a session for Ringo Starr's *Goodnight Vienna* album provided a bigger break for Howard. Elton also appeared on the album, taking note of Howard's talent. In 1975, the keyboardist became part of Elton's new band, recording on *Rock of the Westies*. His relationship with Elton grew. On 1976's *Blue Moves*, Howard began writing with Elton ("One Horse Town"). His arrangement on "Tonight" remains one of the album's highlights. Howard worked with Eric Carmen, Leo Sayer, Kiki Dee, and Boz Scaggs before teaming up with Elton again in 1980 and 1981 for a tour and albums. Sharing an admiration of jazz pianist Keith Jarrett, Howard and Elton even worked together on an instrumental album. At least four songs were finished for the project. Though never fully realized, the promise of such a collaboration was demonstrated on the beautiful "Carla/Etude" on *The Fox*. By the mid-1980s, Howard was producing, arranging, or co-writing with Randy Newman, Chaka Kahn, Earth, Wind and Fire, Barbra Streisand, Bob Seger and Rickie Lee Jones. In 1986 Howard rejoined Elton to conduct the Melbourne Symphony Orchestra for the *Live in Australia* album. He also released a second solo album, *James Newton Howard and Friends*, featuring members of Toto. Married briefly to actress Rosanna Arquette, Howard had already launched his second career — the one in which he would most make his mark: scoring feature films. His first solo effort, *Head Office*, revealed promise and brought work. Howard has scored more than two dozen films, receiving Grammy nominations for *The Fugitive* and *The Prince of Tides* (during which he became romantically involved with director Streisand). "Elton's piano playing is always phenomenal," said Howard. "I didn't know how good he was until I worked with him. He's a rhythm-chord player, using five-note chords and vocals a la Leon Russell." Howard and Elton remain friends, though they have worked together infrequently since 1986.

Huntley, Gordon: Played steel guitar on "Country Comfort."

Hurdie, Les: Played bass guitar on *Elton John*.

Hype: In promoting his own albums, Elton, like other artists, has not shied from hyperbole. He has compared many of his 1980s albums favorably to the classic *Goodbye Yellow Brick Road*. Consider these comments by the star himself:

❖ *Honky Chateau*: "I don't want to say it's the best thing I've ever done because that's what I said and felt about *Madman* but people didn't agree."

❖ *Blue Moves*: "I just love the album."

❖ *Too Low for Zero*: "There have only been a few times I've ever been totally confident about an album — *Yellow Brick Road* and maybe *Captain Fantastic*. And I've got that feeling again with this one."

❖ *Live in Australia*: "It was a very special album to me."

❖ *Reg Strikes Back*: "I feel a lot of the album is like the *Yellow Brick Road* era. ... There are things I like on every one of my albums. But there are only a few of them I think are good all the way through. This one sounds good all the way through."

❖ *Sleeping with the Past*: "I think (it) is the strongest record we've ever made. We went back to our roots and tried to do something special, and I feel we succeeded."

❖ *The One*: "This album is the best one I've done since *Captain Fantastic*. ... No matter how much it sells, for me, in my heart, this is a great album."

❖ *Made in England:* "To me, the album sounds as if it could have been made in that purple patch in the 1970s when I had all that energy."

I

Indigo Girls: The acoustic group credits Elton as an influence and has performed "Mona Lisas and Mad Hatters" in concert.

Influences: When auctioned off in 1993, Elton's record collection rated as one of the world's premier private holdings. Since boyhood, he has savored — and hoarded — the work of others. Even now, it is not uncommon for him to drop a few thousand dollars on a visit to an Atlanta record store. Like all musicians, he has drawn from the music he loves. Many artists have influenced his songwriting. In the first tier would be Leon Russell, the Beach Boys, The Beatles, the Rolling Stones, and The Band. Over time, he has identified numerous artists as influences, including Aretha Franklin, Joni Mitchell, Dusty Springfield, Little Feat, Motown acts, Randy Newman, Laura Nyro, Redbone, Jackson Browne, Sting, James Taylor, Procul Harum, Leonard Cohen, and Creedence Clearwater Revival. Similarly, Elton has influenced a generation of performers, among them George Michael, Axl Rose, Liz Phair, Jon Bon Jovi, Branford Marsalis, and Nik Kershaw.

Piano Men (and Woman): Ten contemporary pianists whose work greatly influenced the style of Elton John:
- ❖ Winifred Atwell.
- ❖ Ray Charles.
- ❖ Fats Domino.
- ❖ Garth Hudson of The Band.
- ❖ Keith Jarrett.
- ❖ Jerry Lee Lewis.
- ❖ Ramsey Lewis.
- ❖ Little Richard.
- ❖ Leon Russell.
- ❖ George Shearing.

Elton's favorite classical composers: Chopin, Bach, Brahms, Handel, Albinoni, Mahler, Prokofiev, Sibelius, and Tchaikovsky.

❖ **Believe it or not!** How much do artists influence each other? In 1972 Leon Russell released a song titled "Don't Let the Sun Go Down." Two years later, Elton had a hit with a similarly titled song. A decade later, Nik Kerhsaw's biggest hit had a strikingly familiar name: "I Won't Let the Sun Go Down on Me."

Interview with the Vampire: In 1986, Elton and Taupin began writing songs for a Broadway musical based on Anne Rice's Vampire Trilogy novels. They penned three or four tracks before the project was scrapped in a legal dispute. The songs remain unreleased. Said Rice, the author, "Elton John wanted to make a musical based on *Interview with the Vampire*, and he wouldn't proceed until he knew I was willing." They met at one of his concerts, where Rice gave the blessing. But because Lorimar Pictures owned the stage rights, the project was put on hold. Then Lorimar was bought by Warner Brothers, delaying the project yet again. Finally, in 1994, a major movie was released, starring Tom Cruise and Brad Pitt. However, Elton had no involvement.

Interviews: After a quarter century in the business, Elton has granted hundreds of interviews to print journalists. From such a body of literature, a handful rate as essential reading for the more-than-casual fan.

❖ *Rolling Stone*, June 10, 1971: "I've got no time for love affairs."

❖ *Rolling Stone*, Nov. 21, 1974: "I won't be around so much. I want to do other things."

❖ *Time*, July 7, 1975: "I didn't start enjoying life until I was 21."

❖ *Playboy*, January 1976: "If you can't solve your own problems, then you're in a bum way."

❖ *Rolling Stone*, Oct. 7, 1976: "I haven't met anyone I would like to settle down with — of either sex."

❖ *Los Angeles Times*, Aug. 23, 1992: "I got to the point where I didn't know how to speak to someone unless I had a nose full of cocaine."

Island Records: Lionel Conway and Muff Winwood, two Elton John boosters with strong ties to Island Records, approached chief Chris Blackwell several times with Elton John demos in the 1960s. Blackwell reportedly offered Elton roughly $15,000 to sign with Island. Both friends also tried to help Elton break his contract with Dick James. In 1969 and 1970 Elton did demo sessions for Island Records projects. By December 1969 Dick James had decided to go ahead with a second *Elton John* album, scuttling the likelihood of Elton jumping. Twenty-six years later, Elton's Rocket Records company became affiliated with Island Records.

Israel: Elton created an international incident in June 1993 when, after being treated rudely at an Israeli airport and mobbed at a hotel, he stormed out of the country, forcing the cancellation of a concert. Feeling snubbed, Israeli officials, including the prime minister's office, blasted the singer. At the urging of the British ambassador, Elton returned to Israel to perform. He apologized and, recognizing he had been portrayed as a pampered star by the Israeli press, opened his show with "The Bitch Is Back."

J

Jackson, Michael: On the surface, few similarities exist between the careers of Michael Jackson and Elton John. There are interesting coincidences, though. Aside from musically dominating the charts in consecutive decades, the two stars shared a friendship with Ryan White, a boy who died of an AIDS-related illness. Also, at different times, they employed Norman Winter as their press agent. Each singer once lived in the Spanish mansion in Los Angeles where entertainment executive Jose Menendez and his wife were murdered in 1989 by their sons. Further, both Jackson and John count actress Elizabeth Taylor as a close friend. In 1993, through Taylor, Elton recommended a counselor to help Jackson through a reported drug addiction and he also allowed him to stay at one of his English residences.

Jackson, Millie: The R&B artist duetted with Elton on "Act of War," after Tina Turner rejected the offer.

James, Dick: A London music publisher, James was credited with helping discover The Beatles — recognition he admitted was only half accurate. But he did play a major role. That good fortune — enough to make one career — struck twice for James. In 1967 he found out that a young songwriter, Reg Dwight, was recording demos after hours in his studio. Caleb Quaye, a friend of Dwight and a James employee, was not charging the aspiring artist for studio time. James listened to Dwight's material and brought the young writer on staff. The Philips label released early singles by Reg Dwight, but balked at risking money on his first album, *Empty Sky*, to be released under his new name, Elton John. On February 28, 1968, James started his own self-named label and Elton and Bernie Taupin became its first official songwriters. With encouragement from employee Steve Brown, James grew to see potential in Elton John as a performer — rather than just a songwriter for other artists. Perhaps his biggest risk, in regard to Elton, was agreeing to pay for his relatively expensive and orchestrated first album and his introduction to America at the Troubadour in Los Angeles. James footed most of the bill, and it paid him back in ways he could not have envisioned. In the early 1970s, Elton's manager, John Reid, began having misgivings about James's contract with Elton and Taupin, a contract that kept James benefiting financially until 1976. Elton once described James as a father figure. "I'm sort of tied to Dick James for everything," Elton told *Jazz & Pop* magazine in 1971. "He's such an honest man and he looks after us both so well." That view would not last. Reid felt James was cheating Elton out of international royalties. Years after leaving James, they filed a lawsuit that put James, Elton, and Taupin on the witness stand. On January 29, 1986, the songwriters won an award that Elton's side estimated at $14 million. Within a week, James died of a heart attack. His son, Steven, blamed Elton for the death.

Jenkins, Karl: Played oboe on "Come Down in Time."

Joel, Billy: Joel's manager and producer, Michael Stewart, hoped to relaunch his artist in 1974 as a more masculine version of Elton John. Though some Elton fans have long contended that Joel has played off John's success, the two rock pianists have offered kind words about each other. They jammed together on "Lucy in the Sky with Diamonds" — with Debbie Gibson — at a 1988 Elton concert in New York. In 1994 and 1995, at Joel's urging, they conducted a joint U.S. stadium tour, titled "Face to Face." Joel even released a promotional single featuring a version of "Goodbye Yellow Brick Road." Both artists have hinted they might collaborate on a song.

Johnstone, Davey: No musician has been more involved in Elton's career than Johnstone, his lead guitarist. Since the late 1980s, he has also carried the title of music director. Born May 6, 1951, in Edinburgh, Scotland, Johnstone studied piano and violin as a child. At age 15, he had become active in a succession of folk groups: Carrick Folk, Fife Reivers, and Draught Porridge. He debated whether to pursue art in college. But by 1970 the lanky musician had established a reputation with Magna Carta, a London group that included Rick Wakeman (later of Yes). Producer Gus Dudgeon had worked with the band and been impressed by Johnstone's versatility. (He plays not only guitar, but mandolin, sitar, banjo, lute, and dulcimer.) Johnstone and Wakeman contributed to 1971's *Madman Across the Water*. But Johnstone might never have gotten the call had folk guitarist Michael Chapman worked out. A solo artist, Chapman appeared on one version of the title track, but found the experience so unenjoyable that Dudgeon could not convince him to return to the sessions. He turned to Johnstone. Later, Elton asked him to be a part of the band. After months of rehearsing, Johnstone joined Elton, Nigel Olsson, and

Solo album: *Smiling Face*, 1973. Songs: "Keep Right On," "Janine," "The Boatman," "Walking Out," "Our Dear Friend," "Island," "After the Dance," "You Are, I Am," "Smiling Face," "Beautiful One," "A Lovely Day," and "A Lark in the Morning with Mrs. McLeod."

Dee Murray onstage Feb. 5, 1972, with the Royal Philharmonic Orchestra. Primarily an acoustic musician, he polished his skills on electric guitar and produced scorching guitar riffs — like the ones on "Funeral for a Friend," "Saturday Night's Alright (for Fighting)," and "All the Girls Love Alice." But equally as memorable is his more subtle work on such songs as "Rocket Man," "Captain Fantastic and the Brown Dirt Cowboy," and "A Word in Spanish." Unlike Olsson and Murray, Johnstone has never been cut from Elton's band. He was absent from albums in the late 1970s and early 1980s, but it was not part of a purge. Johnstone worked with Alice Cooper and Meat Loaf (on *Dead Ringer*, the follow-up to *Bat Out of Hell*) rejoining Elton in 1982. He has been with

What about "Honky Cat"? As music director, Davey Johnstone helps Elton select the song lists for concerts. It's a no-win proposition. More than fifty Elton John singles have charted. But the average two-and-a-half-hour show features only twenty-seven songs. And since tours are designed to promote record sales, a few new songs are always part of the repertoire. That leaves little room for the obscurities that many dedicated fans crave. Further, Elton leans toward his Top 40 ballads, believing that the average fan pays to hear those hits. Johnstone explained the difficulty: "People are always saying why didn't you do 'Crocodile Rock' or why aren't you doing 'Goodbye Yellow Brick Road?' ... That's why it's such a problem to pick the songs."

him ever since. Unlike his earlier band mates, Johnstone has co-written songs with Elton. Among the more memorable ones: "I Guess That's Why They Call It the Blues," "Grow Some Funk of Your Own," "Cage the Songbird," "Passengers," "Wrap Her Up," "Snow Queen," and "Heavy Traffic." At Elton's invitation, Johnstone released a solo album, *Smiling Face*, in 1973 on the Rocket label. Four years later, still on Rocket, he and three others recorded and toured briefly as the group China. Neither release prospered. In 1991 Johnstone formed Warpipes, which included current and past Elton band members Nigel Olsson, Guy Babylon, and Bob Birch. (The failure of their label, Artful Balance, and subsequent litigation sidelined the group until 1995.) Though he has worked with such artists as Bob Seger, Barry Manilow, Stevie Nicks, and the Pointer Sisters, Johnstone will likely remain an integral part of Elton's sound. As music director, he enjoys considerable freedom, picking new band members, organizing rehearsals, dividing musical parts, and helping select concert songs. A married father and resident of California, Johnstone cites The Beatles, Rolling Stones, Jimi Hendrix, Barry McKenna, and John McLaughlin as musical influences. "I have worked with a lot of big, big names, but nobody can touch (Elton) in my mind," said Johnstone. "He is the most consistent and the best performer I have ever worked with."

Jones, Robin: Percussionist appeared on *Tumbleweed Connection*.

Jones, Tom: Elton sings back up on "Delilah," "Daughter of Darkness," and other songs released by Jones from 1968 to 1970.

Jorgenson, John: A member of The Hellecasters, Jorgenson, a guitarist, joined Elton's band in 1995, making his debut at the Commitment to Life awards ceremony in January. He was co-founder of the Desert Rose Band, a country band featuring Chris Hillman, husband of Connie Pappas Hillman, Elton's longtime American tour manager. Elton added a guitarist to help Davey Johnstone replicate the sound of the guitar-laden, 1995 album, *Made in England*.

Jullien, Ivan: Played trumpet on *Honky Chateau* and *Don't Shoot Me, I'm Only the Piano Player*.

K

Kanga, Skaila: Played harp on *Elton John*, *Tumbleweed Connection*, and *Too Low for Zero*.

Kershaw, Nik: The British guitarist describes Elton as "a hero." Kershaw, who has charted over a dozen times in England, said "Your Song" was the first record he purchased. In the mid-1980s, he worked with Elton on *Ice on Fire*. The two even toured together, with Kershaw as the opening act in Europe. In addition, they sang Kershaw's "Old Friend" on 1993's *Duets* album. Kershaw offered a musical nod to Elton in the song "I Won't Let the Sun Go Down on Me."

Key, Robert: A longtime member of Elton's management team, Key handles all non-American releases.

King, Billie Jean: An avid tennis fan, Elton met champion Billie Jean King at a party in 1973. He struck up a friendship with King, playing tennis with her and investing in her new enterprise, a world tennis league, which included the Philadelphia Freedoms, whom he later honored with a song. Their friendship has spanned decades. In September 1993, they co-hosted their first Smash Hits, a team tennis match to raise money for his AIDS foundation. Elton and King defeated Martina Navratilova and Bobby Riggs in an exhibition match. The two-day inaugural event included a concert by Elton and an auction at which the original lyrics sheet to "Skyline Pigeon" sold for $22,000 to Al Teller, president of MCA, who outbid King. The second Smash Hits, held in Boston in 1994, was less grand.

King Crimson: Elton auditioned to be lead singer of King Crimson in January 1968. He was booked to sing on the group's 1970 album, *In the Wake of Poseidon*, but the band disliked his vocals and hired Greg Lake instead.

King, Tony: A record producer and Apple Records employee, King brought together the Bread and Beer Band. The group of top session musicians, including Elton, recorded an album's worth of instrumentals in 1968 and 1969. King later became general manager of The Beatles' American operation of Apple Records. In 1973, John Reid convinced him to serve as executive vice president of Rocket Records. He retained that position into the 1980s when Rocket stopped promoting artists other than Elton.

Kinison, Sam: Elton stunned Kinison and organizers of the Rock Music Awards in 1990. Speaking on a live broadcast, Elton applauded friend Eric Clapton for winning a major award. But he lamented that Clapton had to share the stage with host Kinison, whom he described as "a pig." Elton reportedly disliked the comedian for his AIDS-related jokes. The singer used the same description for U.S. football coach Buddy Ryan, creating a minor controversy in the sports world.

Knebworth: In the summer of 1990, dozens of artists performed at Knebworth, England, to benefit Nordoff-Robbins Music Therapy and BRIT School for Performing Arts. The stars included Paul McCartney, Eric Clapton, Robert Plant, Genesis, Dire Straits, and Elton, whose live versions of "Sad Songs" and "Saturday Night's Alright (for Fighting)" are included on the two-CD Knebworth release.

L

LaBelle, Patti: Elton's friendship with LaBelle has its roots in 1965 when he played keyboards for Bluesology, which backed American artists touring in Europe. LaBelle played cards with the keyboardist, whom she knew as Reg Dwight, and cooked him meals after winning his money. In November 1974 Elton John was in Philadelphia for a concert at the Spectrum. He looked up Patti LaBelle, and, by phone, introduced himself as Reg Dwight and asked if they could get together. LaBelle was unaware that shy Reg Dwight had become Elton John. He had shed many pounds since his days in Bluesology and the costumes further hid his identity. She was shocked when she learned. Later, in 1975, Elton invited LaBelle to sing back up on *Rock of the Westies*.

Larkham, David: His designs played a major role in the look of Elton's albums until around 1974. Larkham, who once illustrated for newspapers, hooked up with Elton through mutual friend Steve Brown. Larkham, Mike Ross, and David Costa worked together on the design for *Goodbye Yellow Brick Road*. Though Larkham still runs a design firm, almost all of Elton's work goes through David Costa's company, Wherefore Art?

Lauper, Cyndi: A childhood fan of Elton, she paid subtle tribute on her autobiographical 1993 album, *Hat Full of Stars*. The song "Sally's Pigeons" contains references to "Tiny Dancer," a song that she has said always makes her cry. It may be coincidence — or not — but Taupin's 1995 "Blessed" plays off the words star and hat.

Laurence, Chris: Played acoustic guitar on "Indian Sunset," "Burn Down the Mission," and "Come Down in Time."

Lennon, John: The former Beatle became close friends with Elton in the 1970s after the younger artist had become a household name. They met in October 1973 in a Los Angeles studio where Lennon was recording with Phil Spector. Friend Tony King thought it would be wise for the new star to talk with a legend who had survived similar adulation. Elton admired Lennon. The two got along well. In July 1974 Lennon asked Elton to contribute to his *Walls and Bridges* album. He sang and played keyboards on "Surprises" and "Whatever Gets You Thru the Night." Lennon gave his blessing to Elton's plan to record "Lucy in the Sky with Diamonds" and "One Day at a Time." Elton convinced Lennon to join him at the Caribou studio in Colorado. Between asthma attacks resulting from the high altitude, Lennon (as Dr. Winston O'Boogie) put down guitar tracks on "Lucy..." From Lennon, Elton secured a promise. If *Walls and Bridges* hit number one, Lennon would appear onstage with Elton. "He didn't believe the album would ever do that well," Elton recalled. It did. Lennon performed on Thanksgiving Day in 1974 with Elton and his band. Racked with stage fright, Lennon was led to the edge of the stage by Bernie Taupin. It turned out to be Lennon's final live appearance. That show also rekindled the relationship between Lennon and Yoko Ono. In 1975 they named Elton godfather to son Sean. While on tour five years later, Elton included "Imagine" in his set, proudly announcing that friend John was back in the studio. On December 8, 1980, Lennon was murdered by Mark David Chapman. Manager John Reid broke the news of Lennon's death to Elton while on a flight from Brisbane to Melbourne, where Elton arranged a special service at St. Patrick's Cathedral in Australia. He read a lesson and sang the 23rd Psalm. Soon after, he wrote an instrumental, "The Man Who Never Died," including a faint line, "Imagine, he's the man who never died." Elton wrote three tributes to Lennon from 1981-82. One has not been released. The best known was "Empty Garden." The song struck an emotional high point when Elton performed it in 1982 in New York on the same stage where Lennon had last appeared. Elton found he could only play it with his eyes closed. Yoko Ono and Sean Lennon walked on stage as Elton finished the song. He heard the roar of the crowd, opened his eyes, and saw them. They embraced.

Lewis, Diana: Played and sang backup on *Madman Across the Water*.

Lewis, Jerry Lee: The southern star inspired Elton, who has described Lewis "as the best rock and roll pianist ever." In 1958 young Reg Dwight played "Great Balls of Fire" at a school talent show. (He performed it in concert in 1970 and 1980, as well.) In the 1970s Lewis asked Elton to make a guest appearance on an album. The younger star declined.

Liberty Records: The British company's 1967 advertisement for songwriters and musicians led to the pairing of lyricist Bernie Taupin with Reg Dwight.

Lindscott, Jody: The percussionist played on the American leg of the 1985-86 tour. She has worked with Robert Palmer, Don Henley, Paul McCartney, and others.

Linn, Roger: Played drum synthesizer on "Nobody Wins."

Live Aid: On July 13, 1985, music artists from throughout the world joined forces at Live Aid concerts in Philadelphia and England in an effort to feed the hungry in Ethiopia. Dozens of acts, from The Who to Paul McCartney, participated. Elton performed "Bennie and the Jets," "Don't Go Breaking My Heart" (with Kiki Dee), "I'm Still Standing," "Can I Get a Witness?," and "Rocket Man." He also played piano for George Michael, who sang "Don't Let the Sun Go Down on Me." The concert introduced his new band.

London, Mark: The American songwriter was working with lyricist Don Black in England in 1967 when Elton John was at Dick James Music. Elton recorded several demos of London-Black compositions. The duo's biggest song was "To Sir with Love." London works as a publisher, writer, and producer in Canada.

London Symphony Orchestra: Played on *Blue Moves* and *The Fox*.

Lopez, Dennis: Played percussion on *Elton John*.

Lord Choc Ice: Like Lady Choc Ice, Lord is a character Elton invented. He has used both names as aliases. One explanation is that the Lord and Lady are a proper, elderly English couple. Another story contends that they evolved from Ike and Tina Choc-Ice. A third traces the alias to an English dessert product, Chocolate English Ices, which the star enjoyed. Regardless, he has had fun with the pseudonyms, releasing a B-side track titled "Choc Ice Goes Mental" in 1983 and co-writing a song with Cher. The video to "I'm Still Standing" included a graffiti message in the background: "Choc Ice Lives." A 1993 program for the Smash Hits tennis benefit noted jokingly that Elton had won the "Choc Ice Award."

Lovelace, Linda: The porn star introduced Elton at his famed September 1973 Hollywood Bowl concert: "Ladies and gentlemen, please welcome the biggest, gigantic, most colossal ... Elton John!"

Lowther, Henry: Played trumpet on *A Single Man*.

Lukather, Steve: A member of Toto, Lukather played lead guitar on *21 at 33* and contributed to new songs recorded for *To be continued...*

Lulu: On her British television show in January and February 1969, Lulu performed six songs that were vying to represent the country in the Eurovision Song Contest. Among the finalists was the John-Taupin tune "I Can't Go on Living Without You." The competition became a national TV event drawing a quarter of the country's population. The viewing public chose the winner, "Boom-Bang-a-Bang." Lulu's version of the John-Taupin entry can be heard on a rare Eurovision release. In the 1980s, Lulu recorded another Elton John song, "I Don't Care."

Lustbader, Eric: Writing for *Cash Box*, he was the first journalist in America to peg Elton John as a future superstar. He made the prediction on the basis of a 1969 imported LP, *Empty Sky*, before the artist set the music world abuzz with his 1970 appearances. Lustbader has become a successful novelist.

Mackie, Bob: The Hollywood designer developed some of the entertainer's most outrageous costumes.

Madame Tussaud Museum: Elton was the first rock star since The Beatles to be immortalized in wax. His likeness has been moved to the Rock Circus, a London museum in Picadilly Square.

Mandel, Fred: A Canadian keyboardist, Mandel served as music director for Alice Cooper, belonged to the jazz group Lighthouse, and worked with Pink Floyd, Queen, Cheap Trick, Supertramp, and Kiki Dee. He played a key role in Elton's band from 1984 to 1990, touring and appearing on several albums. Guitarist Davey Johnstone, who puts together Elton's bands, worked with Mandel while both were with Cooper.

Marsalis, Branford: The jazz artist paid tribute to Elton on his 1994 release, *Buckshot LaFonque*. He not only covered "Mona Lisas and Mad Hatters" but also wrote and recorded two brief tunes, "Shoot the Piano Player" and "Sorry, Elton."

Martin, George: After the release of Elton's first album, *Empty Sky*, Martin, known for his work with The Beatles, was asked to produce the young artist's next album. Martin agreed, but he sought more control than Elton's handlers felt comfortable giving. The deal fell apart. Eventually, Gus Dudgeon was selected to produce the album, with Paul Buckmaster arranging. On 1995's *Made in England*, Martin contributed an arrangement for the song "Latitude." The album was recorded at Martin's AIR Lyndhurst studio.

Martyn Ford Orchestra: Played on *Blue Moves*.

Marx, Groucho: The famed comedian took to Elton when they met in the early 1970s. Marx cracked jokes about Elton's name, prompting the singer to respond, "Don't shoot me, I'm only the piano player." The response became the title for John's 1973 album. The cover featured Elton's name on a theater marquee. Off to the side was a poster advertising the Marx Brothers' movie *Go West*.

Mattacks, Dave: Played drums on *Ice on Fire* and *Leather Jackets*.

Mattea, Kathy: The country star recorded "Ball & Chain."

MCA: In America, Elton has spent most of his career on the MCA label. It has been a colorful on-again, off-again relationship. His first U.S. releases appeared on UNI, an MCA subsidiary. In June 1974, after the mammoth success of *Goodbye Yellow Brick Road* and the release of *Caribou*, MCA re-signed Elton for an $8 million advance and high royalties — the biggest contract of the time. In the late 1970s, when Elton's sales dropped, the relationship soured. After 1980's *21 at 33*, Elton left MCA for Geffen Records. But seven releases later, he would return to MCA, signing in 1986 and releasing *Live in Australia* in 1987. The relationship started strong, but by *Sleeping with the Past* Elton had become disenchanted. At a New Haven, Connecticut, concert on October 18, 1989, Elton rushed through his performance and stewed in silence. Midway through the concert, he said disgustedly that he was not going to perform new material because MCA Records wasn't promoting it. His alcoholism and drug addiction, however, influenced his behavior throughout much of the tour. Though the relationship with MCA improved, Elton signed with PolyGram in 1992, consolidating his worldwide releases. In 1995, he fulfilled his contract obligations to MCA.

McBride, Reggie: Played bass on *21 at 33* and *The Fox*.

McKaie, Andy: Working with Elton and Taupin, MCA's McKaie compiled the tracks on *To be continued...*, the four-CD box set. The 1990 release drew criticism from fans who thought it lacked the rare songs often included on such career retrospectives. "We basically just wanted an accurate portrait of his career," said McKaie. "It's just a case where not everybody, no matter how much of a fan, is going to be pleased." The U.S. release is no longer in print.

McKendrie Spring: The young Decca recording act shared the bill with Elton John and the more established headliner, Leon Russell, at the Fillmore East in November 1970. Like UNI (the label on which Elton's releases appeared), Decca was part of MCA. A feud developed between the two labels. UNI representatives felt Decca was deflecting attention to McKendrie Spring at the expense of Elton John.

McMullen, Sarah: As his publicist, McMullen has been a key part of Elton's behind-the-scenes team in America since the 1980s. Her firm has represented other acts as well, including Billy Idol. She is a key figure in his AIDS foundation.

Mendez, Sergio: At the Champs Elysee Theatre in Paris, France, in 1970, Elton, Dee Murray and Nigel Olsson opened for Sergio Mendez and played a 30-minute set. Neither act was well-received by the French. Elton was to tour Germany, Sweden, and Denmark with Mendez, but he and his management did not like the young rocker. Elton was paid and dismissed.

Menken, Alan: Best known for his songwriting work for Disney (*The Little Mermaid*, *Beauty and the Beast*, and *Aladdin*), Menken wrote "The Measure of a Man." Elton recorded the song for the sound track to Sylvester Stallone's *Rocky V*.

Mercury, Freddie: For a few years in the mid-1970s, Elton and Mercury, the lead singer of Queen, were friendly rivals in pursuit of the glam-rock crown. Briefly, John Reid managed the careers of both men. Elton's Rocket Records Company even tried (unsuccessfully) to lure Queen to the label. Elton visited the flamboyant singer in the final weeks before Mercury succumbed to AIDS in November 1991. His death hit Elton hard. At the Concert for Life, an April 20, 1992, tribute to Mercury, Elton duetted with Axl Rose on "Bohemian Rhapsody" and sung "The Show Must Go On," which he continued to perform on his 1992-93 tour. Elton said he offered nightly prayers for Mercury before taking the concert stage.

Michael, George: In March 1985, when Elton presented Michael with Britain's Ivor Novello award (the Grammy equivalent) for best songwriter, neither could predict the extent of their collaboration. As a youth, Michael was a huge Elton fan, buying his new albums on the day of release. By the mid-1980s, Elton had become a fan, mentor, and strong supporter of George Michael. At Live Aid, he played piano as Michael sang "Don't Let the Sun Go Down on Me." Six years later, in March 1991, Elton joined Michael onstage in England to perform the song as a duet. The recording became a number one hit worldwide, though Elton tried to talk Michael out of releasing it, feeling it would be a diversion for Michael's stalled career. Could Michael have known that the duet might keep alive Elton's pursuit of Elvis Presley's record twenty-three straight years with a Top 40 hit? It did. The two singers have also appeared on each other's albums, with Michael singing back up on "Nikita" and "Wrap Her Up" and Elton playing on Michael's final release as part of the pop duo Wham! He also appeared at their June 1986 farewell concert. They have continued as frequent partners, with Michael singing "Tonight" on *Two Rooms* and in concert, and Elton recording for Michael's unreleased "Trojan Horses" project.

Mid-Summer Music Festival: Elton headlined the June 21, 1975, event at Wembley Stadium in England. It proved noteworthy for two reasons. First, Elton unveiled his new band, without original drummer Nigel Olsson and bassist Dee Murray. Second, he performed the just-released and unfamiliar *Captain Fantastic and the Brown Dirt Cowboy* album in its entirety in running order. Fans had already sat through many hours of music, listening to Stackridge, Joe Walsh, The Eagles, Rufus, and the Beach Boys. His selection of largely unfamiliar material surprised and disappointed critics.

Midler, Bette: They met in the early 1970s. Though asked, Elton could not find time to produce an album for her. They performed together on Cher's TV show in 1974 and were joined by Flip Wilson for a 1960s Motown hits medley.

Mills Music: Roy Dwight, Elton's cousin and a former soccer star, found him a job at Mills Music, a Tin Pan Alley publishing firm in 1964. Cyril Gee hired him as a gofer at four pounds a week. His daily jobs consisted of being the tea boy as well as packing parcels and taking messages to Joe Loss, head of Mills Music. He worked at this day job for almost eighteen months. His nights were spent playing at a Northwood Hills pub and performing gigs with Bluesology at local clubs. Young Elton was unsure of himself, but knew he had to be associated with music, whether selling sheet music or writing songs. He felt certain he would never be a singer or a headline performer.

Mr. Bloe: Record collectors have long wondered whether "Mr. Bloe" was yet another songwriting alias for Elton. It was not, but Elton did play in a group with the same name. In 1969 an American band, Wind, released the instrumental "Grooving with Mr. Bloe" as the B-side to its hit single "Make Believe." The group featured ex-Tommy James studio session men. Both songs were written and recorded by Bo Gentry, J. Levine, Kenny Laguna, and Paul Naumann. Mr. Bloe may have simply stood as a surname for the prominent harmonica player featured on the instrumental. When the single charted, Stephen James of Dick James Music was in New York on business. James could not acquire British rights for the release. He had the song covered and released "Groovin' with Mr. Bloe" as a single. In England in the fall of 1969, Steve Brown produced the song featuring Elton John on piano, Caleb Quaye on guitar, Dee Murray on bass, Roger Pope on drums, and Ian Duck on harmonica. James disliked the end result, and the session was left unreleased. James hired pianist Zack Laurence to arrange the song. The track was re-recorded with the same musicians, except for Elton, whose part Laurence filled. The single became the biggest selling tune on the James label up to that time. It hit number two in England on July 4, 1970. The office of Dick James Music buzzed with touring offers. Mr. Bloe formed briefly as a group, appearing on BBC-TV's "Top of the Pops." The band con-

> **Recording with Mr. Bloe**: The following songs were recorded by Mr. Bloe: "Curried Soul," "71-75 New Oxford," "Get Out of This Town," "Loosen Up" (by Elton John), "Groovin' with Mr. Bloe," "Straight Down the Line," "Smokey Joe La-La," "Land of a 1,000 Dances," "Mighty Mouse," "Dancing Machine," "Chicken Feed," "If You've Got to Make a Fool of Somebody," "Sugar, Sugar," "Doo-Di-Dog-Dad," "Ja-Ja," "Sinful."

sisted of members of Hookfoot with Zack Laurence on piano. The single sold over 100,000 copies in France alone. Two more singles, "Mr. Bloe" and "Curried Soul," were later released in France, as was an album. The "Mr. Bloe" French single featured two instrumentals written by Elton John — "Get Out of This Town" and "71-75 New Oxford." The latter was released in England in August 1970. Elton plays piano on both tracks. To further complicate matters, the group Wind changed its name to Cool Heat and reissued "Groovin' with Mr. Bloe" in August 1970.

Mister Chow's: The London eatery rates as a favorite restaurant in England — and a familiar Elton hangout.

Moffett, Jonathan "Sugarfoot": After working with the Jacksons, Madonna, and Lionel Ritchie, Moffett, a Louisiana native, was invited to join Elton's band in 1988. The drummer stayed for three tours and the recording of *Sleeping with the Past*. In 1991 he joined George Michael's band. Ironically, he was Michael's drummer when the live duet of "Don't Let the Sun Go Down on Me" was recorded.

Money: British newspapers rank Elton as England's second richest rock star, behind Paul McCartney. John's wealth was estimated at $200 million in 1994.

Monroe, Marilyn: "Candle in the Wind" has become an anthem to the American actress. A 1994 coffee-table book of the same name blended the lyric with photos of the former Norma Jean Baker.

Moog, Ebeneezer: Elton used the pseudonym on a non-public Christmas single that appeared on the Rocket Records label in 1975. It featured instrumentals of "God Rest Ye Merry Gentleman" and "Silent Night."

Mooning: At a 1983 event hosted by Cartier Jewelers, Elton dropped his drawers for public view, reportedly in response to a rude audience. A decade earlier, he streaked through the studio to lighten the atmosphere during Kiki Dee's sessions for *I've Got the Music in Me*.

Morgan, Barry: Played drums on *Elton John*, *Madman Across the Water* and *Tumbleweed Connection*.

Morgan, Charlie: Morgan's big break came working with Kate Bush. He has done sessions with Tina Turner, Cyndi Lauper, Johnny Mathis, and Paul McCartney. His drumming with Nik Kershaw drew Elton's attention and prompted an invitation to join the band. He premiered with Elton in 1985 at Live Aid and stayed through 1986, returning in 1992. Morgan has done numerous sessions and owns a small English record label, Bridges. He is not related to drummer Barry Morgan.

Movies: Elton has contributed songs to several sound tracks, appeared in a few films, and been connected to a variety of projects. This extensive listing shows the degree to which his music has become part of the fabric of society:

❖ *Alex: The Life of a Child*: Included "Your Song."

❖ *Alice's Restaurant*: Included "Daniel."

❖ *Aloha Bobby and Rose*: 1974 film featured "Blues for Baby and Me."

❖ *And the Band Played On*: The 1993 HBO movie about AIDS ended with "The Last Song."

❖ *Born to Boogie*: Elton had a cameo appearance in this 1972 release, starring Marc Bolan of T. Rex. Filmed in a studio, Ringo Starr, Bolan, and Elton sang "Children of the Revolution" and "Bang a Gong."

Elton and Maude: Perhaps his most unusual flirtation with the movies came in 1970. Elton was offered the lead male role in *Harold and Maude*, a cult classic about a love affair between a troubled young man and an elderly woman. Elton turned down the opportunity to star in the film and write songs for it so he could concentrate on his blossoming musical career.

❖ *Candle in the Wind*: The TV movie about Marilyn Monroe included the John-Taupin song of the same name.

❖ *Days of Thunder*: "You Gotta Love Someone" appeared on the sound track for the 1990 Tom Cruise film.

❖ *Dog Day Afternoon*: Opened with "Amoreena."

❖ *Driving Me Crazy*: Included "I'm Still Standing."

❖ *Even Cowgirls Get the Blues*: Elton rejected the role of the aging drag queen, offered by director Gus Van Sant.

❖ *Fandango*: The 1987 film included "Saturday Night's Alright (for Fighting)."

❖ *Ferngully*: The sound track for this 1992 animated feature, starring Robin Williams, included "Some Other World."

❖ *Four Weddings and a Funeral*: The 1994 movie featured Elton singing Gershwin's "But Not for Me." The sound track also included his versions of "Chapel of Love" and "Crocodile Rock."

❖ *Friends*: He wrote and performed several songs for the 1971 film, including the charting single of the same name.

❖ *Ghostbusters II*: Sound track featured "Love Is a Cannibal."

❖ *Goodbye Norma Jean*: "Candle in the Wind."

❖ *Ice Castles*: This 1979 Robbie Benson movie featured "We All Fall in Love Sometimes."

❖ *Jet Lag:* The movie was to star Elton John and Rod Stewart in a tale about the life of rock stars. It never materialized.

❖ *Leap of Faith*: Wynona Judd performed Elton's "Stone's Throw from Hurtin' " on the sound track.

❖ *Lethal Weapon 3*: "Runaway Train," a duet with Eric Clapton, appeared on the movie sound track.

❖ *Liberace*: Elton reportedly agreed to play the lead role for the American TV film, but backed out.

❖ *Love on the Orient Express*: Included "Goodbye Yellow Brick Road."

❖ *My Girl 2*: Used "Tiny Dancer" and "Bennie and the Jets."

❖ *My Own Private Idaho*: Featured "Blue Eyes."

❖ *Oh, Heavenly Dog*: "Return to Paradise" and "Song for Guy" were in the 1979 Chevy Chase movie.

❖ *Planes, Trains and Automobiles*: Two days before a planned recording of the title track for the Steve Martin-John Candy film, Elton backed out of the session. The lyric had been written by Gary Osborne.

❖ *Rambo III*: In the summer of 1986, Taupin and Elton wrote three songs for the Sylvester Stallone movie, but they were not used.

❖ *Rocky V*: Elton sang the Alan Menken composition "The Measure of a Man."

❖ *Slapshot*: Included "Sorry Seems to Be the Hardest Word."

❖ *Smokey and the Bandit*: Included "Daniel."

❖ *Summer Lovers*: Elton contributed "Take Me Down to the Ocean."

❖ *The Cat's Eye*: The Stephen King movie, part of a horror trilogy, included a segment where a young girl battled a troll in her bedroom as *21 at 33* revolved on a nearby turntable.

❖ *The Entity*: "Saturday Night's Alright (for Fighting)" appeared in the 1986 release.

❖ *The Games*: The 1971 film included "From Denver to LA," sung by "Elton Johns."

❖ *The Lion King*: Elton and Tim Rice co-wrote songs for the 1994 Disney animated film. The sound track hit number one.

❖ *The Lost Boys*: Roger Daltrey sang "Don't Let the Sun Go Down on Me" for this vampire film.

❖ *The Rainbow*: Elton pulled out of this 1988 movie, based on D.H. Lawrence's book. He was to play Uncle Henry.

❖ *The Ryan White Story*: TV film featured "Candle in the Wind" and "I'm Still Standing."

❖ *To Die For*: The 1995 film used "True Love."

❖ *Tommy*: He starred in the 1975 film version of The Who's rock opera, singing "Pinball Wizard."

❖ *Welcome Home*: Included "Your Song."

❖ *Young Guns II*: Played piano on two Jon Bon Jovi tracks.

Muppets, The: Elton appeared once on the American TV show that featured Jim Henson's famed puppets. In June 1976 he sang "Don't Go Breaking My Heart" with Miss Piggy, as well as "Bennie and the Jets," "Crocodile Rock," and "Goodbye Yellow Brick Road."

Murray, Dee: Murray and drummer Nigel Olsson comprised Elton's first band and remained with him through his most successful years. Born David Murray Oates in Gillingham, Kent, England, on April 3, 1946, he taught himself as a teen to play bass by listening to The Beatles and R&B artists. In 1965 he joined his first professional group, Mirage, which later did sessions for Dick James Music. In the summer of 1968, Mirage disbanded. Murray and Olsson, then with Plastic Penny, joined the Spencer Davis Group cutting an album and touring America. In April 1970 they were asked to back Elton John. "We were on the same wave length," said Olsson. "It's seldom that three guys can gel so well." The trio toured Europe, before coming to America in August. From 1972-75, when Elton dominated the charts, Murray, Olsson, and Davey Johnstone themselves became semi-celebrities. Elton usually pictured them in the album packaging and treated them as more than merely backing musicians. Their vocals became a trademark of his mid-1970s work. When Elton launched Rocket Records, he even invited them to record solo albums. (Murray's never came out.) In 1975 Murray and Olsson were shocked to be fired at the height of Elton's sales success. The singer wanted a new sound. Murray rejoined the band in 1980, staying four years, until Elton again dismissed his rhythm section. Murray did session work for Billy Joel, Jimmy Webb, Rick Springfield, Randy Edelman, Herbie Flowers, Yvonne Elliman, Shaun Cassidy, Barry Manilow, Carole King, and Peter Allen, and he toured with Alice Cooper, Kiki Dee, Procul Harum, and Paul Anka. His musical influences were varied: the Shadows, The Kinks, The Beatles, Leadbelly, Stevie Wonder, Jimmy Reid, and Herbie Flowers. In 1981, Murray and his second wife, Maria, moved from West Hollywood to Brentwood, Tennessee. Having married sisters who were twins, Murray and Olsson lived in the same area. "I never planned to get into country music," said Murray. "I just came to Nashville because I liked it." Led by Roger Cook (whose roots go back to Elton's days with Dick James Music), Nashville was becoming a second home for a breed of British musicians who started their careers in the 1960s. Despite his strong credentials, he found only minor work in country music, backing Johnny Rodrieguz, Vince Gill, and Earl Thomas Conley. In the early 1990s, his professional prospects were looking brighter. Murray seemed certain to tour with Joe Cocker, which would have helped his difficult financial situation. But cancer struck and, eight years after his first battle, Murray suffered a stroke and died days later on January 15, 1992, leaving wife, Maria, their two young children as well as children from earlier relationships.

> **A tribute to a friend**: To raise funds for Murray's family, Elton paid tribute to his former bass player at two solo concerts on March 15, 1992, at the Grand Ole Opry in Nashville, Tennessee. "On tour, Dee was the sort of person who complained about everything," said Elton. "I took that mantle later on in my life. But I never heard Dee complain once he was sick. ... He left a big hole in my life."

Murray, Tony: A bass guitarist, he did sessions at Dick James Music with Elton John in the late 1960s and appeared on *Empty Sky* and *Elton John*.

Muscle Shoals Horn Section: The famed group toured with Elton in 1974 and appeared on his albums.

Musicland: Early in his career, Reg Dwight supplemented his income by working at this London record store on Berwick Street.

My Night with Reg: A West End play by Kevin Elyot, it premiered in 1994 at the Royal Court Theatre Upstairs in England. Aside from the title, this gay work contains numerous references to Elton. Characters are named Dwight, Bennie, Daniel, Guy, Bernie, and John.

N

Name change: Immediately following a gig in Scotland in December 1967, Reg Dwight took on the name Elton John. Reg decided his given name limited him, so he created a new one by combining those of Bluesology band mates Elton Dean and Long John Baldry.

Name dropping: Taupin's lyrics are filled with references to other persons. Though born in Britain, he devoured American culture as a teen. That love is reflected in the selection of celebrities, icons, and figures who are either named or alluded to in John-Taupin songs.

❖ Brigitte Bardot in "I Think I'm Gonna Kill Myself."

❖ The Beach Boys in "Goodbye Marlon Brando."

❖ Marlon Brando in "Goodbye Marlon Brando."

❖ Jackie Collins in "Goodbye Marlon Brando."

❖ Dan Dare, English cartoon character, in "Dan Dare."

❖ James Dean in "Amy."

❖ John Dillinger in "The Ballad of Danny Bailey (1909-34)."

❖ Erroll Flynn in "Teacher I Need You."

❖ Robert Ford, the man who shot Jesse James, in "I Feel Like a Bullet."

❖ The Four Tops in "Where Have All the Good Times Gone?"

Women, women, women: "Wrap Her Up" on *Ice on Fire* was the ultimate name-dropping song, though the women mentioned were probably not suggested by Taupin. In a stream-of-consciousness list, the names of these ladies flowed from the mouths of Elton and George Michael: Brigitte Bardot, Marlene Dietrich, Doris Day, Joan Collins, Samantha Fox, Billie Jean (King), Marilyn Monroe, Little Louise, Princess Caroline of Monaco, Nastasia Kinski, Annie Lennox, Mata Hari, Lulu, Little Eva, Kiki Dee, Nancy Reagan, Rita Hayworth, Julie Andrews, Betty Grable, Katharine Hepburn, Grace Jones, Priscilla Presley, Dusty Springfield, and Nancy Williams.

- ❖ Marvin Gaye in "Club at the End of the Street."
- ❖ Geronimo in "Indian Sunset."
- ❖ Buddy Holly in "Leather Jackets."
- ❖ John Lennon in "Empty Garden."
- ❖ Robert Mitchum in "One More Arrow."
- ❖ Marilyn Monroe in "Candle in the Wind."
- ❖ Dolly Parton in "Goodbye Marlon Brando."
- ❖ Elvis Presley in "Leather Jackets" and "Made in England."
- ❖ Otis Redding in "Club at the End of the Street."
- ❖ Little Richard in "Made in England."
- ❖ Roy Rogers (and Trigger) in "Roy Rogers."
- ❖ Tears for Fears in "Sweat It Out."
- ❖ Tina Turner in "Midnight Creeper."
- ❖ John Wayne in "Teacher I Need You."
- ❖ Tennessee Williams in "Lies."
- ❖ Brian Wilson in "Since God Invented Girls."

Nash, Graham: Nash got to know Elton early in his career, when Elton was a session man for The Hollies. Nash co-owned GRALTO, a publishing company that had a financial interest in Elton's early songwriting. In 1975, Nash and David Crosby appeared on Elton's *Blue Moves* album.

Navarra, Tex: Played percussion on *Elton John*.

New Musical Express: A 1967 advertisement in the *Express* brought Reg Dwight and Bernie Taupin together. Liberty Records was seeking songwriters in the English paper. Keyboardist Dwight and poet-lyricist Taupin responded separately. Ray Williams, a young executive at Liberty, put Dwight in touch with Taupin.

Newman, Del: Orchestral arranger on *Goodbye Yellow Brick Road* and *Caribou*.

Newman, Randy: The American pianist and composer got Elton to sing the part of an angel for his musical treatment of *Dr. Faust*. The session took place in 1993, but the recording was still not scheduled for release in 1995.

Newton-John, Olivia: Elton and Taupin wrote "The Rumour" for her album of the same name, and in 1980 he appeared on her American TV special, performing "Little Jeannie." In the mid-1970s, newspapers erroneously reported that they were brother and sister. They are not related.

Nobody's Child: The 1990 release, organized by The Beatles' wives, raised money for the Romanian Angel Appeal to help orphans. Stevie Wonder, Van Morrison, Billy Idol, Traveling Wilburys, and others performed on the CD. Elton and Taupin contributed "Medicine Man," produced by James Newton Howard.

Norman, Philip: The British journalist authored *Elton John*, a well-researched 1991 release. Norman, whose credits include *Shout!* and *Symphony for the Devil*, met Elton after galleys of the book had been released. Their talk over tea, touching on Elton's multiple addictions, resulted in a *Rolling Stone* story that angered the singer, who claimed the conversation was not intended for publication. Norman said he took notes openly.

Northwood Hills Hotel: Fifteen-year-old Reg Dwight picked up a job as a bar pianist at the Northwood Hills Hotel, playing old standards for thirty-five quid a week. It was good pay for a kid, and the money helped Reg and his mom make ends meet. His stepfather used to pass the hat to collect tips. Playing Thursday through Sunday nights, he earned enough money to buy his first electric piano and microphone. Reg's favorite standards included "He'll Have to Go" and "I Love You Because" by Jim Reeves, as well as Ray Charles's "Let the Good Times Roll," "Don't Let the Sun Catch You Crying," and "What'd I Say." (A few years later, his band Bluesology recorded "What'd I Say.") Reg played at the Northwood Hills pub until the fall of 1965 when evening gigs with his band Bluesology became steady. By that time, Reg had added Roger Miller's "King of the Road" and pop hits by Otis Redding and Jimmy Witherspoon to his usual pub lineup of "Beer Barrel Polka" and other honky-tonk standards.

O

O'Connor, Sinead: On the *Two Rooms* tribute, the Irish singer contributed a stark version of "Sacrifice."

Odgers, Brian: Played bass on "Levon."

Olsson, Nigel: Born in Wallasey, Cheshire, England, on February 10, 1949, Olsson grew up in a musical family. He and brother Kai (who later recorded solo and with the band Longdancer) first studied guitar. Olsson's earliest musical inspiration was skiffle/folk artist Lonnie Donegan, known for "Does Your Chewing Gum Lose Its Flavor on the Bedpost Overnight?" After living in Africa, the result of his father's seafaring work, Olsson and family returned to England where they settled in the northeastern coast port of Sunderland. It was the 1960s, and the Shadows (with Cliff Richard), Graham Bond, Memphis Slim, and The Beatles were influencing a generation of younger musicians. Olsson had been lead singer for a local club band, the Fireflies. On the eve of an important gig, the band's regular drummer quit and Olsson's future was sealed. His most obvious influence was Ringo Starr. The Fireflies disbanded and Olsson joined Jimmy Hall and Mick Grabham in Fallout, which became Plastic Penny in 1966. The band began a mildly successful, two-year career with Dick James Music, scoring a number one British single with "Everything I Am." Olsson briefly crossed paths with Elton John and Bernie Taupin when Plastic Penny recorded the fledgling duo's "Turn to Me" in 1968. The group dissolved that year. Olsson did session work, appearing on Elton's "Lady, What's Tomorrow?" He and bassist Dee Murray, fresh from his work with Mirage, joined the ever-changing Spencer Davis Group in 1969. Olsson also connected with Uriah Heap and recorded two tracks with the band. But within nine days, both he and Dee Murray were in a studio rehearsing with Elton. Olsson knew almost instantly that he had found his niche. Throughout his long association with Elton John, he helped redefine the standards of his profession. He was known to practice four hours a day.

In the studio, he constantly experimented. He and producer Gus Dudgeon discovered a way to broaden his instrument's range through special microphones and digital delays. His lasting imprint can be found on numerous Elton John classics. As a drummer, Olsson worked with Elton from 1970-75 and 1980-84. He has sung backup on more recent albums. Even while with Elton, Olsson maintained a solo career. From 1971 to 1980, he released two hit singles, "Dancin' Shoes" and "A Little Bit of Soap," and six solo albums. His session credits read like a Who's Who in 1970s rock and roll: Billy Joel, Rod Stewart, Stevie Wonder, Neil Diamond, Linda Ronstadt, Neil Sedaka, Bob Weir, Eric Carmen, Olivia Newton-John, Leo Sayer, Rick Springfield, and David Foster. Since 1986, Olsson has lived in Nashville, Tennessee, where he writes songs and works for a music production company. He is married and enjoys driving classic

Olsson's solo albums

❖ *Nigel Olsson's Drum Orchestra and Chorus*, 1971. Songs: "Sunshine Looks Like Rain," "I'm Coming Home," "Nature's Way," "Hummingbird," "Some Sweet Day," "I Can't Go Home Again," "And I Know in My Heart," "We've Got a Long Way to Go," "Weird House," "China."

❖ *Nigel Olsson*, 1975. Features Elton John and his band. Songs: "Something Lacking in Me," "Don't Break a Heart," "Tides," "Only One Woman," "Get It Up for Love," "Songs I Sing," "When You Close Your Eyes," "Girl, We've Got to Keep On," "A Girl Like You," "Give Me Something to Believe In," "Just Another Lie," "Can't You See."

❖ *Drummers Can Sing Too!* 1975. This album is a personal music dialogue with Nigel Olsson.

❖ *Nigel Olsson*, 1978. Songs: "Rainy Day," "You Know I'll Always Love You," "Say Goodbye to Hollywood," "Part of the Chosen Few," "Please Don't Tease," "All It Takes," "Living in a Fantasy," "Right or Wrong," "Cassey Blue/Au Revoir."

❖ *Nigel*, 1979. Songs: "Little Bit of Soap," "You Know I'll Always Love You," "Dancin' Shoes," "Part of the Chosen Few," "Say Goodbye to Hollywood," "All It Takes," "Thinking of You," "Living in a Fantasy," "Cassey Blue/Au Revoir."

❖ *Changing Tides*, 1980. Songs: "Saturday Night," "Fool Me Again," "Only a Matter of Time," "If You Don't Want Me To," "That's How Long," "Showdown," "Should We Carry On?," "Trapeze," "If This Is Love."

❖ Albums with Plastic Penny: *Two Sides of a Penny*, 1968; *Currency*, 1969; and *Heads I Win — Tails You Lose*, 1970.

Singles

❖ "Sunshine Looks Like Rain," 1971.
❖ "Some Sweet Day," 1971.
❖ "Alabama," 1972.
❖ "Only One Woman," 1974.
❖ "Something Lacking in Me," 1975.
❖ "A Girl Like You," 1975.
❖ "Part of the Chosen Few," 1978.
❖ "Dancin' Shoes," 1979.
❖ "Little Bit of Soap," 1979.
❖ "Saturday Night," 1980.
❖ "Do You Want to Spend the Night?," duet with Vickie Carrico, 1989.

race cars. He and Elton remain friends, seeing each other a few times a year. The group Warpipes reunited Olsson with Davey Johnstone. He plans to record a solo album in 1995.

O'Neill, Terry: A photographer, he has been taking shots of Elton for twenty-five years. Perhaps his most famous Elton photo was the one used for the album cover of *A Single Man*.

Onward International Horns: The brass section of Raul d'Oleivera, Paul Spong, Rick Taylor, and David Bitelli toured with Elton in 1985-86 and performed on *Ice on Fire*. The group has also backed Paul McCartney, Wham!, Don Henley, and The Temptations.

Orson, Ann and Carte Blanche: A John-Taupin pseudonym used for "Don't Go Breaking My Heart" and "Hard Luck Story."

Osborne, Gary: When Elton and Bernie Taupin began to work with other songwriters in the late 1970s, Osborne became Elton's primary partner. They met in the 1960s, when Osborne was a teen and Elton was playing the Cromwellian Club with Bluesology. In 1973 Osborne began writing lyrics for Kiki Dee. He and Elton struck up a friendship, playing poker in the evenings. Osborne said that Elton pledged that they would collaborate someday. With 1978's *A Single Man*, he fulfilled the promise. All songs were written by Osborne and Elton. Their relationship continued for several albums, until label chief David Geffen pressured Elton in 1982 to reunite his old band and write exclusively with Taupin. "Elton just said that on the next couple of albums I wouldn't be required," noted Osborne. "Obviously, I was unhappy, but I had to accept, appreciate and understand." Given the vast body of John-Taupin work and the success of that collaboration, Osborne struggled for acceptance with music critics. The Taupin-Osborne comparisons were inevitable, and not flattering to Osborne. "I was only known as the poor man's Bernie Taupin, the guy who wrote some of the lighter things for Elton," he said. Elton found himself defending Osborne and their partnership. He said Osborne's method of writing lyrics to his music — rather than the reverse — gave him greater freedom. "It fills a creative need right now," said Elton in the early 1980s. Aside from his work with Elton, Osborne is best known for writing Jeff Wayne's musical version of *The War of the Worlds*, a multimillion selling release in England.

Charting with Elton: The John-Osborne team produced some forty songs, including several hits. These cracked the Top 40 charts in America:
- ❖ "Blue Eyes."
- ❖ "Little Jeannie."
- ❖ "Nobody Wins."
- ❖ "Part-Time Love."
- ❖ "Chloe."

Oscars: As one of the prime fund-raisers for his AIDS foundation, Elton John hosts an annual post-Oscars party in March in Hollywood. The first event in 1993 was produced by activist

Patrick Lippert, who died four months later of an AIDS-related illness. Attendance is limited to invited celebrities. The 1995 party brought additional reasons to celebrate. Elton won an Oscar for "Can You Feel the Love Tonight?" from *The Lion King*. Three of his songs were nominated.

P

Page, Gene: An arranger for Barry White, he gave "Philadelphia Freedom" a black-1970s sound. He also worked on *Captain Fantastic and the Brown Dirt Cowboy*.

Palladino, Pino: Originally with Paul Young's band, he played bass on *The One* and *Ice on Fire*.

Parker, Alan: Appeared on *Elton John*, playing guitar.

Passarelli, Kenny: He joined the band in 1975 with *Rock of the Westies* and stayed for *Blue Moves*. Earlier, he played with Stephen Stills and formed Barnstorm in 1972 with Joe Walsh. Later, he backed Hall and Oates and Bernie Taupin on a solo 1980 album. Passarelli was a classically trained trumpet player, but got his break playing bass guitar. His credits include co-writing the 1973 hit "Rocky Mountain Way" with Joe Walsh and others.

Paton, David: Former lead singer for the 1970s group Pilot (which charted with "Magic"), Paton played bass in Elton's mid-1980s band, which debuted at Live Aid. Paton has also recorded with the Alan Parsons Project and Kate Bush.

Penny, Greg: The son of singer Sue Thompson ("Norman"), Penny, as a teenager, met Elton in the early 1970s and even visited him at a studio in Europe as he recorded *Goodbye Yellow Brick Road*. Twenty years later, after winning a Grammy for work on k.d. lang's *Ingenue*, Penny was asked to produce Elton's next studio album. He supervised the *Duets* release and co-produced, with Elton, its 1995 follow-up, the critically acclaimed *Made in England*, at AIR Studio in Lyndhurst, England.

Personality: Four traits dominate Elton John's personality:

❖ Generosity: He is legendary for buying extravagant gifts. He has bestowed cars, yachts, and expensive jewelry on casual friends and associates. He can go shopping, drop tens of thousands of dollars and leave Tiffany's or Cartier with a dozen spur-of-the-moment gifts.

❖ Temper: His moodiness is as fabled as his unselfishness. Some friends describe these occasions as "Reggie's little moments." When upset, he has yelled at co-workers onstage, kicked over keyboards, canceled concerts, and stormed away in fits. His sobriety has lessened these occasions, but not eliminated them.

❖ Sense of humor: His wit usually reveals itself in televised interviews and is often risque with references to his sexuality. Band members describe his humor as quick, pointed, and often self-deprecating. He frequently mimics voices and shifts into a variety of characters. On tour in 1988, he made note of his silver hair: "That's about the only thing to go platinum these days."

❖ Competitiveness: Whether playing tennis or watching the music charts, he remains ambitious and aggressive. He admits to enjoying the challenge of competing for radio air time with younger peers.

He is also known among associates and fans for being impulsive, kind, stubborn, impatient, and a perfectionist.

Philips: His first British single, "I've Been Loving You," appeared on the Philips label.

Pinner: Elton grew up in the British town.

Playboy Club: MCA Records showcased young acts in a series of luncheons for media- and music-industry honchos in September 1970. Elton, Nigel Olsson, and Dee Murray appeared at the Playboy Club in New York. Among those attending were key people from radio stations and American TV, including representatives of Ed Sullivan, David Frost, and "The Tonight Show." The event was not the grand success later portrayed. Several acts exceeded their allotted time. When Elton took the stage, many executives were already gone. That same week, Elton appeared at luncheons in Philadelphia and Chicago.

Politics: Though he has never been publicly active in political campaigns, Elton has spoken out on several issues: gay rights, gun control (at the time of John Lennon's death) and the environment. In a 1995 interview, Elton, a British citizen, admitted that he has never voted.

PolyGram: On March 20, 1992, Elton signed a U.S. contract with PolyGram. Beginning with his 1995 album, PolyGram will release his next five albums. The company will gain worldwide control of most of his catalog in the next few years.

Ponty, Jean-Luc: The jazz violinist played on *Honky Chateau*.

Pope, Roger: A session drummer with Dick James Music, Pope appeared on Elton's early albums and joined his band in 1975, when Nigel Olsson was dismissed. Born to musical parents on March 20, 1947, in Whitestable, Kent, England, he began drumming at age 13, and soon began playing in semi-pro rock bands. By 1962, he quit school to go professional with Johnny Keeping and the Lonely Ones, renamed the Soul Agents. He played four years with the band, for which Rod Stewart briefly sang lead. In the late 1960s Pope and Dave Glover formed a session group known as Loot. With the addition of Caleb Quaye, it evolved into Hookfoot. All three were session musicians for Dick James Music. In 1969 and 1970 Hookfoot recorded and performed live with Elton John. After the group disbanded in 1974, Pope worked with Nilsson, Al Kooper, Seals and Crofts, Lou Christie, and Kiki Dee, with whom he toured as drummer when she opened American concerts for Elton. The following year, Elton asked Pope to join his band, where he stayed through 1976. Pope, Quaye, Davey Johnstone, and Cooker Lo Presti comprised the group China, which toured Britain and released a 1977 album before disbanding. Pope and Quaye later toured with Hall and Oates.

Porcaro, Jeff: The drummer for Toto and a top session player, Porcaro played on *Jump Up!* He and keyboardist James Newton Howard were good friends. Porcaro died in August 1992.

Presley, Elvis: Elton appeared at Graceland on February 1, 1975, to help celebrate the birthday of Lisa Marie, a big fan of Elton. Elton and Taupin later met "The King" in June 1976 in Maryland while Elton was on tour. The visit impacted Elton. Presley was bloated, bent on self-destruction, and a shadow of his image. Elton vowed never to let it happen to himself. Yet, by the late 1980s, he found himself in the same situation. In 1993, renewed by his sobriety, Elton broke one of Presley's "untouchable" records with the release of "Simple Life" — the twenty-fourth consecutive year in which he had a Top 40 hit. MCA Records announced the achievement with a full page ad in *Billboard*. The headline: "Sorry, Elvis." The 1976 John-Taupin song "Idol" is believed to allude to Presley.

Press relations: Elton has successfully sued two English newspapers over inaccurate stories. In 1987 the *Sun* falsely accused him of participating in a rent-boy orgy. Six years later, the *Daily Mirror* erroneously reported that an eating disorder was again jeopardizing his health. In both cases, the sources were proven unreliable. The singer has had a love-hate relationship with the press. In several songs — "All the Nasties," "Heart in the Right Place," and "Fascist Faces" — he criticizes journalists. Through press coverage (and his own doing, as well), he has evolved from the critics' darling (1970) to teen idol (1973), from the bespectacled, bisexual superstar (1976) to the hapless has-been (1979), from the 1970s hit-maker trying for another comeback (1982) to the purveyor of pop (1985), from the legend on tour (1989) to the sober statesman of rock (1995). Journalists have pinned a variety of labels on Elton John. Among them: The King of Pop and Circumstance, The Everyman's Underdog, Mr. Rock 'n' Roll Robot, The Keyboard Klown, The Liberace of Rock, and The Conscientious Clown. Since 1978 every new Elton album has been greeted by the press with at least a few stories proclaiming yet another comeback for Elton John.

Wrong songs: Dedicated fans often chuckle at the occasional and inevitable reporting errors that surface. When Elton performs a new or obscure song, the unfamiliar title becomes ripe for a mistake. Two examples: In the early 1970s, a *Boston Globe* critic renamed "Levon" as "Believe On." Decades later, a writer at a major Italian newspaper was impressed by the instrumental "Song for Guy," titled for a youth who died in a crash. But the paper called it "Song for a Gay."

Producers: The bulk of Elton's records have been produced by Gus Dudgeon and Chris Thomas. But he has worked with others, including Greg Penny, Don Was, Steve Brown, and Pete Bellotte. Elton gives his producers considerable freedom. Typically, after he has laid down his parts and vocals, he leaves the session and lets his producer finish the project. Though Elton has the ultimate say, his producer helps pick musicians and songs, sweetens the tunes with various sounds and instruments, suggests restructuring of compositions, develops the order that songs appear on albums, and blends all of the various parts of the tune, many of which are recorded separately. Gus Dudgeon, for example, polished a trademark of Elton's mid-1970s sound: the backing vocals.

Producing: Elton has produced recordings by several artists. Excluded from this list are his own releases, three of which he co-produced with Clive Franks and one for which he teamed with Greg Penny.
❖ *It Ain't Easy*, John Baldry, 1971. Side two only.
❖ *Everything Stops for Tea*, John Baldry, 1972. Side one only.
❖ *Loving and Free*, Kiki Dee, 1973.
❖ *Kiki Dee*, Kiki Dee, 1977.
❖ *Another Night Time Flight*, Blue, 1977.
❖ *China*, China, 1977.
❖ "The Rumour," Olivia Newton-John, 1988. Single release only.

A Greek officer? *Moon Bathing*, a 1975 album by Lesley Duncan, includes a "Colonel Christophoulos Spedaki (deposed)" in the credits. He played the bouzouki, a Greek string instrument. The authors speculate that Spedaki is Elton John, who has known Duncan since the late 1960s.

Pseudonyms: Elton has used more aliases than Butch Cassidy. To discourage overzealous fans, he usually registers at hotels under phoney names. Some interesting ones: Judge Thomas, Bobo Latreen, Sir Brian Bigbum, and Baron Von Kindergarten. Recording with other artists, he also has taken other names. With Sting, it was Nancy Treadlight; with Jackson

Browne, Rockaday Johnnie; with Bruce Hornsby, J.T. Thomas (in 1991, around the time of the Clarence Thomas/Anita Hill hearings); with the band Blue, Redget Buntovan. As songwriters, Elton and Taupin have worked as Ann Orson/Carte Blanche, Tripe and Onions, and Reggae Dwight/Toots Taupin. Musically, the British star has also used Phineas Mchize, Lord Choc Ice, Commodore Orpington, Prince Rhino, and Lady Choc Ice. There have been others, as well: William A. Bong, Sharon Cavendish, Lord Elpus, Lord Elfin, Lord Stillery, Ollie Haircut, and Ebeneezer Moog.

Q

Quarterflash: The band opened for Elton on his 1982 American tour.

Quaye, Caleb: While running errands for Mills Music in the mid-1960s, Elton met Quaye at Paxton's, a collection house and one of his regular stops. Quaye, whose father, Cab, was a well-known jazz pianist, needled Elton about his musical activities. The two became reacquainted when, to Elton's displeasure, Quaye landed as an engineer at Dick James's two-track studio. Eventually, they became close friends. Around 1967 Quaye used his job to sneak Elton into Dick James Studios to record demos. Quaye produced demos for the Troggs, Al Kooper, P. P. Arnold, Pete Townshend, and The Hollies. However, it was his early work with Elton that would be his most remembered association. They both played with the Bread and Beer Band. Quaye produced Elton's first solo single, becoming his biggest booster at Dick James Music. Though he quit Dick James in 1968, he would remain active in Elton's career. Born in England in 1949, Quaye learned to play piano, drums, and guitar, joining a neighborhood band, the Sound Castles, in high school. Quaye's early influences included Fats Waller, Charlie Parker, and Art Blakey. After a stint in Bluesology, Quaye landed with Hookfoot, a critically acclaimed band, and appeared on Elton's first three albums. In 1968 he also released a solo single, "Your Phrasing Is Bad." Elton asked Quaye to join his band in May 1975. He stayed a year, even co-writing several tracks on *Blue Moves*. In late 1976, with Elton taking time off, Quaye returned to Chicago to play with Bill Quateman. In 1977 he joined the group China, a short-lived alliance on the Rocket label. He has worked with Hall and Oates, Willie Dixon, Long John Baldry, and others. Now less involved in the industry, Quaye has become a pastor in America. He appeared onstage in 1986 to encore with Elton on "Saturday Night's Alright (for Fighting)."

> **Songwriting**: Caleb Quaye co-wrote several songs with Elton, Taupin, and others. His contributions included "Between Seventeen and Twenty," "Boogie Pilgrim," and "Your Starter For..."

R

Rainforest Foundation: Sting founded the charity. Elton has supported his friend's passion by performing at four of the fund-raisers. In 1992, Elton sang "Your Song" and "Sacrifice" and duetted with Sting on "Come Down in Time" and "The Girl from Ipanema." On March 12, 1993, he joined Sting, Natalie Cole, Don Henley, James Taylor, and others. Elton performed an unusual mix of songs, including Jim Reeves's "He'll Have to Go," Carole King's "Will You Still Love Me Tomorrow?," "I Put a Spell on You," and Gilbert and Sullivan's "Mad Dogs and Englishmen" (a duet with Sting). On April 9, 1994, he shared the stage with Sting, Taylor, Luciano Pavarotti, Tammy Wynette, Aaron Neville, Whitney Houston, Larry Adler, Antonio Carlos Jobim, and Branford Marsalis, singing the opera classic "La Donna e Mobile" and works by himself, Charlie Chaplin, and others. The 1995 cast included Sting, Elton, Bruce Springsteen, Paul Simon, James Taylor and Billy Joel.

Ramone, Phil: Best known as producer of Billy Joel's classic albums, Ramone served as recording engineer for the live New York radio broadcast that became Elton's *11-17-70* album.

Raphael, Mickey: Played harmonica on "The Fox."

Reagan, Ronald: The U.S. President collected belt buckles and exchanged one with Elton when they met in 1984 during his U.S. tour.

Record companies: In America, Elton has signed recording contracts with (in chronological order) MCA, Geffen, MCA, and PolyGram. His releases also have appeared on UNI, Rocket and Rocket-Island, affiliated with MCA and PolyGram.

Regan, Russ: As head of UNI Records in 1970, he received a share of the credit for launching Elton. Regan grew to be an enthusiastic early supporter.

Regimental Sergeant Zippo sessions

Demoed in June through December of 1967, these songs were written by Elton and Taupin and likely meant for an album. None appeared on official releases: "Angel Tree," "Annabella," "Color Slide City," "A Dandelion Dies in the Wind," "I Can't Go on Living Without You," "I Want to See You Smile," "Lemonade Lake," "Mirrors of My Mind," "Mr. Lightning Strike a Man," "Nina," "One Time, Sometime or Never," "Queen of Diamonds," "Regimental Sergeant Zippo," "Scarecrow," "Season of the Rain," "Swan Queen of the Laughing Lake," "Tartan Colored Lady," "The Tide Will Turn for Rebecca," "Velvet Fountain," "Watching the Planes (Go By)," and "Year of the Teddy Bear."

On the following songs, Taupin did not contribute. Except where noted otherwise, they were written by Elton alone: "Can't You See It?," "Countryside Love Affair," "Here's to the Next Time," "I Could Never Fall in Love with Anybody Else," "I Get a Little Bit Lonely," "A Little Love Goes a Long, Long Way," "I've Been Loving You," "The Witch's House," "Thank You for All of Your Loving" (with Caleb Quaye), "Where It's At" (with Nicky James), and "Who's Gonna Love You?" (with Kirk Duncan).

The following songs, written for the likes of Tom Jones, were demoed from January through August 1968: "And the Clock Goes Round," "Baby, I Miss You," "Cry, Willow, Cry," "I Love You and That's All That Matters," "I'll Never Let You Go," "I'll Stop Living When You Stop Loving Me," "If I Asked You," "My Bonnie's Gone Away," "Not the Man I Used to Be," "Reminds Me of You," "Sing Me No Sad Songs," "Sitting Doing Nothing" (John-Quaye), "Taking the Sun from My Eyes," "There's Still a Little Love," "There's Still Some Time for Me," "Trying to Hold on to a Love That's Dying," "Turn to Me," "When I Was Tealby Abbey," "When the First Tear Shows," and "You'll Be Sorry to See Me Go" (John-Quaye).

Regimental Sergeant Zippo: Named informally by fans, this collection of songs was never released, though an acetate was used to promote the John-Taupin team. Elton intended to extract a first album from this work. The material was recorded in 1967, about a half year before Elton and Taupin officially signed with Dick James Music. With help from Caleb Quaye, Elton recorded these songs after hours at James's studio. Quaye, Roger Pope, and Tony Murray backed Elton on almost all of the tunes. Some sources have referred to this body of work as the *I've Been Loving You* sessions. *Regimental Sergeant Zippo* better fits the style of songs. The best of these ("A Dandelion Dies in the Wind," "Regimental Sergeant Zippo," "Tartan Colored Lady," "The Tide Will Turn for Rebecca," "Turn To Me" and "Reminds Me of You") hinted at the duo's promise as writers of ballads and Top 40 pop music. They were signed by Dick James Music on the basis of these sessions. Later, James obtained the rights for some of these songs from GRALTO Music, which was owned by The Hollies. "I've Been Loving You" and "Here's to the Next Time" were released by Dick James Limited in association with Philips Records. Unlike these two songs, most of the material was inspired by The Beatles' *Sgt. Pepper's*

Lonely Hearts Club Band and the flower power movement. The influence of John Lennon can be heard in the title track, The Hollies in "There's Still Time for Me" and even a psychedelic Donovan in "Annabella" and "Season of the Rain." "Swan Queen of the Laughing Lake" resembles the title of Bob Dylan's "Sad-Eyed Lady of the Lowlands." Dylan's epic makes up a side of his 1966 *Blonde on Blonde* album, a John-Taupin favorite at the time. In the spring of 1968, propelled by Dick James's insistence and their own desire to be known, Elton and Taupin began writing commercial pop tunes for the likes of Cilla Black, Tom Jones, and Engelbert Humperdinck. (Of that bunch, only Black released one.) "Taking the Sun from My Eyes" and "The Tide Will Turn for Rebecca," done in that vein, were covered by other artists. By mid-July 1968, at the urging of James's employee Steve Brown, Elton and Taupin began to write more personal songs, including "Lady Samantha," "Skyline Pigeon" and "First Episode at Hienton." Those songs displayed the influence of such folk/rock acts as The Band, Leonard Cohen, and Joni Mitchell. Though these songs were often awkward and naive — Taupin was still, after all, a teenager — they represented the birth of one of the most successful songwriting teams of the twentieth century.

Rehearsals: The task of preparing the band for a tour falls largely to guitarist and music director Davey Johnstone. Before joint practices, Johnstone tells band members to learn their parts for specific songs. Later, the band rehearses as a unit with Johnstone, who works out major kinks. Finally, Elton joins the group for a few days of practice, narrowing the song selection and polishing the sound.

Reichenbach, Bill: Played trombone on *21 at 33*.

Reid, John: Elton's longtime manager, confidant, and ex-lover was born in September 1949 in Paisley, Scotland. The son of a laborer, Reid performed in a local folk group. For two years, he studied to be a marine engineer, but abandoned that career for music. At age 20, Reid went to work for Ardmore-Beechwood, a publishing interest of EMI. He advanced quickly, becoming EMI's label manager for Motown's distribution firm. Reid selected Motown releases for Britain and helped promote them. One of his picks, "Tears of a Clown" by Smokey Robinson and the Miracles, became a number one hit in England before its American release. Earlier in 1970 Elton and Reid had crossed paths. An avid record collector, Elton picked up new releases at EMI. He was also a friend of David Cocker, whose office was next to Reid's. Reid and Elton became acquainted and grew to be flatmates and lovers. Through Reid, Elton met Stevie Wonder in 1970, picking him up at a English airport. Reid accompanied Elton on his first U.S. tour. In March 1971, at age 22, he became Elton's manager, succeeding Ray Williams. A year later, he founded John Reid Enterprises, which over the years has been affiliated with Queen, comedian/singer Billy Connolly, Kiki Dee, Simple Minds, Barry Humphries (Dame Edna), and many others. His career is inextricably entwined with Elton John's. A dapper dresser, gourmet chef, and keen businessman, "Reidy," as several associates call him, has built himself a fortune estimated at over $100 million. He has a reputation as a fierce competitor and protective associate. He has not been shy about using his fists on persons who mistreat his top client. (Reid even served three weeks in jail for one such encounter in New Zealand.) Months before Elton sought treatment for multiple addictions in 1990, English newspapers reported that Reid was addressing

> **1968-71 B.R. (Before Reid)**: Before John Reid became Elton's manager in 1971, five other men played manager-like roles in his career: Lionel Conway, Muff Winwood, Dick James, Ray Williams, and Steve Brown.

his own alcohol-abuse problem. Though their romantic involvement has long since ended, Elton and Reid remain loyal and unquestionably close.

Renwick, Tim: A guitarist, he played on *A Single Man* and toured with Elton in 1980. Renwick belonged to Sutherland Brothers and Quiver, a group that warmed up for John in 1973. A session man, he has also played with Al Stewart and Pink Floyd.

> **"I'm retiring"**: Years in which Elton has proclaimed onstage that "this concert" would be his last:
> ❖ 1976.
> ❖ 1977.
> ❖ 1982.
> ❖ 1984.
> ❖ 1986.
> ❖ 1989.

Retirement: Because of his hectic work pace, Elton has several times collapsed from physical exhaustion. To get his life in order, he has twice retired temporarily, in 1977 and 1990. But several other times, in moments of anger and depression, he has announced onstage that the current concert would be his last. Such pronouncements have not occurred since he became sober in 1990.

Rettore, Donatella: A well-known Italian singer, Rettore and Elton are mutual fans. He asked her to record "Remember," a song written for Frank Sinatra. Her version appears on a 1981 album, *Estasi Clamorosa*. They met that year. "Elton was my idol," she said. "He told me that he liked my voice and style a lot and that he had written a song he thought suited me well. ... We passed several days just drinking beer and talking about music." Two years later, Rettore recorded another Elton song, "Sweetheart on Parade," for the *Far West* album. Elton later worked with Rettore's brother, designer Gianni Versace.

Revolution Club: Dick James Music held its first major press conference for Elton John at this London club on March 26, 1969.

Rice, Tim: A lyricist, Rice co-wrote the songs for *Jesus Christ Superstar*, *Evita*, and *Aladdin*. He teamed up with Elton for "Legal Boys" on 1982's *Jump Up!* album, and again for the 1994 Disney movie, *The Lion King*, for which they wrote six songs. They are collaborating on a Disney production of Verdi's *Aida* for Broadway.

Richard, Cliff: Richard has long been an oddity in the music business. He is a mammoth star in England, where his chart success is surpassed only by Elvis Presley. Richard has released more than 100 singles and starred in stage productions and on television. His band, the Shadows, influenced a generation of British pop musicians. Yet, Richard has had little luck in America. He and Elton have known each other for years, with Elton appearing on his TV show ("Cliff from the Hip"), Richard recording for Rocket Records and the two dueting on "Slow Rivers."

Richard, Little: As a piano player and performer, Little Richard greatly influenced Elton. At a December 11, 1966, show at the Seville Theater in London, Bluesology (with Elton) opened for Little Richard. Fourteen years later, the two stars performed together at a Lupus Foundation benefit in Los Angeles, and, in 1993, recorded "The Power" for Elton's *Duets* album. "When I was a kid, I used to go and see Little Richard at Harrod's Granada," recalled Elton early in his career. "He used to jump up on the piano and I'd think, 'I wish that was me.' " The 1995 song "Made in England" acknowledges Little Richard's inspiration.

Richmond, Dave: Played bass on *Elton John*.

Ricotti, Frank: Played percussion on *Ice on Fire* and *Leather Jackets*.

Ritts, Herb: A photographer of the stars, he has worked extensively with Elton and Taupin. His 1992 book, *Notorious*, includes a portrait of Elton. He and Elton are friends, and Ritts sits on the board for his AIDS foundation.

Rivers, Joan: Elton appeared on her first show in 1986 with Cher. They discussed their song collaboration for *Leather Jackets*. Rivers duetted with Elton on "The Bitch Is Back."

Robinson, Tom: In the late 1970s, Robinson emerged as an outspoken and thoughtful singer-songwriter on the British new wave scene. Up front about his homosexuality, he wrote the anthem "Glad to Be Gay" and other songs that demonstrated his commitment to equal rights. Around the same period, he and Elton co-wrote at least three songs: "Sartorial Eloquence" and "Never Gonna Fall in Love (Again)" on *21 at 33*, and "Elton's Song" on *The Fox*. As a video, the latter focused on a boy who had a crush on an older male at school. Robinson released "Never Gonna Fall in Love (Again)" on his 1979 album — prior to Elton's version. He also recorded "Elton's Song" in 1994. Robinson charted in England with "2-4-6-8 Motorway" and "War Baby." He participated in several political movements, including concerts put on by Rock Against Racism and the Anti-Nazi League. In the mid-1990s, Robinson, who became a father, continued to perform, record, and speak out.

Rock and Roll Hall of Fame: Elton was inducted into the hall on the first ballot. In January 1994, Axl Rose bestowed the honor in New York, citing the artist

Artists once signed to Rocket:

❖ Blue.
❖ Colin Blunstone (formerly of the Zombies).
❖ Mike Boreham.
❖ Casablanca.
❖ China (with Davey Johnstone).
❖ The Classics.
❖ Sheri Dean.
❖ Kiki Dee.
❖ Dramatis.
❖ Flyover.
❖ Donny Gerrard.
❖ Dick Graves.
❖ The Hudson Brothers.
❖ Alan Hull.
❖ Davey Johnstone.
❖ Lambretta.
❖ Joe LeMaire and Flouze.
❖ Longdancer (with Kai Olsson and Dave Stewart).
❖ Lulu.
❖ Hugh Nicholson.
❖ Nigel Olsson.
❖ Maldwyn Pope.
❖ Radiator.
❖ Brian and Brenda Russell.
❖ The Five Sapphires.
❖ Neil Sedaka.
❖ Mike Silver.
❖ Mutter Slater.
❖ Solution.
❖ Stackridge.
❖ The Stingrays.
❖ Peter Straker.
❖ Bernie Taupin.
❖ Judie Tzuke.
❖ R. J. Wagsmith Band.
❖ Johnny Warman.
❖ Howard Werth and The Moonbeams.
❖ Andy and David Williams (nephews of the famed singer).
❖ Lorna Wright.

as an inspiration musically and personally. "When I first heard 'Bennie and the Jets,' I knew I had to be a performer," said Rose. In accepting, Elton thanked his own idols, early American rock pianists like Jerry Lee Lewis, Little Richard, and Fats Domino. Elton gave the award to his writing partner, Bernie Taupin, saying he would not have made it without Taupin. Among the other 1994 inductees were John Lennon, Rod Stewart, Bob Marley, The Band, The Animals, Willie Dixon, and Duane Eddy. Though scheduled to perform, Elton did not take the stage for the final jam.

Rocket Records: By 1973 all that Elton John touched turned to gold. Like The Beatles and Rolling Stones before him, Elton sought to use his influence and money to launch other talented artists. Rocket Records was the vehicle. The label was started in May 1973 by Elton, manager John Reid, Bernie Taupin, producer Gus Dudgeon, and associate Steve Brown. Each man was to have equal influence, and, so, the label represented their individual interests. It also made producers out of most of them. Aside from Elton, whose British releases from late 1976 and after appeared on Rocket, the label's greatest success was in America. The mid-1970s comeback of Neil Sedaka, highlighted by two number one hits, came as a result of Elton's support through Rocket. The label produced the first-ever top ten U.S. hit by Cliff Richard, "Devil Woman." It also carried Elton protege Kiki Dee and her several hits, including "I've Got the Music in Me." In England, Rocket introduced Judie Tzuke, Blue, and Lambretta, all of which charted, as well as Longdancer, featuring future Eurythmics leader Dave Stewart. Rocket allowed Elton's band members to pursue solo careers. Davey Johnstone's *Smiling Face* appeared on the label, and

Johnstone, Nigel Olsson and Dee Murray recorded a single as trio for Rocket, though it was never released. When Elton left his American label, MCA, in 1980, Rocket artists, such as Judie Tzuke, suffered in the United States because MCA stopped distributing their releases. Consequently, when Tzuke opened for Elton John at Central Park in 1980 before 450,000 fans, her records were not available in local stores. Despite spotty success, Rocket failed to attract and keep a major artist. In the mid-1970s, the label was offered Queen and 10cc but found both too expensive. Over time, Rocket Records became precisely what Elton vowed it would not: a label for his own releases. In 1995, Elton and Reid resurrected Rocket, under the wing of Island Records, which is part of PolyGram. The label's first release was Elton's *Made in England*. Other artists will be signed to the label.

Off with a bang: Prior to officially launching Rocket Records, Elton celebrated with a March 24, 1973, birthday bash aboard the Sloop John D in Edmonton, Canada. The affair began at midnight following one of his concerts. Among those attending were the Beach Boys, Paul Simon, George Harrison, Ringo Starr, Rod Stewart, and Cat Stevens.

Rockford Files, The: Numerous television shows, ranging from "Seinfeld" to "The Simpsons," have included Elton in jokes or skits, but none as consistently as the "The Rockford Files," a 1970s detective series. In three consecutive segments in 1979, actor James Garner mentioned the singer in gag lines.

Rogers, Kenny: The country singer is also a photographer. He shot Elton for a book of star portraits released in the late 1980s. Earlier, as a member of the First Edition, Rogers recorded "Border Song."

Rolling Stones: The Stones were an early influence, so it was a thrill for Elton in 1970 when he was asked to sign on as their opening act. He wanted to do it, but his management convinced him otherwise. Opening acts for the Stones typically face an unappreciative audience, and Elton's career was ballooning without the added exposure. Elton recorded "Honky Tonk Women" live on *11-17-70* and jammed with the Stones at their July 19, 1975, Colorado concert. During his 1993 tour, he performed "Jumpin' Jack Flash" as part of his encore.

It's only rock 'n' roll: Seven John-Taupin songs inspired by the Rolling Stones:
- ❖ "Restless."
- ❖ "Empty Sky."
- ❖ "No Shoe Strings on Louise."
- ❖ "Saturday Night's Alright (for Fighting)."
- ❖ "The Bitch Is Back."
- ❖ "Dirty Little Girl."
- ❖ "Pain."

Romo, Olle: A drum programmer who has worked with the Eurythmics and others, Romo performed on Elton's late 1980s and early 1990s recordings. He even co-wrote a few songs, including "Runaway Train."

Ronson, Mick: Known for his work with David Bowie, guitarist Ronson appeared on an alternate version of "Madman Across the Water."

Rose, Axl: Elton slammed the group Guns 'n Roses at a June 1988 music industry gathering, probably for what he considered homophobic lyrics. But he and Axl Rose grew to be friends. Rose has cited Elton as an inspiration, describing his work as "my classical music." On 1992's *Use Your Illusion II*, the band paid tribute with the song "You Could Be Mine," thanking Taupin and John in the credits. At the Freddie Mercury tribute, Rose and Elton duetted on "Bohemian Rhapsody." While on tour, Rose has used the chorus of "The One" as an intro to "Sweet Child o' Mine." Further, the band's "November Rain" has been described as a tribute to the songwriters. Elton accompanied the band on a performance of it at an MTV awards show. Rose was selected in 1994 to induct Elton into the Rock and Roll Hall of Fame, which he did articulately.

Rose, Howard: He is Elton's longtime agent. Rose worked for Chartwell Artists in 1970 when the agency booked Elton for under $300 at the Troubadour. He later came to work for the artist.

Rosner, David: Rosner represented Dick James in America in 1970 when Elton was launched in the United States. He is a music publisher for several artists, including friend Neil Diamond.

Royal Academy of Music: Elton qualified to attend the prestigious school part-time from age 11 to 15. He sometimes skipped his Saturday sessions and didn't practice religiously, but he learned the rudiments before leaving the school for a gofer's job at a music house. His early classical training can be detected in the chord structure of his compositions.

Royal family: With his stature in England and friendship with the royal family, Elton could be knighted this decade by the Queen of England — though his status as a gay activist could prevent the honor. He has enjoyed a long-running relationship with the royals, not only performing at their events but socializing with them. He has danced with the queen, gone to the cinema with Princess Margaret, and been a frequent party guest at royal gatherings. He performed at the twenty-first birthday and bachelor party for Prince Andrew and wrote a song as a wedding gift when Andrew married Sarah Ferguson. The Duke and Duchess of York have attended his birthday bashes and eaten dinner at his home.

Ruislip-Norwood Music Festival: It was the first true public appearance by 12-year-old Reg Dwight. He played "Les Petites Litanies de Dieu" by Groylez.

RuPaul: Elton and the celebrated drag queen appeared together on Valentine's Day 1994 on the Brit Awards. They did several joint promotions for their "Don't Go

Breaking My Heart" dance single.

Rush, Jennifer: They duetted on "Flames of Paradise" in 1987, and he appeared as a taxi driver in her video for the song.

Russell, Leon: When Elton came to America in 1970, he was already an admirer of rock pianist Leon Russell — a solo artist, top session musician, member of the Asylum Choir, and a standout on Joe Cocker's Mad Dogs and Englishmen tour. Hard to miss in his long hair and beard, Russell showed up for Elton's first American performances at the Troubadour in Los Angeles. They even jammed together at Russell's house in a phenomenal demonstration of talent witnessed by a few friends. Within months, at Russell's request, they were sharing the bill at concerts in New York and California. With his album receiving strong air play, Elton upstaged his idol, as well as the lesser known McKendree Spring, at the Fillmore East. Russell has worked with Eric Clapton, Bob Dylan, George Harrison, and many others, but his chart success ("Tight Rope" and "Lady Blue" in the early 1970s) never matched the respect given by fellow musicians. Several of his songs, including "Delta Lady" and "This Masquerade," surfaced as hits for other artists. The early work of Elton and Taupin revealed a strong influence by Leon Russell. "Razor Face" is but one example. As a tribute to Russell, Elton has performed his classic "Song for You" in concert.

Russo, Toni: Bernie Taupin's second wife, a model.

S

Saturday Sun: While trying to launch his solo career in early 1970, Elton continued to do session work for other musicians. *Saturday Sun* was one such project. At the time, Warlock Music publisher Joe Boyd was grooming a network of young songwriters and wanted to put together a promotional album to encourage other artists to record their songs. Boyd hired Elton and others for the session. The result is a rare treasure. Less than ten vinyl copies of the recording exist, most supposedly owned by the musicians. A few have made it into the hands of British collectors. *Saturday Sun* (the name given it by Elton fans) features songs by folk singer Nick Drake, Mike Heron of the Incredible String Band, and the husband-wife duo of John and Beverly Martyn. The sessions were rumored to have been recorded with six or seven

> **Saturday Sun demos**: Songs from the *Saturday Sun* session: "The Day Is Done" (Drake), "Time Has Told Me" (Drake), "Saturday Sun" (Drake), "Way to Blue" (Drake), "Stormbringer" (Martyn), "Go Out and Get It" (Martyn), "Sweet Honesty" (Martyn), "You Get Brighter" (Heron), "This Moment" (Heron), "I Don't Mind" (Ed Carter), "Pied Pauper" (Carter). (Elton sang lead on the first six and played piano on all others.)

musicians, including Drake, Martyn, Caleb Quaye, and Roger Pope. Elton played piano and sang lead vocals on most songs. Linda Peters, the future wife of Fairport Convention's Richard Thompson, sang female leads. (She was then a member of Fotheringay, a group that appeared on the same concert bill with Elton at the Roundhouse Chalk Farm in May 1970.) Elton recorded four Nick Drake songs, all from the 1968 *Five Leaves Left* album. In interviews, Elton has rarely mentioned Drake. But a listen to the Drake album reveals lush string arrangements, strong piano playing and a melancholy mood not unlike that captured by Elton. Drake overdosed on Tryptizol, a sleeping pill, and died on November 25, 1974, at age 26. Many past associates have spoken of his depression and frustration as an unrecognized musician and composer, The Martyns' three numbers appeared on the 1970 *Stormbringer* album. In a 1971 French interview, Elton listed the album among his favorites. In 1986, Rykodisc, which Joy Boyd directs in Europe, released *Fruit Tree*, a box set focusing on Drake's work. Boyd hopes to put together a Drake tribute album, with Elton's demo of "Time Has Told Me" as the centerpiece.

Scaffold: While pursuing his solo career in March 1969, Elton did session work with this British band. Scaffold had several English hits in the late 1960s, including the chart-topping "Lily the Pink." Paul McCartney's brother, Michael McGear, belonged to the group. Elton performed on Scaffold's "Gin Gan Goolie."

Scarlett Pimpernel: In 1986 Elton and Tim Rice were to begin work on writing a musical of the same title. The project was scrapped.

Scott, John: The Atlanta real estate agent helped Elton locate his Georgia condominium. They became close friends. Scott co-directs the artist's AIDS foundation. Elton's 1993 *Duets* album was dedicated to him.

Sedaka, Neil: After a string of pop hits from 1959 to 1962, Sedaka entered the 1970s with hopes of a comeback. He found success in England, where air play on two BBC radio stations could make a career. In America, record labels remained uninterested. U.S. executives viewed him as "a ghost from the '60s," said Sedaka. After two well received British albums, backed by the group 10cc, Sedaka was invited to meet Elton, a fan from the 1960s. "We became friends and played each other new songs," said Sedaka. "One day at a party in my flat, he told me he was starting a record label, Rocket Records." Sedaka suggested Rocket carry his work. Elton was elated. "He said, 'It's like handing me gold bricks,' " recalled Sedaka. In 1975, Rocket released *Sedaka's Back* in the United States. The album, originally titled *The Tra La La Days Are Over*, included cuts from Sedaka's previous albums in Britain, as well as new material. It took off, cracking the top 30, due initially to the number one single "Laughter in the Rain." "It was a remarkable comeback for me," he said. "But I had the top artist in the world promoting me in interviews. In one year, I went from making $50,000 to $6 million." The hits continued with "The Immigrant" and "That's When the Music Takes Me." In September 1975 Sedaka released "Bad Blood," his best-selling single, with Elton singing backup prominently and David Foster playing keyboards. "I thought it was an unusual song for me," said Sedaka. "It was courageous and different." The single topped the charts, dislodged by Elton's "Island Girl." In 1976, after charting with a remake of

Bad Blood: Elton sings backup prominently on this 1975 number one hit by Neil Sedaka. After keeping Sedaka waiting at the studio for two hours, Elton showed up and laid down his backing track in seven takes. Sedaka said he knew after hearing their voices together it would be a hit. "It was full of energy," he said.

"Breaking Up Is Hard to Do" and "Love in the Shadows," Sedaka released "Steppin' Out," another tune featuring Elton. But it fizzled, competing for play time with "Don't Go Breaking My Heart," the Elton-Kiki Dee duet. When Sedaka's three-album contract with Rocket expired, he asked the label for an advance to re-sign. "They said we should be grateful for what they had done for my career," Sedaka remembered. "I went to Elektra Records. I'm not sure it was the best decision, but I got a nice advance." The contractual dispute left a riff in Sedaka's relationship with Elton, whom he describes as a "genius." Though he has not charted in America since 1980, Sedaka had a top ten album, *Timeless*, in Britain (1991).

Sessions: Like many aspiring rock stars, Elton John supported his fledgling career by doing sessions for other artists. From 1968 to 1970, he was active playing backup on songs by better known artists, laying down demos of other writers' songs and recording sound-alike versions of hit tunes for budget releases. In 1969, for example, he worked with The Hollies, Barron Knights, and Scaffold. Also appearing in these sessions were such artists as Lesley Duncan, Liza Strike, Herbie Flowers, Hookfoot, and members of Blue Mink. Throughout 1969, Elton spent much time putting down lead vocals, background vocals, piano and organ on demos. Most were songs by other struggling writers who didn't have the

> **One demo's story:** Elton demoed and recorded many songs that were never released. The case of "Apache" is but one example. Originally, the song was an instrumental piece written by Jerry Lordan. He toured England in 1960 on the same bill as Cliff Richard and the Shadows, who chose to record the song. It went to number one in July 1960, setting off a string of instrumental hits. In 1968, Lordan reworked the song, adding lyrics. Elton cut a demo of it, singing lead and playing piano. It remains unreleased. Incidentally, Burt Weeden, the guitarist who led the Millermen (which included Elton's father), also charted with "Apache."

talent to polish their own demos. Elton credited Lesley Duncan and Madeline Bell, two prominent female backup singers, with throwing session work his way. Among his most interesting sessions were those for copycat recordings on "not-by-original-artist" releases. They not only padded his income from Dick James Music but allowed him to work with others who would achieve success, including David Byron (later of Uriah Heap), Doris Troy, Perry Ford, Russ Stone, and Donna Gillespie. Many sessions were produced by Alan Caddy (an ex-member of the Tornados) at Pyet Studios in Marble Arch. Elton made over two dozen cover versions — or carbon copies — for the popular, mass-marketed records. "They were a blast," he recalled. "I can remember singing the oohs and ahs on a song like '(I'll Be Your) Jack in the Box.' Just a line like that would set us all off, and we'd have to stop the tapes because we'd all be laughing so hard." The songs — many recorded just a month before his American debut — appeared on a variety of labels: Marble Arch, Music for Pleasure, Gallery, Hallmark, Boulevard, Deacon, and Avenue. The session artists were not credited on these releases.

Soundalike recordings: These cover versions featured Elton prominently on lead vocals or piano. Also noted are the acts that charted with the original versions:
❖ "The Best of Both Worlds," Lulu.
❖ "Cotton Fields," Beach Boys.
❖ "Don't Forget to Remember," Bee Gees.
❖ "Good Morning Freedom," Blue Mink.
❖ "I Can't Tell the Bottom from the Top," The Hollies.
❖ "In the Summertime," Mungo Jerry.
❖ "Lady D'Arbanville," Cat Stevens.
❖ "Love of the Common People," Nicky Thomas.
❖ "My Baby Loves Lovin'," White Plains.
❖ "Natural Sinner," Fair Weather.
❖ "Neanderthal Man," Hotlegs.
❖ "Saved by the Bell," Robin Gibb.
❖ "She Sold Me Magic," Lou Christie.
❖ "Signed, Sealed, Delivered," Stevie Wonder.
❖ "Snake in the Grass," Paul Martin.
❖ "Spirit in the Sky," Norman Greenbaum.
❖ "Travelin' Band," Creedence Clearwater Revival.
❖ "United We Stand," Brotherhood of Man.
❖ "Up Around the Bend," Creedence Clearwater Revival.
❖ "Yellow River," Jeff Christie.
❖ "Young, Gifted and Black," Aretha Franklin.

He sang backup on these versions:
❖ "All in the Game."
❖ "Back Home," Cup Football Squad.
❖ "Down the Dust Pipe," Status Quo.
❖ "Everybody Get Together," Youngbloods.
❖ "Goodbye Sam, Hello Samantha," Cliff Richard.
❖ "I Will Survive," Arrival.
❖ "(I'll Be Your) Jack in the Box."
❖ "I'll Say Forever My Love."
❖ "It's All in the Game," Four Tops.
❖ "Jingle, Jangle," Archies.
❖ "Knock, Knock, Who's There?," Mary Hopkin.
❖ "Lola," The Kinks.
❖ "Love Grows," Edison Lighthouse.
❖ "Rainbow," Marmalade.
❖ "Si Tu Dois Partir," Fairport Convention.
❖ "Soul Deep," The Box Tops.
❖ "Too Busy Thinkin' About My Baby," Marvin Gaye.
❖ "What Does It Take?," Junior Walker and the All Stars.

These versions were rumored to feature Elton on backing vocals, but the final mix disguised his appearance:
❖ "All Right Now," Free.
❖ "Come and Get It," Badfinger.
❖ "Early in the Morning," Vanity Fair.
❖ "Sugar, Sugar," Archies.
❖ "The Wonder of You," Elvis Presley.

Sexuality: In an October 1976 *Rolling Stone* interview, Elton admitted publicly that he enjoyed male companions. The announcement did not surprise friends, but it made them worry for his popularity. By the time stardom arrived in 1971, Elton had been open with associates about his preferences. They need have looked no further than his manager, John Reid, with whom Elton had a long relationship. Though Elton now downplays the price he paid for coming out, the revelation did impact his sales and airplay, especially in America. Despite the cost, he continued to talk openly about being gay. Two years later, as if to reinforce the point, he titled his new album *A Single Man*. It included "Big Dipper," a campy, sexual song featuring his male soccer team on backing vocals. His 1980 tour program offered a cover drawing of Elton in heavy makeup. *The Fox* album in 1981 featured "Elton's Song," written by gay activist Tom Robinson, about one boy's crush on another. Even in concert, Elton occasionally inserted the words "young stud" in the slow love song "Blue Eyes." "The gay business really hurt me a lot," he said. "But I had to learn to take (it) well. If you take your seat at a football ground and 20,000 people are singing, 'Elton John is a homosexual,' you learn fairly quickly." Given his openness, friends were startled when Elton married Renate Blauel in 1984. Some said he genuinely hoped to father children. Others said he wanted to ease pressure from his mother. Later, Elton said he had hoped foolishly that the union would settle his wild life. The marriage ended in 1988. Elton has since expressed remorse at hurting Blauel, whom he said genuinely loved him. As the AIDS crisis grew, Elton became even more open about his sexuality. In the 1990s, he has dedicated albums to his boyfriends, proclaimed his love to one on a Barbara Walters interview, recorded "The Last Song" about a gay man with AIDS, and granted numerous interviews to the gay press.

Seymour, Adam: Played guitar on *The One*.

Shepherd, Jim: Played trombone on *A Single Man*.

Sinatra, Frank: In 1976 Frank Sinatra appeared at the Royal Albert Hall in London. During his concert performance, he sang "Sorry Seems to Be the Hardest Word." Afterward, he had Elton and Taupin take a bow. Both songwriters were so honored that they promised to write a song for Sinatra. "Remember (I'm Still in Love with You)," composed in 1977, features a Sinatra-like melody and appropriate words. The Chairman's version has never been released. It probably remains as one of several studio sessions Sinatra aborted in 1977 and 1978. The Elton piano demo of "Remember" has surfaced, however, and the song was later recorded by Italian artist Donatello Rettore.

Smith, "Legs" Larry: A former member of the Bonzo Dog Doo-Dah Band, Smith tap danced on "I Think I'm Gonna Kill Myself," subbing for Elton's stepfather, who was to play the spoons. On a 1972 concert tour, Smith also performed to Elton's rendition of "Singing in the Rain" while dressed as a bearded bride.

Smith, Michael: The contemporary Christian singer grew up listening to Elton and credits him as an influence.

Songwriters Hall of Fame: Elton John and Bernie Taupin were inducted in May 1992. The hall was founded in 1969 by Johnny Mercer and others with the National Academy of Popular Music. The museum is located in New York.

Soul Train: In 1974 Elton became the first white star to perform on the long-running American TV show.

Soulosophey: The rap group sampled "Take Me to the Pilot."

Spedding, Chris: Played slide guitar on "Rotten Peaches."

Speedy Gonzales: Elton lost a lawsuit because of the similarity between the end of "Crocodile Rock" and "Speedy Gonzales."

Stacey, Bob: A band roadie in 1970, Stacey remains part of Elton's entourage. He is in charge of the star's massive wardrobe.

Stallone, Sylvester: The American actor and the British singer are friends and frequently attend each other's events. Stallone has been supportive of Elton's anti-AIDS efforts and presented him with his 1995 Oscar.

Starr, Ringo: Elton and Taupin wrote "Snookeroo" for the ex-Beatle. Starr recorded it on his 1974 *Goodnight Vienna* album, with Elton playing keyboards. At the time, he was one of Elton's closest pop star friends.

Starship One: Elton's leased Boeing 720 carried band and crew in 1974 and 1975 and included a bedroom, den, bar, sofas, and room for forty passengers. The jet had previously been owned by Led Zeppelin.

Stern, Howard: Stern was just a New York disc jockey in 1986 — a popular one, but still just a DJ — when Elton appeared on his live show. He presented Elton with the lyrics to "Why Won't They Let Howard Stern Go on TV," and Elton wrote a melody on the air. Then he sang the song, which described Stern's "small penis."

Stevens, Cat: He and Elton recorded a duet, "Honey Man," in October 1970, but a dispute over royalties prevented its release. Lionel Conway organized the session. He was a friend of Elton and, as a top official at Island Records, worked with Stevens. Elton covered Stevens's "Lady D'Arbanville" in a 1970 session. He also made a brief appearance in the promotional video for "Banapple Gas."

Stewart, Rod: None of Elton's friendships with other stars has lasted as long as his relationship with Rod Stewart. In the late 1960s, their paths crossed frequently. Both worked separately with Long John Baldry. They shared a love not only for music, but also for soccer and, until the 1990s, wild parties. Stewart recorded "Country Comfort" on *Gasoline Alley* in 1970, before Elton released it. Later, Elton and Taupin wrote "Let Me Be Your Car" specifically for Stewart, who included it on his 1974 *Smiler* album, with Elton on piano. The November 12, 1973, recording session evolved into a late-night jam with the two stars performing tunes by Sam Cooke and Aretha Franklin. "We just played and played," recalled Elton. "That session was one of those nights where you go into the studio and all you want to do is just play for a long time." Their friendship has always included a dose of jovial competitiveness. Frequently in interviews, they mention each other in jest. In 1983 the two stars talked of a joint stadium tour. The tour was called off. Elton later joked that it was to feature a battle-of-the-bands format, but that Stewart lacked enough hits. When Elton got married, Rod sent this telegram: "You're still standing, but we're on the floor." On April Fool's Day in 1991, Elton, wearing a dress and wig, surprised Stewart onstage at Wembley Stadium. He kissed his pal and sat on his leg as Rod sang "You're in My Heart." Two months later, Stewart presented Elton with a music box. Its inscription: "To my dear Sharon, my left leg has never been the same. Love Phyllis." (The feminine names are explained in the box at right.) In interviews, they have sniped at each other repeatedly through the years. In a European publication, Elton injected Stewart into a description of RuPaul: "He's almost seven feet tall. His clothes are rather feminine, a bit like Rod Stewart." Musically, the Scotsman paid tribute to Elton and Taupin (with whom Stewart wrote occasionally in the 1980s) on the *Two Rooms* project. Stewart's version of "Your Song" was a hit on the adult contemporary charts in 1992. Given their friendship and other parallels in their careers, it seemed fitting that both men were inducted into the Rock and Roll Hall of Fame in 1994.

> **Sharon and Phyllis**: Elton and Stewart have referred to each other by feminine names, Sharon and Phyllis. The practice began in the late 1960s when Elton was touring with Bluesology as part of Long John Baldry's band. At the Eel Pie Island Club, the marque announced the appearance of "Ada Baldry and the Hoochie Coochie Ladies, featuring Phyllis Stewart." The nickname stuck, and Elton got tagged as Sharon Cavendish, after the Sheffield Cavendish Club, where Bluesology also played. Later, others in the inner circle, including manager John Reid, were tagged with feminine names as part of the ongoing joke.

Sting: The ex-Police singer is among Elton's closest music-star friends. They met in 1980 and have performed together at several benefits, including fund-raisers for Sting's Rainforest Foundation. Sting turned in one of the sterling performances on the *Two Rooms* tribute with his version of "Come Down in Time."

Suicide attempts: At least twice, Elton has tried to take his own life. The first occasion was in 1968 when he was depressed over a proposed marriage. He attempted (half-seriously) to gas himself to death. The second attempt came at the peak of his popularity in the mid-1970s, when he swallowed a handful of pills, jumped into a swimming pool occupied by family members, confessed that he had taken the drugs, and ended up in a hospital.

Sun Newspaper: In February 1987 the British tabloid published lurid allegations that Elton attended sex parties with rent boys. Friends encouraged him to let the matter die, but the singer vigorously fought the report. He won in court after airline records showed that Elton was elsewhere on the date of the alleged orgy. The *Sun* paid up, apologized, and admitted the stories were false.

T

Taupin, Bernie: When the Rock and Roll Hall of Fame inducted Elton John in 1994, the British star gave the award to Taupin, his longtime lyricist. There would be no Elton without Taupin, he proclaimed. Their partnership rates with the most prolific and popular of the twentieth century. In rock music, their only peers in terms of success are John Lennon and Paul McCartney. Their alliance began in 1967, when both young men responded to a talent ad in *New Musical Express*. An aspiring executive, Ray Williams, paired Taupin, a 17-year-old country boy who wrote poetry, with Reg Dwight, the shy, classically trained piano player who would become Elton John. Born May 22, 1950, Taupin grew up in the English countryside near Lincolnshire. He was raised in a Catholic home, with French as a second language. Taupin's mother, Daphne, and grandfather Leonard Patchett Cort instilled in him a love for literature that would become apparent in his earliest lyrics. Educated at Cambridge, Cort taught classics and passed that affection — as well as his knowledge of nature — on to his grandson. As a rebellious teen, Taupin hung out in pool halls and grew discouraged at the prospect of a farming-related career similar to that of his father, Robert Taupin, who worked for Britain's ministry of agriculture. The younger Taupin, the middle of three sons, read Coleridge and Longfellow. He was fascinated with America, from its icons to the Old West. His interest in music evolved from Marty Robbins's "El Paso" to Woody Guthrie songs of the

A few facts about Taupin.

❖ He doesn't think of his lyrics as poetry; he writes both.

❖ Literary figures like Oscar Wilde, Christopher Isherwood, and Somerset Maugham have influenced him as much as contemporary songwriters.

❖ His songs reflect his almost "religious experience" with America.

❖ He comes up with titles first, then writes a few lines before fleshing out the entire song.

❖ He is partially deaf in one ear due to touring with Elton.

land to Jimi Hendrix, Bob Dylan, and The Band. Still, he had no idea that his career would relate to music. Leaving school at 16, Taupin worked as an apprentice in the print department at the *Lincolnshire Chronicle*. Unemployed for long spells, he also labored on a chicken farm. In heading to London to meet up with Reg Dwight in the summer of 1967, Taupin figured he would kick around for a year or two, eke out a living while staying with an aunt, and eventually head back to Lincolnshire — a little richer for the experience. He suspected he would end up as a blue-collar worker. In time, he shared a room with Elton at the latter's family flat. They struggled for three years while writing songs for Dick James Music, but everything changed when Elton exploded onto the American scene in 1970. Taupin was 20, and, suddenly, because Elton focused attention on their partnership by picturing Taupin on albums and doing joint press interviews with him, the introspective, nonperforming lyricist found himself in the spotlight. Early in the experience, Taupin toured with the band and hung out at the studio when albums were being recorded. Lyrics often were written at the studio. But with no musical role to play at the sessions or onstage, Taupin eventually found little reason to spend time in either place. The songs Elton John sings have always been more about the lyricist. Elton writes the melodies; Taupin, the words. In 1971, for example, Taupin married an American woman, Maxine Feibelman, honoring her with a song, "Tiny Dancer." Their relationship fell apart in the mid-1970s, unable to survive his drinking or the rock and

> **The Alice Cooper album:** Taupin and close friend Alice Cooper confronted their addictions to drugs and alcohol around 1977, and they decided to write about the experience. Though critically slammed in 1978, Cooper's *From the Inside* painted a disturbing, though honest, indictment of the rock and roll lifestyle. It even produced a top 20 hit, "How You Gonna See Me Now?." (With Elton exploring other avenues, Cooper not only worked with Taupin but also with other Elton associates such as Davey Johnstone and Kiki Dee.) Songs on the album: "From the Inside," "Wish I Were Born in Beverly Hills," "The Quiet Room," "Nurse Rozetta," "Millie and Billie," "Serious," "How You Gonna See Me Now?," "For Veronica's Sake," "Jacknife Johnny," "Inmates." Outtake: "No Tricks."

> **Books by Taupin**
> ❖ *The One Who Writes the Words for Elton John*, 1976. Taupin's lyrics and poems were illustrated in black and white. Among those contributing artwork were John Lennon, Charlie Watts, Alice Cooper, and Joni Mitchell.
> ❖ *Burning Cold*, 1979. A Taupin poem accompanied by photographs, many of nude women.
> ❖ *A Cradle of Haloes*, 1988. An autobiography of his childhood.

roll lifestyle. He told of its disintegration in "Tonight" and, in another song, described himself as a nicely tanned drunk. As would be expected, his lyrics draw on his experiences, his literary influences, his childhood memories, and his interests. Several topics surface repeatedly. Nearly every album he

Taupin's solo sessions

❖ *Bernie Taupin*, 1971. Wanting to be known as more than Elton's lyricist, Taupin recited his poems while guitarists Davey Johnstone, Shawn Phillips, and Caleb Quaye provided impromptu music. Today, Taupin would just as soon the album be forgotten. Songs: "Birth," "The Greatest Discovery," "Flatters (a Beginning)," "Brothers Together," "Rowston Manor," "End of a Day," "To a Grandfather," "Solitude," "Conclusion," "When the Heron Wakes," "Like Summer Tempests," "Today's Hero," "Sisters of the Cross," "Brothers Together Again," "La Petite Marionette," "Ratcatcher," "The Visitor."

❖ *He Who Rides the Tiger*, 1980. Taupin collaborated with Dennis Tufano (an ex-member of The Buckinghams), formed a group (the Altar Boy Band), sang his own words, and even posed for a teen-idol photo in *Cream* magazine. His second wife, Toni Russo, modeled for the album cover. Though the tunes were average, a few songs offered compelling lyrics. In "Approaching Armageddon," Taupin addressed a failed marriage, a new relationship, his alcoholism, and his collaboration with Elton John. "The Whores of Paris," a riveting epic in the tradition of "Ticking," is the unquestionable highlight of the album, rivaling lyrically the best songs he wrote with Elton John. Songs: "Monkey on My Back," "Born on the Fourth of July," "Venezuela," "Approaching Armageddon," "Lover's Cross," "Blitz Babies," "Valley Nights," "Love (the Barren Desert)," "The Whores of Paris."

❖ *Tribe*, 1987. With Elton at a low point creatively and personally, Taupin teamed up with Martin Page for another solo effort. He and Page also wrote hits for Starship and Heart, and in 1995 Page had a solo hit with "In the House of Stone and Light." In support of *Tribe*, Taupin released two singles, "Friend of the Flag" and "Citizen Jane," which did not chart. Songs: "Friend of the Flag," "Corrugated Iron," "Citizen Jane," "Hold Back the Night," "She Sends Shivers," "Billy Fury," "I Still Can't Believe That You're Gone," "Conquistador," "The New Lone Ranger," "Desperation Train." Outtakes: "Backbone" and "White Boys in Chains."

❖ Unreleased. In Toronto November 1-14, 1976, Taupin recorded a solo album with producer Robert Appere for Rocket Records. It featured a few original tracks, country western covers, and songs by Tony Snow, Mickey Newbury, and Tom Waites. The project never made it to fruition. The musicians included Kenny Passarelli, Davey Johnstone, James Newton Howard, Jim Keltner, Phil Everly, and Ringo Starr.

has written with Elton John contains references to God or religion, guns or bullets, and death. Farming, drinking, and railroad imagery also emerge regularly. With the exception of a few major hits (like "Your Song"), Taupin avoids typical, straightaway love songs. More often, his lyrics deal with the darker or more ambiguous side of relationships. Living in America, he has often had a long-distance relationship with Elton,

The Hornsby songs: In the early 1980s, Taupin collaborated with Bruce Hornsby, who had not yet hit the big time. They wrote several songs that have never been released: "But Then Again," "Adult Magic," "The Kids Are Loose," "Fly on the Wall," and "The Last Note." Hornsby ended up heading in a different direction, writing songs with his brother.

though less so in the 1990s. While close, they aren't best friends. They don't hang out together. Their interests are different. They are different, as much so, Taupin has said, as town mouse and country mouse, as cheese and chalk. They go months without seeing each other. Writing lyrics just a few weeks out of the year leaves Taupin time for other projects. He has released three records: *Bernie Taupin*, 1971 (spoken poems put to music), *He Who Rides the Tiger*, 1980, and *Tribe*, 1987. He has produced a few others: David Ackles's *American Gothic*, 1971, and the Hudson Brothers's *Totally Out of Control*, 1974, and *Ba-Fa*, 1975. He has directed song videos, emceed a televised tribute to Roy Orbison (1990), produced a live show of musical stars singing songs from *West Side Story* (1992), and written three books. Independent of Elton, Taupin has co-authored two number one hits, "We Built This City" for Starship and "These Dreams" written for Stevie Nicks but recorded by Heart, as well as songs with Rod Stewart, Melissa Manchester, Cher, and others. In

---

The other songs: Taupin songs written without Elton John or Alice Cooper and not included on Taupin's solo albums.

❖ "Lover Come Back to Me," Hudson Brothers, 1974.
❖ "Lonely School Year," Hudson Brothers, 1975.
❖ "Broken Woman," China, 1977.
❖ "Savage," China, 1977.
❖ "If I Weren't So Romantic I'd Shoot You," Derringer, 1978.
❖ "For the Working Girl," Melissa Manchester, 1980.
❖ "Julie," Cher, 1980.
❖ "Never Give up on a Dream," Rod Stewart, 1981. (The song commemorated 18-year-old cancer activist Terrance Fox's attempted run across Canada with the aid of an artificial leg.)
❖ "Sonny," Rod Stewart, 1981.
❖ "Guess I'll Always Love You," Rod Stewart, 1982.
❖ "Johnny and Mary," Melissa Manchester, 1982.
❖ "Hey Ricky (You're a Low Down Heel)," Melissa Manchester, 1983.
❖ "Satisfied," Rod Stewart, 1983.
❖ "White Rose," Melissa Manchester, 1983.
❖ "Into the Heartland," The Motels, 1984.
❖ "Love Rusts," Starship, 1985.
❖ "We Built This City (on Rock and Roll)," Starship, 1985.
❖ "Hard Lesson to Learn," Rod Stewart, 1986.
❖ "I Engineer," Animotion, 1986.
❖ "These Dreams," Heart, 1986.
❖ "When the Phone Stops Ringing," Boomerang, 1986.
❖ "The Burn," Starship, 1989.
❖ "Deal for Life," John Waite, 1990.
❖ "Light in Your Heart," Martin Page, 1990.
❖ "Dip Your Wings," Peter Cetera, 1992.
❖ "The Rain," Carlene Carter, 1993.
❖ "Monkey in My Dreams," Martin Page, 1994.

1978, he and Alice Cooper collaborated on an album, *From the Inside*, which probed their alcoholism. It marked a brief period during which Taupin and Elton did not work together. The separation was neither formal nor bitter, but it was competitive. By 1982 they were again working extensively as a team. From their sexuality to their reading interests, Taupin and Elton offer contrasting portraits. (Taupin has been married three times.) Their differences extend to music as well. Taupin prefers jazz and blues. Elton is keenly aware of new

---

Whatever happened to: Taupin projects that never materialized.

❖ A movie treatment of outlaw Sam Bass.

❖ An animated feature film titled *Captain Fantastic and the Brown Dirt Cowboy*, but about neither Elton nor Taupin.

❖ A novel, *Warlord of the Marshland.*

❖ A 1976 album recorded in Toronto.

❖ A book of poems, *The Devil at High Noon.*

---

music. "I don't listen to anything modern at all now," said Taupin. "Whenever I get into (Elton's) car, he's playing stuff by these groups with initials for names." With 1989's *Sleeping with the Past*, which honored American soul artists who inspired both men, Taupin got as much say musically as he had had on any earlier Elton John album. Essentially, he had veto power over songs. The *Two Rooms* tribute that in 1991 heralded their collaboration combined with Elton's self-discovery to bring Taupin and John closer. Their mutual respect and love have grown in recent years. The 1995 album, *Made in England*, saw Taupin once again writing in the studio, rather than faxing lyrics overseas.

Taylor, Alvin: Played drums on *21 at 33* and *The Fox.*

Taylor, Mark: A keyboardist, he toured with Elton in 1992 and 1993 and played on *The One*. He has also worked with Simple Minds and Sinead O'Connor.

Television appearances: Though shy, Elton does appear on television for interviews, usually a few times a year. Selected TV appearances are noted chronologically:

❖ A Henry Mancini special: Appearance recorded November 15, 1970, at Santa Monica Civic Center concert.

❖ "The Andy Williams Show," 1971: Ray Charles and Elton played dueling black and white pianos, performing "Your Song" and "Georgia on My Mind." Joined by Mama Cass Elliot, they performed Stevie Wonder's "Heaven Help Us All."

❖ "The David Frost Show," 1971: Performed "Your Song" and "Take Me to the Pilot" with his band.

❖ "Soul Train," 1974. "Philadelphia Freedom" and "Bennie and the Jets" solo.

❖ *Elton John and Bernie Taupin Say Goodbye to Norma Jean and Other Things*, 1974. An ABC special.

❖ Rock Music Awards, 1975. Hosted the event with Diana Ross.

❖ "Cher," 1975: Performed "Bennie and the Jets" with Cher and premiered "Lucy in the Sky with Diamonds."

❖ "Tomorrow" with Tom Snyder, 1976.

❖ Elton in Edinburgh, Scotland, 1976. An ABC special.

❖ "The Mike Douglas Show," 1977. Interview.

❖ David Frost special, 1978. Interview.

❖ "The Muppet Show," 1978. Miss Piggy duetted with Elton.

❖ American Music Awards, 1980. Hosting the show, he performed "Sorry Seems to Be the Hardest Word" and debuted "Elton's Song."

❖ Olivia Newton-John special, 1980. Duetted with her on "Candle in the Wind" and premiered "Little Jeannie."

❖ "Tomorrow" with Tom Snyder, 1980. "Little Jeannie" and "Sartorial Eloquence" live.

❖ "The Phil Donahue Show," 1980. Audience questions. "Your Song" solo.

❖ "The Tonight Show Starring Johnny Carson," 1980. Played "Sorry Seems to Be the Hardest Word."

❖ "Tomorrow" with Tom Snyder, 1981. Performed "Nobody Wins," "Just Like Belgium," and "Breaking Down the Barriers" with a band.

❖ "Saturday Night Live," 1982. "Empty Garden" and "Ball & Chain."

❖ "The Joan Rivers Show," 1986. "Your Song," "The Bitch Is Back," and "Twist and Shout."

❖ "The Return of Bruno," 1987. Elton had a cameo in the HBO Bruce Willis special.

❖ "CBS This Morning," 1987. Four-part interview.

❖ MTV "Stand By Me" concert, 1987. Performed "Will You Still Love Me Tomorrow?" and "I Guess That's Why They Call It the Blues."

❖ "A Royal Gala" on ABC, 1988. "Candle in the Wind" and "Saturday Night's Alright (for Fighting)."

❖ "Dionne & Friends" on HBO, 1988. Performed "That's What Friends Are For."

❖ MTV Music Awards, 1988. "I Don't Wanna Go on with You Like That."

❖ "The Arsenio Hall Show," 1990. "Sad Songs" and "Sacrifice."

❖ "Unplugged," 1990. Brief seven-song set.

❖ International Rock Awards, 1990. Called Sam Kinison a pig.

❖ MTV "Rockumentary," 1990. Brief but rare clips.

❖ David Frost special, 1991. Interview.

❖ "Good Morning America," 1992. Interview.

❖ Whoopi Goldberg show, 1992. Interview.

❖ "The Arsenio Hall Show," 1992. Taupin and Elton do a brief skit.

❖ Aretha Franklin special, 1993. Recorded April 27 at Radio City Music Hall. Elton duetted with Franklin on "Border Song."

❖ "The Tonight Show Starring Jay Leno," 1993. With Billie Jean King and Dame Edna.

❖ Barbara Walters special, 1994. Interview.

❖ "Late Night with David Letterman," 1995. Performed "Made in England."

Elton has appeared frequently on British TV. Among the highlights are a 1976 appearance on the Morecombe and Wise comedy show and a guest role as a priest who kills a British comedian in "Hysteria 3," an AIDS benefit.

Teller, Al: Despite leaving MCA for PolyGram, Elton enjoys a good relationship with Teller, vice president of MCA. They support each other's pet charities.

Tennis: It ranks as his favorite recreational sport. His lengthy friendship with Billie Jean King has brought his affection for the sport into the public eye, though he has been playing since the late 1960s. John has performed in exhibitions with King, Martina Navratilova, Bobby Riggs, Bill Cosby, and others.

Thatcher, Les: Played acoustic guitar on *Madman Across the Water* and *Tumbleweed Connection*.

Thomas, Chris: Like Elton and arranger Paul Buckmaster, Thomas attended the Royal Academy of Music as a child, studying violin. In 1968, he produced an unreleased instrumental album by the Bread and Beer Band, a group of session musicians that included Elton. Thirteen years later, Elton would select him to produce most of his 1980s work. Born in 1947, Thomas worked with George Martin at AIR Studios in Montserrat in the late 1960s, playing horns on The Beatles' white album. His first solo effort as a producer came in 1969 with the Climax Blues Band. He also supervised and mixed Pink Floyd's *Dark Side of the Moon*. In the two decades since then, he has evolved into one of Britain's top producers. He has worked with INXS, Paul McCartney, the Sex Pistols, The Pretenders, Roxy Music, Pete Townshend, Human League, John Cale, Brian Eno, Badfinger, and Procul Harum. His work with Elton has brought him a Grammy nomination. Despite their history, Elton chose Greg Penny over Thomas for his 1995 album.

Thompson, Andrew: Played sax on *Breaking Hearts*.

Thompson, Chester: Played organ on *Caribou*.

Three Dog Night: The Los Angeles-based band had a reputation for recording the work of up-and-coming songwriters. Laura Nyro, Harry Nilsson, and John Hiatt were among them. In 1969, as Elton was releasing *Empty Sky*, Three Dog Night included his "Lady Samantha" on *Suitable for Framing*. Later, the band recorded "Your Song."

Throat surgery: In January 1987 Elton had a nonmalignant lesion removed from his vocal cords. The surgery was at St. Vincent's Hospital in Sydney, Australia.

Tommy: The movie *Tommy*, based on the rock opera by Pete Townshend of The Who, premiered in 1975, six years after The Who album and at the peak of Elton's sales. Wearing a four-foot-high pair of Doc Marten boots, Elton played the Pinball Wizard. Though his bespectacled flamboyance seemed a perfect match for the part, he was not the first choice for the role. Rod Stewart was. Stewart had played it in a 1972 performance with the London Symphony. He asked his friend Elton whether or not he should appear in the movie. Elton discouraged him, and Stewart turned down the part. Later, at the urging of Townshend (and because Ken Russell was directing the movie), Elton agreed to do *Tommy*. Stewart was upset. "He was really furious and quite rightly so," recalled Elton. The movie also featured Roger Daltrey, Ann-Margret, Eric Clapton, Tina Turner, and Jack Nicholson. Because of his film role, Elton became the subject of a Bally pinball machine, now a collector's item. On August 24, 1989, Elton returned to the role during a charity performance of *Tommy* with The Who in Los Angeles.

Tower of Power: The horn section performed on *Caribou*.

Traveling Wilburys: Elton inspired George Harrison and Jeff Lynne to form the group. During the sessions for Harrison's *Cloud Nine* album, Elton joked about starting an exclusive forty-and-older rock band. They followed through with the idea.

Tribe: Bernie Taupin's third solo album, released in 1987.

Trojan Horses: Aretha Franklin, Anita Baker, and Elton were among the singers scheduled to perform on the George Michael-produced all-star album. Michael wrote all of the songs for the project, which punctuated a legal dispute with his record label. The project has not been released.

Opening-night reviews

"Rejoice! Rock music, which has been going through a rather uneventful period lately, has a new star. He's Elton John ... whose U.S. debut was in almost every way magnificent." Robert Hilburn, *Los Angeles Times*.

"He was a major star before the end of his first set. ... The future seems incredibly bright for John." Kathy Orloff, *Chicago Sun Times*.

"He had hardly opened his mouth when it was apparent that he is going to be a very, very big star." John L. Wasserman, *San Francisco Chronicle*.

"It's not often that someone gets a standing ovation at the Troubadour, but Elton John did — twice." John Gibson, *Hollywood Reporter*.

Troubadour: The West Hollywood club hosted the American premiere of Elton John — an event that instantly changed his life. It's the stuff of which legends are made. In 1990, *Rolling Stone* rated it among the twenty concerts that changed rock and roll. Overnight — literally — Elton was transformed from a struggling act in England to the industry's most-talked-about newcomer. He debuted on Tuesday, August 25, 1970. The next day, Robert Hilburn of the *Los Angeles Times* proclaimed, "He's going to be one of rock's biggest and most important stars." Others were equally as enthusiastic. Elton did not foresee the impact. He and band mates Dee Murray and Nigel Olsson had just begun to make gains in England. They had been touring England,

Scotland, and Wales nearly five months. Elton viewed his American trip as premature, and he feared disaster. But with his U.S. record label and Dick James Music paying the bill, he went along with it. Besides, America held another attraction for the 23-year-old record collector: an opportunity to buy U.S. albums. Though Elton had doubts, his American boosters did not. They were working diligently to make the Troubadour show an event. Elton's early manager, Ray Williams, hired publicist Norm Winter in the summer of 1970. His enormous task was to break a virtually unknown act from Pinner, England. Winter spent the week before Elton's discovery cajoling the press and preparing a red London Transport double-decker bus with the slogan "Elton John Has Arrived." It would transport an embarrassed Elton and entourage from the airport. David

On video, somewhere: Publicist Norm Winter filmed at least part of one Troubadour show and apparently still owns the recording. Footage was used by UNI and MCA in a 28-minute montage called "Where We're At." The promo film, tracing the history of UNI Records, aired September 5, 1970, at a business convention. Other snippets from the Troubadour have appeared in various projects. But a full-show video has yet to surface.

Rosner, who represented Dick James in America, worked to create excitement within the industry. He persuaded friend Neil Diamond to introduce Elton at Doug Weston's Troubadour, a social mecca of the West Coast record industry. The 350-seat club was celebrating its twentieth anniversary, and Elton was co-headlining with folksinger David Ackles, who got lost in Elton's shadow. The anticipation built through the

Troubadour song list: "Your Song," "Sixty Years On," "I Need You to Turn To," "Border Song," "Country Comfort," "Take Me to the Pilot," "Burn Down the Mission" (with "Get Back"), "Honky Tonk Women," and "Bad Side of the Moon."

week. "The club was packed, filled with record industry people, the media and fans," recalled Weston. "Every celebrity in town turned out." Among them was an idol, Leon Russell. Elton appeared on stage at about 10 P.M., wearing a beard and dressed in bell-bottom jeans and a red shirt with white letters that declared "Rock 'n Roll." (The cover for 1972's *Honky Chateau* album featured a photo taken backstage at the club.) Elton opened with his future hit "Your Song." Bass player Dee Murray joined in on the tag line and Nigel Olsson exploded on drums on the second number, "Bad Side of the Moon." "We knew, man, within about 45 minutes that we had a superstar," said Russ Regan of UNI Records. "It was electrifying. It was a charged evening." Elton performed his one-hour show nightly through August 30. "His debut was all people talked about both before and after it happened," noted *Times* critic Hilburn. A week later, promoter Bill Graham offered Elton $5,000 for late-fall concerts at Fillmore East and West — the highest amount the Fillmore had paid a new act.

Trump, Donald: Several years before the opening of his Taj Mahal in Atlantic City, Trump worked to secure Elton for the celebration. Elton came and performed.

Turner, Tina: On his first visit to America, Elton met Turner, whose work he admired, backstage at the Greek Theatre in California. She rates as the only entertainer to release two versions of a John-Taupin song. Turner contributed "The Bitch Is Back" to the *Two Rooms* effort in 1991 — more than a decade after releasing another version of the song on a solo album. The latter rendition earned Turner a Grammy nomination. She also recorded "Philadelphia Freedom" on a 1980 album. Elton dressed as Turner for some 1984 concert appearances.

Two Rooms: Steve Brown, a member of Elton's inner circle since 1969, pursued the idea for this tribute to the twenty-five-year-long collaboration between Elton John and Bernie Taupin. It included an October 1991 release on PolyGram, a video, a hardcover book (in Britain only), and a network television special. For this effort, sixteen artists covered John-Taupin songs. *Two Rooms*, named for their method of writing lyrics and music in separate rooms, aimed to enhance their image as songsmiths and put them in a league with Lennon and McCartney. "This project is a way for Elton and Bernie to get the credit they deserve," said Brown. Over six years in discussion, the tribute helped elevate the pair to the status of rock statesman. It also

Songs and artists on *Two Rooms*
- ❖ "Border Song" by Eric Clapton.
- ❖ "Rocket Man" by Kate Bush.
- ❖ "Come Down in Time" by Sting.
- ❖ "Saturday Night's Alright (for Fighting)" by The Who.
- ❖ "Crocodile Rock" by the Beach Boys.
- ❖ "Daniel" by Wilson Phillips.
- ❖ "Sorry Seems to Be the Hardest Word" by Joe Cocker.
- ❖ "Levon" by Jon Bon Jovi.
- ❖ "The Bitch Is Back" by Tina Turner.
- ❖ "Philadelphia Freedom" by Hall and Oates.
- ❖ "Your Song" by Rod Stewart.
- ❖ "Don't Let the Sun Go Down on Me" by Oleta Adams.
- ❖ "Madman Across the Water" by Bruce Hornsby.
- ❖ "Sacrifice" by Sinead O'Connor.
- ❖ "Burn Down the Mission" by Phil Collins.
- ❖ "Tonight" by George Michael.

allowed PolyGram, which had obtained rights to the early John-Taupin catalog, to recoup some of its investment. Polygram Records promoted *Two Rooms* heavily, and it entered the charts at #28 and peaked at #19. The record, praised by the press, received broad airplay. Rock stations picked up Eric Clapton's "Border Song," Phil Collins's "Burn Down the Mission," Bruce Hornsby's "Madman Across the Water," and The Who's "Saturday Night's Alright (for Fighting)." Sting's "Come Down in Time," the Beach Boys' "Crocodile Rock," and Rod Stewart's "Your Song" drew attention on adult contemporary formats, while Sinead O'Connor's "Sacrifice" and Kate Bush's "Rocket Man" were featured on alternative stations. Many musicians were approached for *Two Rooms*. Mark Knopfler, the Eurythmics, Bonnie Raitt, Kool and the Gang, Paul Young, and others expressed interest but did not appear. Most artists strayed little from Elton's original interpretations of the songs. Bon Jovi's "Levon" was nearly identical to Elton's. Seven artists — Kate Bush, Joe

---

Discordant notes on _Two Rooms_

❖ Elton asked the Beach Boys to perform "Harmony" but they felt it lacked their trademark up-tempo flavor.

❖ Steve Winwood played organ on Phil Collins's contribution.

❖ Elton played on two tracks, "Come Down in Time" and "Madman Across the Water," using the pseudonyms Nancy Treadlight and John "J.T." Thomas.

❖ George Michael recorded his live version of "Tonight" in March 1991, the same night Elton joined him onstage for their duet of "Don't Let the Sun Go Down on Me," which would hit number one in Europe and America.

❖ For a tribute album, Daryl Hall took great liberties with the words to "Philadelphia Freedom," changing "road" to "run," "never" to "always," "zapped" to "got," and adding his own line: "You gotta go home to get back."

❖ A _Two Rooms_ tribute concert was scheduled for December 13, 1991, at the Paramount Theatre in New York. It was canceled.

Cocker, Sinead O'Connor, Bruce Hornsby, Sting, Hall and Oates and Oleta Adams — took their interpretations of John-Taupin classics in new directions. Early in their career, Elton and Taupin wrote songs primarily for other artists. "I've always wanted to write a hit song for somebody else," he said in 1974.

Tyler, Bonnie: For a project involving producer George Martin, Elton set Dylan Thomas lyrics to music for "I Loved a Man." Tyler recorded the song for the 1988 _Under Milk Wood_ album.

Tzuke, Judie: A Rocket Records artist, she opened for Elton on his 1980 tour and co-wrote "Give Me the Love" on his _21 at 33_ album. She has had ten album releases.

U-V

UNI: Elton's first U.S. releases appeared on this MCA-affiliated label.

Unplugged: MTV aired a brief, seven-song unplugged episode with Elton on July 15, 1990. He planned to do a second segment in 1993 to be released as an album. The project progressed to the point where song lists were drawn up. Plans were scrapped because of a glut of similar projects by the likes of Eric Clapton, Rod Stewart, Neil Young, and Paul McCartney. The proposed play list included many songs that Elton has rarely performed, including "Amoreena," "Dixie Lily," "Breaking Hearts," "Too Low for Zero," "Mellow," "Amazes Me," "Emily," "Hoop of Fire," "Shoot Down the Moon," "Cry to Heaven," "Roy Rogers," "Cage the Songbird," "High Flying Bird," and Tab Hunter's "Young Love."

Van Derek, Johnny: Played violin on "Country Comfort."

Versace, Gianni: The Italian designer counts Elton among his clients and friends. Versace's involvement grew from clothing the star in the mid-1980s to helping design his stage, album cover, and merchandise for *The One*.

Very Best of Elton John, The: The two-CD project was released only in Europe and Japan, topping the charts in Britain in 1990.

Vickery, Graham: Played harmonica on *Empty Sky*.

Videos: MTV, VH1 and the home video industry have revolutionized the music business. Since the early 1980s, Elton has kept a constant flow of videos available for fans. Most of the following official releases are still in distribution:
❖ *From Russia with Elton*. It documented his historic 1979 tour of the Soviet Union with percussionist Ray Cooper.

❖ *Central Park.* The 1980 concert was before 450,000 music fans. It included "Imagine."

❖ *Visions.* It consisted of artistic videos for each of the eleven songs on 1981's *The Fox* album.

❖ Day and Night. This 1984 Wembley Stadium concert was taped for Showtime, but sold as two videos: the daytime portion as *The Breaking Hearts Tour*, the other as *The Nighttime Concert.*

❖ *Live in Australia*: Recorded in December 1986, it was released in two parts. One featured Elton John with his band. The other included Elton, his band and the Melbourne Symphony Orchestra. His approaching throat surgery was evident in the quality of his voice.

> **In the director's seat**: Some who have filmed Elton song videos:
> ❖ Gus Van Sant (*My Own Private Idaho*), "The Last Song."
> ❖ Russell Mulcahy (*Highlander* and *The Shadow*), *Visions*, "Blue Eyes," "I'm Still Standing," and others.
> ❖ Ken Russell (*Tommy*, *Altered States*), "Nikita" and others.
> ❖ Michael Lindsay-Hogg (*Brideshead*, *Let It Be*), "Ego."
> ❖ Bernie Taupin, "In Neon" and others.

❖ *Two Rooms*: Honoring twenty-five years of the John-Taupin collaboration, it featured interviews with the songwriters, rare studio footage, and appearances by Phil Collins, Eric Clapton, Sting, both writers' mothers, and others.

❖ *The Very Best of Elton John*: Available in Europe and Japan, this 1990 video was released at the same time as his import album of the same name. It is a greatest hits collection, bringing together old BBC footage with newer cable-TV song videos.

❖ Video tourbook: In 1992, rather than publish traditional souvenir books, a tour video was sold. It focused on the making of the tour and included interviews with band members.

❖ *World Tour 1992.* Live in Barcelona, Spain.

❖ *The Last Song.* This brief video, benefiting AIDS charities, featured the single, a short interview with Elton, and a public service announcement.

Numerous other official releases include snippets with Elton, among them *Tommy* (the movie), the Freddie Mercury tribute, *Knebworth*, *Live Aid*, *The Prince's Trust Concerts*, *Lean on Me*, *The Who Live*, *John Lennon: Imagine*, and *John Lennon: A Tribute*. Videos, of course, have spawned a whole new field for collectors, who search out bootleg recordings of TV appearances and live concerts. A wealth of such material is available. Among the common favorites is a 1973 television documentary, *Elton John and Bernie Taupin Say Goodbye Norma Jean and Other Things*. One rarity: a 1986 Australian video in which Elton performs "Music Change the World," a YMCA benefit song written by an eight-year-old boy. In addition, Elton has recorded MTV-style videos for over forty songs. By far the most savored release among devout fans would be a video of his U.S. premiere at the Troubadour in 1970. The show was recorded, but only small segments have been aired.

W-Z

WABC Studio: *11-17-70* was recorded live at this New York radio station.

Waldon Woods: The September 6, 1993, Massachusetts benefit featured organizer Don Henley, Aerosmith, Jimmy Buffett, Sting, Melissa Etheridge and Elton.

Warner-Chappell Music: The publishing firm signed Elton and Taupin to a $35-39 million songwriting deal, gaining control of their vast catalog.

Warpipes: The group formed in 1991 with current and past Elton band members Davey Johnstone, Nigel Olsson, Guy Babylon, and Bob Birch, plus vocalist Billy Trudel. Artful Balance released the group's debut album, *Holes in the Heavens*, but the label died months later, leaving the band in limbo after one single, "Back a' Ma Buick." Johnstone, who wrote most of the music (with lyricist Steve Trudell), co-produced the album with Babylon at the latter's studio. The album received good reviews and some airplay, with the band promoting it by performing a live acoustic version of "Goodbye Kemosabe" at radio studios. In 1995, Charlie Morgan's label, Bridge, released the album in Europe, replacing "Back a' Ma Buick," "Divided City," and "Satellite City" with "One Love True," "Dust on My Boots," and "Little Persuader."

> *Holes in the Heavens*, 1991. Songs: "Rock 'n' Roll Condition," "Mr 2 U," "Tear Jerker," "Son of a Loaded Gun," "Holes in the Heavens," "Back a' Ma Buick," "Duty to Dance," "Divided Heart," "Satellite City," "Goodbye Kemosabe." Outtakes: "Dust on My Boots," "Friction," "Ton o' Bricks," "Little Persuader."

Warwick, Dionne: She asked Elton to sing on "That's What Friends Are For." He surprised her onstage for a live version of the song at a late 1980s concert. Elton performed the song solo only at the 1992 tributes to Dee Murray.

Was, Don: Aside from being co-leader of the band Was (Not Was), he has produced many recordings, including Bonnie Raitt's Grammy winner, *Nick of Time*, and the B-52s' "Love Shack" single. Elton sought out Was to produce new songs for the 1990 *To be continued...* box set. "He did all of the vocals in about three hours," said Was, "not only perfect lead vocals, but doubling vocals and singing harmonies with himself."

Washington, Larry: Played percussion on *The Complete Thom Bell Sessions*.

Watford Football Club: One of the few fond memories Elton has of his father revolves around trips to Watford soccer games. Elton enjoys the sport, in which his cousin, Roy Dwight, was a national star. In 1971, Elton became vice president of the Watford Hornets. Five years later, he bought control of the team and ascended to the chairmanship. His interest and money helped to drastically improve Watford, under the leadership of coach Graham Taylor. By 1984 the team had risen from the basement league to the first division. On tour, Elton regularly phoned from hotels to listen to Watford games and check on scores. He was a visible booster, attending games and banquets. The Hornets even sang backup on a few songs. In the 1990s, Elton sold his interest in the team. He retains an honorary title, but is not involved in the decision making. At his concerts, you can often see fans waving Watford scarves.

Webber, Andrew Lloyd: Elton has revealed his intention to write a Broadway musical that will teach Webber a few things about composing melodies.

Weighill, Alan: Played bass on *Elton John*.

West Side Story: Bernie Taupin produced an all-star performance of the music from *West Side Story* on November 18, 1992. The AIDS Project benefit in Los Angeles featured Barbra Streisand, Johnny Mathis, Kenny Loggins, Lyle Lovett, Aaron Neville, Billy Joel, Patti Austin, Clint Black, and Liza Minnelli. But the highlight was Elton dressed in drag singing "I Feel Pretty." Taupin received praise for his effort. Wrote a *Los Angeles Times* reviewer, "Someone hire Bernie Taupin to produce the Oscars. Quickly."

Weston, Doug: He owned the Troubadour in Los Angeles where Elton launched his American career in August 1970. "For years and years, we had folk singers twanging their guitars. ... It was basic, simple music," Weston recalled. "All of a sudden we book Elton, a virtual unknown who'd been seriously struggling in London. Elton got on stage with his band and with just one song enraptured the entire audience." During the weeklong gig, as Elton drew strong reviews, Weston negotiated several options that brought the budding star back to his clubs.

Westwood, Paul: Played bass on *Ice on Fire* and *Leather Jackets*.

Wet, Wet, Wet: The popular British group opened for Elton in 1988 on the U.S. leg of the *Reg Strikes Back* tour.

White, Ryan: The American youth fought a public battle against AIDS. Contracting HIV through a blood transfusion, Ryan was scorned by his schoolmates and forced to move to another town. The story touched Elton. He befriended the boy in 1986, regularly talking and visiting with him. Their friendship grew over time. In Ryan's final days, Elton was at the teen's bedside with family members, running errands for Ryan's mom, Jeanne White, who remains an AIDS activist. At her urging, Elton took a break from his hospital vigil and performed at Farm Aid IV, dedicating "Candle in the Wind" to Ryan and breaking down onstage while performing "I'm Still Standing." At the youth's April 1990 funeral, Elton sang one of his earliest songs, "Skyline Pigeon." He later said that the family's dignity helped him realize his own shortcomings and, combined with other factors, prompted him to fight his multiple addictions.

Whitten, Bill: Though Bob Mackie is the clothes designer most often associated with Elton's flamboyant mid-1970s, Whitten also contributed many classic outfits. Among the better-known creations: a beaded *Goodbye Yellow Brick Road* ensemble, a feathered gorilla suit, and a black space outfit wired with colorful cork balls. Whitten also hatched the idea for Michael Jackson's sequined glove.

Who, The: The group covers "Saturday Night's Alright (for Fighting)" on the *Two Rooms* tribute, tucking a snippet from "Take Me to the Pilot" into the song. The Who was just returning the favor. When Elton covered "Pinball Wizard" in 1975, he ended the song with a taste of the band's "Can't Explain."

Williams, Hugh: The Atlanta, Georgia, ice cream store manager persuaded friend Elton to seek help for his multiple addictions. The four-CD, 1990 boxed set *To be continued...* is dedicated to "Hugh."

Williams, Larry: Played sax on *21 at 33*.

Williams, Ray: As a 19-year-old, Williams was working for Liberty Records when he paired Taupin with Reg Dwight after they responded to a talent ad in a trade publication. Williams said he felt sorry for Reg Dwight. Williams managed Elton for a short time, working through Dick James. As Elton's career took off and his relationship with John Reid blossomed, Williams got left behind. He resents that James later took credit for a lot of his work. Williams went on to a successful career in music and films, managing Jeff Lynne, Stealer's Wheel, serving as press agent for Sonny and Cher and Cream, and winning a Grammy for the score to *The Last Emperor*.

Williams, Romeo: With drummer Jonathan Moffett, Williams served as Elton's rhythm section from 1988 to 1990, playing on *Sleeping with the Past*. He has also worked with Aretha Franklin, Gladys Knight, Natalie Cole, and The Temptations.

Wilson, Brian: The architect of the Beach Boys sound, Wilson inspired Elton musically. In his autobiography, *Wouldn't It Be Nice*, he recounted a 1970 meeting with an insecure Elton, who doubted his abilities as a singer. Wilson encouraged him. "Elton asked if I were still writing. I said not much, which was hard considering how jealous I was of Elton at that moment," Wilson wrote. "Listening to his songs, I knew he was hot, that he was tapped into the great source. I'd been there myself."

Wilson Phillips: The trio covered "Daniel" on *Two Rooms*.

Winter, Norman: He was head of MCA's publicity department when Elton was launched. Winter formed his own company with Elton as the prime client. Winter was responsible for the red English double-decker bus that picked up Elton and his small entourage when they flew into Los Angeles in August 1970 for his U.S. debut. A banner on the bus proclaimed, "Elton John Has Arrived." The artist was embarrassed by the gimmick. But Winter stayed on for several tours. A decade later, he had the good fortune to be with Michael Jackson when *Thriller* became the best-selling album in history. In fact, Winter introduced Elton to Jackson.

Wonder, Stevie: In 1969, Elton did sound-alike records for a British label. Among the artists he mimicked was Wonder doing "Signed, Sealed, Delivered." In 1970 Elton met the Motown star through the label's British representative, John Reid, who had borrowed Elton's car to pick up Wonder at the airport. Elton tagged along. When introduced, Wonder recalled greeting Elton as the "It's a little bit funny" singer, alluding to "Your Song." Fourteen years later, Wonder contributed harmonica to "I Guess That's Why They Call It the Blues." In between, they became acquainted. In the mid-1970s, Wonder joined Elton on stage twice. In 1985 they sang with Dionne Warwick and Gladys Knight the number one hit "That's What Friends Are For." Later, for *Duets*, Wonder wrote, produced, and played all the instruments on "Go On and On."

Woodrow, Linda: Elton met Woodrow on December 24, 1967, at the Sheffield Cavendish Club while in Bluesology. He and Taupin came to share a flat at 29 Furlong Road, Islington, with Woodrow, Elton's fiancee. Feeling trapped by the prospect of marriage, Elton tried half-seriously to take his own life, turning on a gas stove in the flat — but leaving the window open. (The incident was memorialized in "Someone Saved My Life Tonight.") Taupin and Long John Baldry (who was to be the best man) talked Elton out of marrying Woodrow. In the years since, she has talked to the British media about the relationship, describing Elton as a mundane lover.

Woodside: Elton's mansion in England.

Wrather, Steve: Played guitar on *21 at 33*.

Wynette, Tammy: The queen of country music asked Elton to appear on her album of duets. John and Taupin collaborated on the song "A Woman's Needs," which was recorded in Atlanta. But Elton used it on his 1993 album, *Duets*, before Wynette's 1994 collection was released. While promoting the album, Wynette noted that Elton autographed a photo to her: "To the queen of country, from the queen of England."

Young, Neil: Elton was an early admirer of Young's work. He joined James Taylor and Shawn Colvin for a 1992 benefit organized by Young for a San Francisco-area school. Young offered kind words about Elton on the *Two Rooms* video, but the two couldn't get together to record for the *Duets* album.

Zito, Ritchie: An ex-member of Eric Carmen's band, Zito recorded with Neil Sedaka in 1974-75 when Sedaka was on Elton's Rocket label. In the late 1970s, through session work, he came to know Dee Murray and Nigel Olsson, appearing on the drummer's *Changing Tides* album. That work brought him to Elton in 1980 and 1981 for two records and a tour. Zito is a top producer, working with Heart, White Lion, Cher, and Eddie Money.

Photos by Donna Vela

As a teen, Reg Dwight played piano at the Northwood Hills Inn, near his mother's home (below) on Frome Court.

Photos by Sharon R. Fox

Backstage at a 1971 Chicago concert, Elton (above) poses with drummer Nigel Olsson and bass player Dee Murray. A year later (lower right), the star jokes with guitarist Davey Johnstone and manager John Reid.

Photo by Susan Canty

The 1976 tour, at the peak of his popularity, was a record-breaking sellout.

Photo by Sue Guzman-Kirby

Photo by Fran Morreale

Even on his most subdued tours, Elton has dressed colorfully. These shots were taken in New York in 1982 (above) and in Chicago in 1976.

Photo by Susan Canty

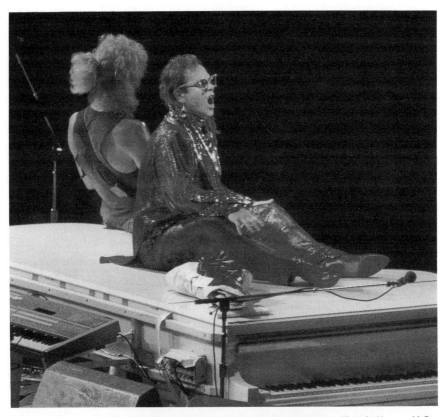

Photo by Nannette M. Bac

In 1984 Elton toured with his original band, including Nigel Olsson (at left). However, by 1986 (above) he had another new band, including Davey Johnstone.

Photo by
Dr. Christau O'Boogie

Photo by Nannette M. Bac

The 1986 tour saw Elton return to outrageous stage costumes.

Albums

Elton John has kept a river of albums flowing toward the buying public. Since 1970, only one year has passed in which he has not issued at least one studio album or compilation in America. This section explores his U.S. albums, except for a few bargain-buy hit collections.

Empty Sky
Released June 1969 in England and January 1975 in America.
Peaked at #6 in 1975.
Producer: Steve Brown.
Studio: Dick James, England.
Recorded: December 1968 through April 1969.
Songs: "Empty Sky" (8:29), "Valhalla" (4:09), "Western Ford Gateway" (3:12), "Hymn 2000" (4:30), "Lady, What's Tomorrow?" (3:06), "Sails" (3:39), "The Scaffold" (3:13), "Skyline Pigeon" (3:31), "Gulliver/Hay Chewed/Reprise" (6:58).
Outtakes: "Lady Samantha," "All Across the Havens," "Just Like Strange Rain," "It's Me That You Need," "Reminds Me of You," "The Flowers Will Never Die," "First Episode at Hienton," "Child," "The Last to Arrive."

       This album, the first by Elton John, holds fond memories for the singer and the lyricist Bernie Taupin, the latter then in his late teens. In their 1975 song "We All Fall in Love Sometimes," they refer lovingly to the album. The 1969 recording, especially the simple, hymn-like ballad "Skyline Pigeon," offered a glimpse of the pair's promise. *Empty Sky* also reflected the influence of The Band and the Rolling Stones on the aspiring songwriters. Among the first songs written and recorded during these sessions was "Lady Samantha," in December 1968. It was released January 17, 1969, as a single, after early manager Lionel Conway and producer Steve Brown convinced music publisher Dick James of the song's potential. James wanted Elton to release a recording of a pop song by Don Black and Mark London, but James was convinced otherwise. The song gave the industry an accurate pre-

Their introduction, too: *Empty Sky* featured drumming by Roger Pope and Nigel Olsson, who between them would keep beat on most of Elton's albums in the 1970s. Session guitarist and friend Caleb Quaye would join the band in 1975. Two others listed among the credits — Steve Brown as producer and Clive Franks as tape operator — remain active in Elton's career.

view of the upcoming album — though it was not included on *Empty Sky*. London radio stations played the single, but it did not chart. In the four months after the album's release, *Empty Sky* sold about 2,500 copies. The record, costing $2,500 to produce, featured session musicians with whom Elton had worked. It included the Elton debut of drummer Nigel Olsson, who appeared on "Lady, What's Tomorrow?" and would join Elton's first band a year later. Six years passed before *Empty Sky* was officially distributed in America.

Originally, UNI Records intended a U.S. release in the fall of 1971, presuming that this older LP would give the pair time to relax after promoting *Elton John* and *Tumbleweed Connection* on the road and before cutting the next album, *Madman Across the Water*. However, with songs already written for *Madman*, the U.S. issue was postponed until 1975. Elton played harpsichord on some tracks, mirroring the psychedelic sound of the time. His voice was reedy and high-pitched, and he had not yet begun to extract catchy lyrical riffs for song choruses. Taupin's thick lyrics drew on mythical and biblical images. The album introduced Elton as a talented musician and thoughtful performer, an image he would build on with his next release.

Elton John

Released April 1970.
Peaked at #4.
Producer: Gus Dudgeon.
Studio: Trident, England.
Recorded: December 1969 through January 1970.
Songs: "Your Song" (4:00), "I Need You to Turn To" (2:30), "Take Me to the Pilot" (3:48), "No Shoe Strings on Louise" (4:30), "First Episode at Hienton" (4:52), "Sixty Years On" (4:33), "Border Song" (3:19), "The Greatest Discovery" (4:11), "The Cage" (3:28), "The King Must Die" (5:09).
Outtakes: "All the Way Down to El Paso," "In the Morning," "Bad Side of the Moon," "Into the Old Man's Shoes," "Ballad of a Well-Known Gun," "Rock and Roll Madonna," "Big Circle of Stone," "She Sings Rock and Roll," "Son of Your Father," "Come Down in Time," "Talking Old Soldiers," "Country Comfort," "Thank You, Mama," "Grey Seal," "I'm Going Home."

With this album — Elton John's introduction to America — critics hailed the Brit as one of music's brightest new stars. Robert Partridge of *Record Mirror* called him "Britain's first real answer to Neil Young and Van Morrison." Some went so far, less than a year into the decade, to predict that Elton John would be to the 1970s what The Beatles were to the 1960s. In preparation for the album, Elton and Taupin wrote forty songs between September and December 1969. Many later appeared on *Tumbleweed Connection*. The *Elton John* album took a month of careful planning, eighteen days to record and fifty-five hours of studio time. At $15,000, it was a costly effort for the time, partly because of the use of an orchestra. Instrumentation was painstakingly planned, and Elton recorded with a string section. Paul Buckmaster and new producer Gus Dudgeon, who had worked together with David Bowie, labored over the arrangements. Buckmaster's sweeping strings were inspired by the classical pieces of Dvorak. "Paul Buckmaster is a genius," said Elton in 1990. "He revolutionized string playing with this album. People still ... talk about the production, the drum sound, the strings on that album." Despite strong reviews, U.S. Top 40 radio was not easily persuaded to pick up the album or its first single, "Border Song." The record label hyped the release, scheduling industry luncheons and concerts — including the now famous Troubadour shows in Los Angeles in August 1970. By November, album-oriented stations were saturated with Elton John. That airplay, combined with glowing concert and album reviews, piqued public interest. The album became so popular on FM radio that it was not uncommon to hear several of its songs on the same station on the same day. The album spawned classics, including the soft "Your Song" — the songwriting duo's standard — and the raucous "Take Me to the Pilot." Some lyrics are autobiographical for Taupin, especially "The Greatest Discovery" (about his younger brother) and "First Episode at Hienton" (about coming of age). In a 1991 interview with David Frost, Elton recalled composing the songs: "In those days it took me about 15 to 20 minutes to write a song and half an hour to an hour to memorize it because I didn't put it on tape. I didn't put any of the songs on tape. So at one point, I had about 30 or 40 songs stockpiled in my head that I'd written by memory." The album showcased Elton's substantial musicianship. His intricate, percussive piano work gave drama to each song. A test of a song's structure and substance is how well it can be performed live. Into his mid-1990s concerts, Elton has continued to play "Sixty Years On," "I Need You to Turn To," "Border Song," and "The Greatest Discovery." Stripped of all other instruments, the songs are even more intimate and expressive. Elton's classical training as an adolescent shows on the *Elton John* album, as do the influences of Jerry Lee Lewis and the Rolling Stones. This moody album, recorded with session musicians, is defined by the orchestral arrangements, Elton's acoustic piano playing, and

> **Experiments on tape:** Demo versions exist of many songs on this and the next two albums. The material is both fascinating and uniquely revealing. "Grey Seal" was recorded twice in demo form, once with just piano and once with full band. The piano demo is an under-stated, three-minute recording with Elton's vocals youthful and unrefined. The mysterious tone of the finished studio recording is absent from the demo, which ends almost cheerfully. So many songs from these sessions were vying for inclusion on the album that "Grey Seal" became an obscure B-side, re-recorded for *Goodbye Yellow Brick Road*, where it gained substantial acceptance as a classic rock track.

Taupin's lyrics, which had become more rhythmic. The album set the stage for a bright future.

Tumbleweed Connection

Released October 1970.
Peaked at #5.
Producer: Gus Dudgeon.
Studio: Trident, England.
Recorded: March-October 1970.

Songs: "Ballad of a Well-Known Gun" (4:59), "Come Down in Time" (3:25), "Country Comfort" (5:08), "Son of Your Father" (3:46), "My Father's Gun" (6:19), "Where to Now, St. Peter?" (4:12), "Love Song" (3:40), "Amoreena" (4:57), "Talking Old Soldiers" (4:06), "Burn Down the Mission" (6:21).

Outtakes: "Into the Old Man's Shoes," "Can I Put You On?," "Honey Roll," "Rolling Western Union," "Madman Across the Water," "Indian Sunset," "Michelle's Song," "Rock Me When He's Gone."

Many songs on this album were actually written for *Elton John* in November and December 1969. ("Ballad of a Well-Known Gun," for example, was written long before "Your Song.") Because their mood was more raw, the songs were saved for *Tumbleweed Connection*. From its title to its sepia-toned cover to its opening song, with references to stagecoaches and bank robberies, *Tumbleweed Connection* focuses on Taupin's fascination with America's Old West. The work was heavily influenced by The Band's *Music from the Big Pink*, including "The Weight." It reflected a change for Elton. Unlike the previous album, *Tumbleweed* lacked lush orchestral arrangements. The music had room to breathe. Its sound was sparse, rustic, and dominated by piano. *Tumbleweed* produced several gems, but no singles were released. "Burn Down the Mission," "Where to Now, St. Peter?" and "Country Comfort" all received solid FM airplay. "Talking Old Soldiers," though more obscure, stands as one of Elton's most poignant ballads. The song balances Elton's solo piano play with one of his strongest vocal performances, giving a remarkable treatment to Taupin's lyrics. The song was recorded in one take, vocals and piano together. Many ideas were tried and scrapped on *Tumbleweed*. Joined by friends and session musicians, Elton sometimes recorded four or five songs a day, only to re-record them differently. On the whole, an average studio session for this album was three hours long, ending with two to three songs on tape. The Leon Russell-like "Amoreena" was the first recording to feature Elton with drummer Nigel Olsson and bass player Dee Murray, his touring band. They had been performing the song live for nearly a year, so Elton used them in the session, initially against producer Gus Dudgeon's wishes. "Love Song," written by Lesley Duncan, marked the first non-Elton composition to appear on one of his albums. In concert, he jokingly introduced it as a "Crosby, Stills, Nash and John" performance. Two of the songs when later covered by other artists ("Country Comfort" by Rod Stewart and "Come Down in Time" by Sting) received more airplay than the Elton versions. Fan surveys have consistently ranked *Tumbleweed Connection* among Elton's most popular albums. It put him firmly on album-oriented rock stations. Critically acclaimed, Elton had not yet become a Top 40 hit maker. But that would occur soon enough, to the ire of rock purists.

Friends
Released March 1971.
Peaked at #36.
Producer: Gus Dudgeon.
Studio: Trident, England.
Recorded: October 1970.
Songs: "Friends" (2:20), "Honey Roll" (3:00), "Variations on Friends" (1:45), "Variations of Friends Theme (The First Kiss)" (3:52), "Seasons" (3:52), "Variations on Michelle's Song" (2:44), "Can I Put You On?" (5:52), "Michelle's Song" (4:16), "I Meant to Do My Work Today" (1:33), "Four Moons" (10:56), "Seasons: Reprise" (1:33).

On October 9, 1969, ten months before their big break in America, Elton and Taupin signed to write three songs — "Seasons," "Michelle's Song," and "Friends" — for this movie sound track. They finished writing in August 1970. The *Friends* sessions took four weeks to complete, including a re-recording, which resulted in the film and sound track containing different versions of some songs. The vocals on "Seasons," for example, vary greatly. The original recordings were raw. The album includes "Honey Roll" and "Can I Put You On?," outtakes from *Tumbleweed Connection* that were intended for *Madman Across the Water*. Several sound track instrumentals were written by Paul Buckmaster, not Elton. Paramount released the film in March 1971, and the title song, a ballad, became a hit in America. Despite a hideous pink cover (designed by Universal Studios), the album also charted. If Elton could have foreseen his upcoming transformation into a star, he would have turned down this project.

11-17-70
Released April 1971.
Peaked at #11.
Producer: Gus Dudgeon.
Studio: A&R, New York.
Recorded: Live November 17, 1970, at radio station WABC in New York.
Songs: "Take Me to the Pilot" (6:43), "Honky Tonk Women" (4:09), "Sixty Years On" (8:05), "Can I Put You On?" (6:38), "Bad Side of the Moon" (4:30), "Burn Down the Mission" medley including "Get Back" and "My Baby Left Me" (18:20). Outtakes: "Your Song," "Border Song," "I Need You to Turn To," "Indian Sunset," "My Father's Gun," "Amoreena."

Elton, drummer Nigel Olsson, and bassist Dee Murray performed live on a radio broadcast for WABC in New York. A strong-selling bootleg of the November 17, 1970, show prompted the release of an official album. The U.S. album mix, done at Trident Studios in London, eclipses the U.K. mix from Dick James Studios.

Live albums usually pull together the best performances over several nights. *11-17-70* featured a single appearance. Elton said he was unaware the performance was being taped. Originally set for September, the event was rescheduled because of the excitement over the August Troubadour shows and trouble obtaining a work permit in America. New York DJ Dave Herman introduced the concert. Joe DiSabato, a John-Taupin fan who worked for WABC, planned it. The 125 tickets went to fans, press, friends, record executives, and contest winners. Elton premiered "Indian Sunset," performing a riveting version, which did not make the album. A studio rendition later appeared on *Madman Across the Water*. No singles were released off the live album. With *11-17-70*, Elton had a glut of fresh material on the market — three new albums within seven months.

Madman Across the Water

Released November 1971.
Peaked at #8.
Producer: Gus Dudgeon.
Studio: Trident, England.
Recorded: February 27, 1971, and August 9-14, 1971.
Songs: "Tiny Dancer" (6:12), "Levon" (5:17), "Razor Face" (4:36), "Madman Across the Water" (5:46), "Indian Sunset" (6:36), "Holiday Inn" (4:14), "Rotten Peaches" (4:55), "All the Nasties" (5:08), "Goodbye" (1:48).
Outtakes: "Salvation," "Rock Me When He's Gone," "Suzie (Dramas)."

Friends and *11-17-70* provided brief diversions for Elton's career. But *Madman Across the Water* picked up musically where *Tumbleweed Connection* left off. It spotlighted Elton's piano work and pensive compositions, but, unlike *Tumbleweed*, also featured Paul Buckmaster's powerful arrangements, best exemplified on the title song and "Levon." Though Elton had been touring for a year with Dee Murray and Nigel Olsson, this album contained little of their work, but did introduce future lead guitarist Davey Johnstone, who appeared with fellow Magna Carta band member Rick Wakeman. (Producer Gus Dudgeon had worked with Magna Carta.) The LP took six days to record and one week to mix. Few songs were written specifically for it. One can detect the influence of The Band, Leon Russell, Bob Dylan, Joni Mitchell, and Jefferson Airplane. Though blasted by music critics (partly because it marked Elton's fifth release in eighteen months), *Madman* sold well, due to interest generated by "Tiny Dancer," "Levon," and the title track. The artist became his own critic, displeased with his vocal performance. Over time, *Madman Across the Water* has become one of his most

Madmen on guitar: An alternate, nine-minute version of the title song was recorded, featuring guitarists Mick Ronson and Michael Chapman. The recording has a hard edge, consisting of numerous guitar and piano solos. With both guitarists, echo effects on guitars, and even some back-masking, the wall of sound nearly drowned out Elton's lead vocals and piano. The version was left in the cans until the 1992 *Rare Masters* release.

popular U.S. albums. That is fitting given Taupin's lyrical attention to the country. Written after their 1970 U.S. tour, most songs relate to the United States, most noticeably "Holiday Inn," "Indian Sunset," and "Rotten Peaches." The songs were composed sporadically: "Madman Across the Water" and "Indian Sunset" in October 1970; others in August 1971; and several in between. With a piano intro for nearly every song and bold solos accenting several tunes, *Madman* rates as the quintessential Elton John piano album. "Tiny Dancer," a minor hit about Taupin's first wife, has grown in stature over the years. Though its six-minute length hindered its chart success, in concert Elton almost always performs the ballad of a "blue jean baby." "Levon," a bigger single, has evolved into a standard. Despite his good fortunes, Elton had just begun to reveal his hit-making capabilities.

Honky Chateau

Released May 1972.
Peaked at #1.
Producer: Gus Dudgeon.
Studio: Strawberry, France.
Recorded: January 1972.
Songs: "Honky Cat" (5:12), "Mellow" (5:30), "I Think I'm Gonna Kill Myself" (3:32), "Suzie (Dramas)" (3:24), "Rocket Man (I Think It's Going to Be a Long, Long Time)" (4:40), "Salvation" (3:26), "Slave" (4:20), "Amy" (4:02), "Mona Lisas and Mad Hatters" (5:00), "Hercules" (5:20).
Outtakes: "I'll Be There Tomorrow," "I'm Going to Be a Teenage Idol," "Elderberry Wine," "Midnight Creeper," "Hi-Heel Sneakers."

> **Sharing the sound**: Fans of the John-Taupin song "Slave" should check out the 1972 John Baldry album, *Everything Stops for Tea*. Side one, produced by Elton and featuring his band, contains the Ross Wilson song "Come Back Again." The similarities between that track and "Slave" are striking, especially in the handling of Johnstone's guitar and banjo work. All of side one resembles *Honky Chateau* musically.

A change would do them some good. That line, paraphrased from "Honky Cat," sums up the impact 1971 had on Elton and Taupin and the direction of their next work. After the serious *Madman Across the Water*, Elton relaxed and had some fun. The result was *Honky Chateau* — and its frivolous feel, exhibited most outrageously on the tap dance punctuated "I Think I'm Gonna Kill Myself." The album introduced Nigel Olsson, Dee Murray, and Davey Johnstone as a recording unit. An acoustic artist, Johnstone learned to play electric guitar during this session. "Suzie (Dramas)" represented his first effort. The album, also introducing Elton on electric piano, unfolded quickly. The band waited for Maxine Feibelman, Taupin's first wife, to shuttle lyrics from Taupin to Elton. He would immediately begin composing and within two hours the track would usually be recorded as a demo. The release revealed the influence of Van Morrison, Ray Charles, and the Rolling Stones. Originally to be recorded at the Stones' mobile studio, the album took five days to write (nine songs in the first three days), nine days to rehearse, and, after a two-week break, ten days to record. Some songs appeared later on *Don't Shoot Me, I'm Only the Piano Player*. Elton has described

Honky Chateau as one of his "happiest" albums, owing to the fun he and the band had while recording in France. Contrasting earlier work, Elton played saloon-style piano, complementing a rowdy, drinking mood. There were exceptions, though. The ballad "Mona Lisas and Mad Hatters" alluded to a shooting in the streets of New York. It and other songs drew consistent radio play. "Rocket Man" and "Honky Cat" became Elton's first top 10 singles. The album expanded Elton's following and shot to number one — a spot to which he would grow accustomed.

Don't Shoot Me, I'm Only the Piano Player

Released January 1973.
Peaked at #1.
Producer: Gus Dudgeon.
Studio: Strawberry, France.
Recorded: June-July 1972.
Songs: "Daniel" (3:52), "Teacher I Need You" (4:08), "Elderberry Wine" (3:34), "Blues for Baby and Me" (5:38), "Midnight Creeper" (3:53), "Have Mercy on the Criminal" (5:55), "I'm Going to Be a Teenage Idol" (3:55), "Texan Love Song" (3:33), "Crocodile Rock" (3:56), "High-Flying Bird" (4:10).
Outtakes: A new version of "Skyline Pigeon," "Tell Me What the Doctor Said."

Recovering from infectious mononucleosis, Elton recorded the album under severe strain. Twelve songs were written in the two days before the recording sessions. Three other songs were left over from the *Honky Chateau* sessions. When the album was released, Elton and Taupin were riding a wave of success. Elton's live concerts were sellouts, and the mass appeal of *Honky Chateau* fed the success of *Don't Shoot Me, I'm Only the Piano Player*. "Daniel" and "Crocodile Rock" became massive hits (the latter his first number one single). Album-oriented FM stations picked up on "Teacher I Need You," "Elderberry Wine," "High-Flying Bird," and "Have Mercy on the Criminal," with Paul Buckmaster's clever arrangements, which were becoming less frequent on Elton's albums. Elton came to view the album as forgettable — a pleasant and short-lived pop record. But he underestimated his work. "Daniel," the first song written and recorded (in three takes), grew to be a standard, though his label balked at releasing it as the first single. The B-side is a remake of the 1968 John-Taupin song "Skyline Pigeon." *Don't Shoot Me* spotlighted strong performances, including Davey Johnstone's 1950s-style guitar on "Crocodile Rock" and Elton's stunning piano on "I'm Going to Be a Teenage Idol." Elton had begun to nurture his reputation for outrageous eyeglasses and stage

King of the scene: When Elton sang "I'm Going to Be a Teenage Idol," he was paying tribute to Marc Bolan of T. Rex. Ironically, 1973 marked the year Elton became an object of fascination. His face graced the covers of heartthrob magazines. High school girls mobbed his police escorts and dominated his concerts with their screams. His image had taken a turn. He evolved from an album rock hero to the bespectacled boy-next-door who sang "Crocodile Rock."

costumes. Further, Taupin's writing style had become less contemplative and more rhythmic and pop-oriented. *Don't Shoot Me* marked Elton's second straight number one album, but it would be eclipsed by its successor.

Goodbye Yellow Brick Road
Released October 1973.
Peaked at #1.
Producer: Gus Dudgeon.
Studio: Strawberry, France.
Recorded: May 1973.
Songs: "Funeral for a Friend/Love Lies Bleeding" (11:05), "Candle in the Wind" (3:41), "Bennie and the Jets" (5:10), "Goodbye Yellow Brick Road" (3:13), "This Song Has No Title" (2:18), "Grey Seal" (4:03), "Jamaica Jerk-Off" (3:36), "I've Seen That Movie Too" (5:59), "Sweet Painted Lady" (3:52), "The Ballad of Danny Bailey (1909-34)" (4:24), "Dirty Little Girl" (5:03), "All the Girls Love Alice" (5:13), "Your Sister Can't Twist (But She Can Rock 'n' Roll)" (2:41), "Saturday Night's Alright (for Fighting)" (4:50), "Roy Rogers" (4:10), "Social Disease" (3:45), "Harmony" (2:49).
Outtakes: "Jack Rabbit," "Whenever You're Ready (We'll Go Steady Again)" "Screw You (Young Man's Blues)," "Supercool," "Lonnie and Josie," "The Last Good Man in My Life," "Let Me Be Your Car," "Gotta Get Back to England," "Good Morning."

    Goodbye Yellow Brick Road has become synonymous with Elton John. The double album is a classic, widely considered the plateau of his career. Originally to be recorded in Jamaica, it had two working titles: *Vodka and Tonics* and *Silent Movies, Talking Pictures*. Taupin wrote the lyrics in two and a half weeks. Elton composed most melodies in three days at the Pink Flamingo Hotel in Kingston, Jamaica, during the time of the famous Joe Frazier/George Foreman boxing match on January 22, 1973. The fight combined with political turmoil to make Jamaica an uncomfortable place for Elton and the band. Though the Rolling Stones had just recorded *Goat's Head Soup* at Dynamic Sounds Studio in Kingston, Elton and his entourage found the production equipment inadequate. Struggling for three days with a bad piano and poor sound system, the group abandoned Jamaica for the familiarity of Chateau d' Hierouville in France, the recording site of two earlier albums. Completed in two weeks, the album offered a rollicking, rocking taste of American culture, with lyrics touching on icons like Marilyn Monroe and Roy Rogers and alluding to gangsters and classic movies. Melodies flaunted the influences of the Beach Boys, The Everly Brothers, Frankie Valli, and Freddie Cannon. In all, twenty-two songs were written and recorded specifically for the release. Two were outtakes from the earlier album and three were written for future projects. *Goodbye Yellow Brick Road* not only produced several hit singles, but tracks that remain rock standards, like the title release, "Bennie and the Jets," "Candle in the Wind," "Funeral for a Friend," and "Saturday Night's Alright (for Fighting)." Critics raved about the album, and nearly all of the songs received airplay. Fans and rock historians alike regard it as the John-Taupin masterpiece. "We could have taken singles off that album for years to come," Elton told BBC disc jockey Andy Peebles. The album excelled in many areas, including packaging, with illustrations accompanying the lyrics. The technical production shone as well, with impeccable attention to detail. Unobtrusive song arrangements (by Del Newman) and background vocals added to the fullness of sound. *Goodbye Yellow Brick Road* succeeded in helping Elton recapture early fans who felt abandoned by the pop nature of his previous two albums. Those releases expanded his audience but were viewed as less musical than their predecessors. "This album's got to be good," said Elton in 1973. "It's an important album for me and my career at this point." He couldn't have hoped for more. *Yellow Brick Road* anchored the number one spot on the U.S. charts for eight weeks and spent forty-three weeks among the forty best-selling albums. None of his studio albums was more successful. Across the Atlantic, it performed as well. "It's only in these later years," said bass player Dee Murray in 1991, "that I'm realizing the full impact of it. People come up and tell me they were influenced in high school by *Goodbye Yellow Brick Road*." Oddly, Elton's band now includes members like keyboardist Guy Babylon and bass player Bob Birch who as teens were inspired by this album. Unfortunately, many music critics used *Goodbye Yellow Brick Road* as the standard by which to judge most later Elton John albums. The comparison was unfair. Elton has been a consistently good songwriter, but albums of this quality are rare. Still, *Goodbye Yellow Brick Road* cemented his place in rock history — and made fans think, erroneously, that band members Davey Johnstone, Nigel Olsson, and Dee Murray would always be part of the musical equation.

Caribou

Released May 1974.
Peaked at #1.
Producer: Gus Dudgeon.
Studios: Caribou Ranch, Colorado; Record Plant, California; and Brother, California.
Recorded: January 1974, remixed in February 1974.
Songs: "The Bitch Is Back" (3:42), "Pinky" (3:53), "Grimsby" (3:47), "Dixie Lily" (2:48), "Solar Prestige a Gammon" (2:50), "You're So Static" (4:49), "I've Seen the Saucers" (4:45), "Stinker" (5:16), "Don't Let the Sun Go Down on Me" (5:33), "Ticking" (7:34).
Outtakes: "Sick City," "Cold Highway," "Hard Luck Story," "Snookeroo," "I'll Make You Smile," "Here Comes Miss Hurt Again," "Cadillac," "Ducktail Jiver."

Early on, Elton envisioned the album as *Ol' Pink Eyes Is Back*, with a cover featuring him dressed as Sinatra with a fedora, cigarette in mouth, and jacket slung over his back. When the idea was dropped, Ringo Starr suggested the title *Caribou*, the name of the Colorado studio at which it was recorded. The album was written in two days, mostly at the studio, and recorded in six. Fourteen songs were reportedly written and recorded, two of them country/western. Elton took the tapes to the Record Plant in Los Angeles for remixing. As the follow-up to *Goodbye Yellow Brick Road*, the album was destined to face criticism. Realizing that, Elton did a musical about-face. He and the band returned to the much looser, rocking feel of 1972's *Honky Chateau*. Percussionist Ray Cooper joined the group, and a horn section embellished several songs. But the album inevitably reflected numerous compromises. Producer Gus Dudgeon admitted disappointment at the inconsistencies. *Caribou* was made under intense stress. Stardom had begun to exact its price. The band wasn't getting along, Dudgeon and Elton were arguing, and the group had just ten days to work before touring Japan. "The Bitch Is Back" and "Don't Let the Sun Go Down on Me" charted. The whole album

Discord over vocals: The vocals for "Don't Let the Sun Go Down on Me" took so many takes that Elton wanted to drop the song. Frustrated and angry, he intentionally missung the word "discard" — pronouncing it "discord." He told Dudgeon to scrap the song or give it to Lulu or Engelbert Humperdinck. He didn't anticipate such problems when composing the tune. Drummer Nigel Olsson said he knew the song would be a hit. "It was early morning and I was upstairs in my room, half awake, and I could hear Elton downstairs in the breakfast room at Caribou sort of plunking out the first few verses," Olsson said. "He seemed to be struggling with the first line of the chorus when all of a sudden he got it and the whole chorus started to come out. Man, it hit me, and I ran downstairs right to him and said that it would be a number one hit."

received airplay, but that was more a sign of Elton's popularity than of the work's quality. (Even a B-side, the marvelous "Sick City," received radio play.) Decades later, the two hits and the riveting piano masterpiece "Ticking" remain a proud part of Elton's legacy. Despite the conflict and criticism, *Caribou* reached number one.

Greatest Hits
Released November 1974.
Peaked at #1.
Producer: Gus Dudgeon.
Songs: "Your Song" (4:00), "Daniel" (3:52), "Honky Cat" (5:12), "Goodbye Yellow Brick Road" (3:13), "Saturday Night's Alright (for Fighting)" (4:55), "Rocket Man" (4:40), "Bennie and the Jets" (5:10), "Don't Let the Sun Go Down on Me" (5:33), "Border Song" (3:19), "Crocodile Rock" (3:54).

This compilation is the best-selling album in the Elton John catalog. Its popularity spans the world. In America, it became the first hits package to reach number one. The Diamond Club in Canada honored it in 1988 as one of the few albums to ever ship more than one million copies to Canada. The American and British releases differed. In the United Kingdom, "Candle in the Wind" replaced "Bennie and the Jets." The album gave Elton and Taupin time to compose another masterpiece.

Captain Fantastic and the Brown Dirt Cowboy

Released May 1975.
Peaked at #1.
Producer: Gus Dudgeon.
Studio: Caribou Ranch, Colorado.
Recorded: June-August 1974.
Songs: "Captain Fantastic and the Brown Dirt Cowboy" (5:45), "Tower of Babel" (4:28), "Bitter Fingers" (4:32), "Tell Me When the Whistle Blows" (4:20), "Someone Saved My Life Tonight" (6:45), "(Gotta Get a) Meal Ticket" (4:00), "Better Off Dead" (2:35), "Writing" (3:38), "We All Fall in Love Sometimes" (4:15), "Curtains" (6:12).
Outtakes: "Planes," "House of Cards," "Dogs in the Kitchen" (probably just a poem), "Philadelphia Freedom," "Lucy in the Sky with Diamonds," "One Day at a Time."

Though many view *Goodbye Yellow Brick Road* as Elton's definitive work, the less-commercial *Captain Fantastic and the Brown Dirt Cowboy* is its artistic equal. After 1974's disappointing *Caribou*, *Captain Fantastic* reestablished the songwriters with professional critics. From its autobiographical nature to the impeccable writing, musicianship, and outstanding packaging, the album reflected the genius of John and Taupin at their pinnacle. It entered the album charts at number one — a feat that eluded even The Beatles and Elvis Presley. For some critics, Elton would never again measure up to this album. The release also sealed Elton's glitter-rock image as Captain Fantastic. He would work for more than a decade to shed that caricature, which limited him as a live performer and detracted from the music. (Taupin, however, seemed at peace with his portrayal as the "brown dirt cowboy.") Ironically, *Captain Fantastic* itself defied the glitter-rock image. The songs were serious and introspective and tinged with nostalgia, probing the songwriters' early years. Their success gave them the freedom to write an album that blatantly avoided their hit-making formula. The idea for the concept album came to Taupin while writing a poem called "Dogs in the Kitchen." John and Taupin preplanned the running order of the album lyrically before Elton wrote melodies. During the session, Elton was listening to Joni Mitchell's *Court and Spark*, and he drew musical and vocal inspiration from it. Elton wrote four songs, including "Meal Ticket," while on a five-day cruise on the *S.S. France* from Southhampton, England, to New York (in July 1974). He used the ship's piano daily from noon to 2 P.M., when it was not in use by the boat's entertainer. The songs touched on the childhood of Elton and Taupin, their frustration at trying to write hit songs for Dick James, their fledgling partnership, and other experiences. "Someone Saved My Life Tonight," the lone single, revisited Elton's depression over a poten-

Oh, by the way: During the sessions for *Captain Fantastic*, several songs were recorded that had little to do with the album's autobiographical story line. They were intended as non-album singles. Among them were two number-one hits, "Philadelphia Freedom" and "Lucy in the Sky with Diamonds."

tially disastrous near-marriage early in his career. "*Captain Fantastic* was, for me, one of the best albums we ever recorded," Elton said in a 1990 radio interview. "I felt more involved in the lyrics. I didn't write them, but they were all about Bernie and I." Taupin selected the photos and diary excerpts for the booklets that accompanied the release. The album took one month to record and two months to mix. Producer Gus Dudgeon came up with four separate mixes of each track, and Elton chose which ones to release. Dudgeon maintains that *Captain Fantastic...* is Elton's best work. "There's not one song on there that is less than incredible," he said. "From every conceivable point of view, it adds up to being the best." Given the accolades, fans had trouble understanding why months after its release Elton fired longtime drummer Nigel Olsson and bassist Dee Murray.

Rock of the Westies

Released October 1975.
Peaked at #1.
Producer: Gus Dudgeon.
Studio: Caribou Ranch, Colorado.
Recorded: June-July 1975.
Songs: "Medley: Yell Help; Wednesday Night; Ugly" (6:30), "Dan Dare (Pilot of the Future)" (3:25), "Island Girl" (3:45), "Grow Some Funk of Your Own" (4:45), "I Feel Like a Bullet (in the Gun of Robert Ford)" (5:30), "Street Kids" (6:30), "Hard Luck Story" (5:05), "Feed Me" (4:00), "Billy Bones and the White Bird" (4:25).
Outtakes: "Chameleon," "Sugar on the Floor," "Tonight," "Sorry Seems to Be the Hardest Word," "Desperation," "Boogie Pilgrim," "Cage the Songbird," "Between Seventeen and Twenty," "The Wide-Eyed and Laughing," "If There's a God in Heaven."

The album was originally to be titled *Bottled and Brained*, a line from "Street Kids," a piece about Taupin's teen years. *Rock of the Westies* refers to the Los Angeles session men whom Elton picked from for his new band, as well as the group's West Coast sound, influenced by Little Feat, the Doobie Brothers, and The Eagles. And, of course, with the recording taking place in Colorado, it also played on the phrase "west of the Rockies." Most of the project was written and recorded in one week. In fact, it contains more one-take recordings than any of his other albums. *Rock of the Westies* and its outtakes bear musical comparisons with one of Elton's favorite albums of 1974, Little Feat's *Feets Don't Fail Me Now*. Many songs for the following *Blue Moves* project also were written during these sessions. The new band included Davey Johnstone and Ray Cooper, along with Roger Pope and Caleb Quaye (who worked on Elton's earliest albums), bass player Kenny Passarelli and keyboardist James Newton Howard. Most backing tracks were recorded in one week on single takes with few overdubs. The lineup offered an up-tempo, rock and roll sound. Elton wanted to contrast his earlier album, *Captain Fantastic*, to deter comparisons. But critics did not want a *Caribou*-style follow-up to the much-praised *Captain Fantastic*. For a recording that entered the charts at number one, *Rock of the Westies* gets little respect. Elton rarely performs material from it, and both MCA and Geffen labels have overlooked the album in publicity biographies. Oddly,

Rolling Stone magazine, rarely an admirer of Elton, ranks this as among his best works. Though *Rock of the Westies* boasts fine musicianship, the songs are inconsistent. What holds the album together is the energy of Elton's vocal and instrumental performance. The chart-topping single "Island Girl" paled next to songs like the ballad "I Feel Like a Bullet (in the Gun of Robert Ford)" and "Billy Bones and the White Bird." Arguably, the best song from the *Westies* session did not appear on the album. "Sugar on the Floor," a Kiki Dee composition, surfaced as a B-side, reminding fans of Leon Russell's influence on Elton. Though one of the less memorable albums from his commercial plateau, *Rock of the Westies* holds lasting significance for one reason: Not since then has an Elton John album — *The Lion King*, with extensive work by arranger Hans Zimmer, does not qualify — hit number one in America or rocked as hard.

Here and There

Released May 1976.
Peaked at #4.
Producer: Gus Dudgeon.
Recorded live at Royal Festival Hall, London, on May 18, 1974, and at Madison Square Garden, New York, on November 28, 1974.
Songs: "Skyline Pigeon" (4:44), "Border Song" (3:23), "Honky Cat" (7:32), "Love Song" (Lesley Duncan) (5:41), "Crocodile Rock" (4:04), "Funeral for a Friend/ Love Lies Bleeding" (11:47), "Rocket Man" (4:48), "Bennie and the Jets" (6:17), "Take Me to the Pilot" (5:55).
Outtakes: "Country Comfort," "Holiday Inn," "I Need You to Turn To," "Your Song," "Take Me to the Pilot," "Honky Cat," "I Saw Her Standing There," "Goodbye Yellow Brick Road," "Daniel," "Don't Let the Sun Go Down on Me," "Crocodile Rock," "The Bitch Is Back," "Grimsby," "Lucy in the Sky with Diamonds," "Candle in the Wind," "Whatever Gets You Thru the Night," "Grey Seal," "Burn Down the Mission," "Saturday Night's Alright (for Fighting)."

The album's sole purpose was to fulfill Elton's record contract with Dick James Music. James wanted an album of twelve unreleased songs (eight of which were said to be "great"), but a live album was delivered instead. Some of the unreleased songs would appear on the next project.

Blue Moves

Released October 1976.
Peaked at #3.
Producer: Gus Dudgeon.
Studios: Eastern, Canada; Abbey Road, England; Brother, California; and Sunset Sound, California.
Recorded: March-June 1976.
Songs: "Your Starter For..." (1:25), "Tonight" (8:02), "One Horse Town" (5:47), "Chameleon" (5:27), "Boogie Pilgrim" (6:03), "Cage the Songbird" (3:28), "Crazy Water" (5:42), "Shoulder Holster" (4:20), "Sorry Seems to Be the Hardest Word"

Missing songs: If you're looking for the entire *Blue Moves*
album on CD, you can't find
it — yet. MCA put the two-
album set onto a single CD,
eliminating four songs: "Cage
the Songbird," "Shoulder
Holster," "The Wide-Eyed
and Laughing," and "Where's
the Shoorah?" A complete re-
release is planned.

(3:43), "Out of the Blue" (6:10), "Between Seventeen and Twenty" (5:10), "The Wide Eyed and Laughing" (3:20), "Someone's Final Song" (4:00), "Where's the Shoorah?" (4:10), "If There's a God in Heaven" (4:20), "Idol" (4:10), "Theme from a Non-Existent TV Series" (1:20), "Bite Your Lip (Get up and Dance)" (6:37).

Outtakes: "The Man Who Loved to Dance," "Flinstone Boy," "Don't Go Breaking My Heart," "Snow Queen," "City of Blue," "Shine On Through," "Ego."

With *Rock of the Westies* and *Captain Fantastic*, Elton John had peaked in sales and airplay. *Blue Moves*, the album that followed in 1976, marked a decline in popularity. "I think people had enough of me by the time *Blue Moves* came out," said Elton in a 1978 *Billboard* interview. "I'd put out an awful lot of product." Exhausted, he did little to promote it. "Sorry Seems to Be the Hardest Word" cracked the top 10, the last Elton release to do so for three years. Songs such as "Tonight," "One Horse Town," "Chameleon," "Crazy Water," and "Cage the Songbird" received limited play. Originally intended to be a single album (called *Black Moves*), MCA officials insisted on a two-album set when they discovered enough songs existed. Producer Gus Dudgeon protested, but to no avail. "I am proud of this album, because there are eight or nine songs which sound exactly as I wanted them to sound when I wrote them at the piano," said Elton in 1976. The release contained eighteen tracks; two others were written for the project, which was recorded in three weeks. However, eight or nine tracks had been recorded during the *Rock of the Westies* sessions and were reworked for *Blue Moves*. As for the lyrics, many are personal to Taupin. "Tonight" and "Someone's Final Song" allude to his marital problems. "Cage the Songbird" was to be the title track for Kiki Dee's next album, but instead she received "The Man Who Loved to Dance." "Chameleon" was written two years earlier for the Beach Boys, who rejected it. "Tonight," the album's centerpiece, irritated some critics who saw its eight-minute length as a sign of artistic excess. But they were off base. In the spirit of "Ticking," "Have Mercy on the Criminal," "Indian Sunset," and "Madman Across the Water," "Tonight" represented the less commercial and arguably more substantial songwriting of John-Taupin — a welcome relief from the three-minute radio format. The song served as an epitaph for such lengthier album work. In the 1980s, John and Taupin released nothing comparable. Elton's inevitable fall from the pinnacle of rock — a fall accelerated by his admission that he enjoyed sex with men — painted *Blue Moves* as a failure. On his 1980 solo album, Taupin lamented in song that the album had strangled him. With Taupin battling alcoholism and Elton burned out by the rock and roll lifestyle, it was indeed a blue period for the two. But in time, *Blue Moves* would gain respect for its maturity.

Greatest Hits Volume II

Released October 1977.
Peaked at #21.
Songs: "The Bitch Is Back" (3:42), "Lucy in the Sky with Diamonds" (5:58), "Sorry Seems to Be the Hardest Word" (3:43), "Don't Go Breaking My Heart" (4:23), "Someone Saved My Life Tonight" (6:45), "Philadelphia Freedom" (5:38), "Island Girl" (3:45), "Grow Some Funk of Your Own" (4:45), "Levon" (4:59), "Pinball Wizard" (5:08).

The release marked the album premiere of four songs: "Philadelphia Freedom," "Lucy in the Sky with Diamonds," "Don't Go Breaking My Heart," and "Pinball Wizard." All were singles, but none had yet appeared on an Elton album. When PolyGram rereleased the package in 1992, it lacked the rights to two songs: "Sorry Seems to Be the Hardest Word" and "Don't Go Breaking My Heart." They were replaced by "Tiny Dancer" and "I Feel Like a Bullet (in the Gun of Robert Ford)."

A Single Man

Released October 1978.
Peaked at #15.
Producers: Elton John and Clive Franks.
Studio: The Mill, England.
Recorded: January-September 1978.
Songs: "Shine on Through" (3:40), "Return to Paradise" (4:12), "I Don't Care" (4:20), "Big Dipper" (4:00), "It Ain't Gonna Be Easy" (8:23), "Part-Time Love" (3:12), "Georgia" (4:47), "Shooting Star" (2:43), "Madness" (6:07), "Reverie" (0:52), "Song for Guy" (6:34).
Outtakes: "Smile That Smile," "Trying Too," "Lovesick," "I Cry at Night," "Strangers," "Dreamboat," "Can't Get Over Getting Over Losing You," "Earn While You Learn," "Ego," "Flinstone Boy," "I'll Try," "Remember (I'm Still in Love with You)."

The album title reflected Elton's state of mind. He had dropped his band, was co-producing himself, and even suggesting lines for lyrics. Elton and Taupin drifted apart after *Blue Moves*. Though the separation was neither formal nor permanent, each worked more freely with other songwriters. For *A Single Man*, Elton collaborated with lyricist Gary Osborne. Their writing method offered Elton a change, with Osborne fitting words to Elton's melodies and Elton contributing to the lyrics. (With Taupin, Elton wrote the melodies after receiving lyrics.) Initially when Elton went into the studio in the winter of 1978, he planned only to record a single, "Ego," which he had earlier demoed, along with "Shine on Through," "Flinstone Boy," and "I'll Try." Co-producer Clive Franks remembered, "Elton was tinkling away on the piano between takes, and by the time we had finished recording the single, he had ideas for six songs." Other tunes had been composed earlier. With melodies written, Osborne was called in to do lyrics. In all, twenty-eight songs were recorded. The work was initially titled *Shine on Through*. Elton considered putting out a double album, but the other songs did not fit the mood of *A Single Man*. Further, Elton was having problems with his record company, MCA. The troubles became more apparent when MCA fought the single release of the instrumental track "Song for Guy." (The artistic struggle frustrated Elton and later he signed with Geffen Records.) On the strength of Elton's reputation, the album charted respectably in the top 20. But music fashion was changing, and Elton found himself out of style. Disco dominated the charts. Though the album's sound was contemporary, it produced no major hits. The single "Part-Time Love" died quickly. Critics were cold to the album, one proclaiming that it left Elton "a single man, without any fans." In Europe, bolstered by the "Song for Guy" instrumental, the album did well. Except for percussionist Ray Cooper and co-producer Clive Franks, Elton relied on studio musicians. The project marked the return of arranger Paul Buckmaster, though his work was less prominent than on early albums. Elton promoted the LP heavily. In fact, one day he did twenty press interviews over a seven-hour period while visiting Los Angeles. He wanted to show his star power had not waned, though clearly it had. In early October 1978, Elton surprised 250 MCA executives at their national convention by performing live for the first time in a year. He did a two-hour solo set that included much of *A Single Man*. The album is regarded now as an interesting experiment on Elton's part. Several songs are pleasant, but only the instrumental "Song for Guy" has demonstrated longevity. The artist who once released five albums within eighteen months had deliberately slowed down. "I've gotten in the routine of doing albums," he said. "You can't maintain huge selling albums. There must be a break sometime."

The split: When *A Single Man* debuted, critics and fans focused on one question: Where is lyricist Bernie Taupin? Since 1967, his and Elton's names had been entwined. For a non-performing lyricist, Taupin received tremendous credit on Elton's albums. Often, he was pictured prominently in the album packaging and always mentioned in interviews. And, so, his absence received attention, and it became more pronounced two months later when Alice Cooper released *From the Inside*, co-written with Taupin. Years later, Elton and Bernie would downplay their separation, painting it alternately as no big deal and a distancing that reignited their partnership. But there was more to it. Each needed to test his talents individually. They lived in different countries, but were aware of the other's projects — competitive, in fact. Further, Elton was getting more heavily involved in drugs and alcohol, as Taupin was drying out. While Elton's homosexuality was never a surprise to Taupin, it began to impact him as Elton became public about it. In two songs around the time of their separation, Taupin made clear that he and Elton were not lovers. On "Approaching Armageddon," Taupin referred to the gossip and said he never tried the "swings," alluding to bisexuality. The irony of their brief separation is that to this day, several critics greet each new Elton John album with the pronouncement that he has reunited with Taupin. In fact, Taupin's work appears on all but two of Elton's releases.

Victim of Love

Released October 1979.
Peaked at #35.
Producer: Pete Bellotte.
Studios: Musicland, Germany, and Rusk Sound, California.
Recorded: August 1979.

Songs: "Johnny B. Goode" (8:06), "Warm Love in a Cold World" (3:22), "Born Bad" (6:20), "Thunder in the Night" (4:40), "Spotlight" (4:22), "Street Boogie" (3:53), "Victim of Love" (5:02).

Widely regarded as Elton's worst album, *Victim of Love* marked his disco debut. Originally titled *Thunder in the Night*, the project was proposed by producer Pete Bellotte after he attended an April 1979 Elton concert at London's Drury Lane Theatre. The men had known each other since the late 1960s, when Bluesology, with Elton on keyboards, played the Top Ten Club in Germany. Bellotte belonged to another group on the bill. The two fell out of touch. When Elton picked up a Donna Summer album, he was surprised to see his old friend listed in the credits. Elton agreed to do the album, stipulating that he would supply only vocals. Bellotte did the songs. The vocals for the album were recorded in eight hours. Elton was writing songs for *21 at 33* at the time but flew to Munich to record. Elton has maintained that *Victim of Love* was not a serious musical departure. Fans and critics promptly dismissed the effort. The title single not withstanding, the album became better known among fans for its dreadful disco version of "Johnny B. Goode." Coupled with the single release months earlier of a Spinners song, Thom Bell's "Mama Can't Buy You Love" (off an extended-play single), *Victim of Love* left fans unsure where Elton would go next.

21 at 33

Released May 1980.
Peaked at #13.
Producer: Elton John and Clive Franks.
Studios: Superbear, France; Sunset Sound, California; and Rambo, California.
Recorded: August 1979; January-March 1980.

Songs: "Chasing the Crown" (5:36), "Little Jeannie" (5:18), "Sartorial Eloquence" (4:44), "Two Rooms at the End of the World" (5:37), "White Lady, White Powder" (4:35), "Dear God" (3:45), "Never Gonna Fall in Love Again" (4:07), "Take Me Back" (3:52), "Give Me the Love" (5:19).

Outtakes: "Steal Away Child," "Tactics," "Love So Cold," "Tortured," "The Retreat," "Bobby Goes Electric," "Conquer the Sun," "Cartier," "White Man Danger," "Free the People" (it evolved into "Breaking Down the Barriers"), "Reach Out to Me" (it became "Les Aveux"), "Can't Get Over, Getting Over Losing You," "Heart in the Right Place," "Carla/Etude," "Chloe," "Elton's Song," "Basque," "Fanfare."

The title stood for the twenty-one albums (counting double albums as two) that Elton had released by age 33. Intended as a two-album set, the release was pared down to two separate LPs, the latter being *The Fox*. When *21 at 33* was released, it was rumored that Elton had a better album in the can and was looking for a new record label. In September 1980, Elton performed on Tom Snyder's "The Tomorrow Show." Playing solo, he hinted at his bitterness with MCA when introducing the song "Sartorial Eloquence." "Well, over here they're calling it 'Don't You Wanna Play This Game No More.' I don't know why!" After his 1980 tour, Elton signed with David Geffen's label. Most of the songs on *21 at 33* were written in August 1979 in Grasse, France — six of them, including "Little Jeannie," on one day. Elton wrote with four lyricists, including Taupin, who explained their separation on the song "Two Rooms at the End of the World." Similarly, Elton called on many musicians: members of Toto, The Eagles, Beach Boys, Peter Noone, Toni Tennille, session players, and, on a few songs, ex-band mates Nigel Olsson, Dee Murray, and James Newton Howard. Thanks to a sizzling performance by Steve Lukather, the album had more of an edge than *A Single Man*, with the synthesizers and electric pianos playing a large role. Polite critics welcomed Elton's return to his musical roots — as well as his reunion with Taupin. With "Little Jeannie," a Gary Osborne song, Elton launched the decade with a major hit. Even album-oriented stations gave *21 at 33* a chance. Through most of the 1970s, Gus Dudgeon produced Elton. *A Single Man* and *21 at 33* were co-produced by Elton and longtime associate Clive Franks. The next album would introduce a new partnership.

The Fox
Released in May 1981.
Peaked at #21.
Producer: Chris Thomas.
Studios: Sunset Sound, California; Davlen, California; Village Recorders, California; Superbear, France; and EMI Abbey Road, England.
Recorded: August 1979; January-June 1980.
Songs: "Breaking Down the Barriers" (4:35), "Heart in the Right Place" (5:15), "Just Like Belgium" (4:05), "Nobody Wins" (3:42), "Fascist Faces" (5:10), "Carla/ Etude" (4:45), "Fanfare" (1:39), "Chloe" (4:38), "Heels of the Wind" (3:37), "Elton's Song" (3:03), "The Fox" (5:13).
Outtakes: "The Retreat," "Fools in Fashion," "The Man Who Never Died," "Can't Get Over, Getting Over Losing You," "Sweetheart on Parade," "Love So Cold," "Tortured," "Lonely Boy."

Elton's first record for his new label, Geffen Records, brought controversy within the industry. It was thought that Elton had already recorded another album of tracks while with MCA. After Elton signed with David Geffen and released *The Fox*, MCA sued, charging that it owned distribution rights. The label contended that MCA had paid for the studio time that resulted in *The Fox*. Geffen and Elton won the battle. *The Fox* was jokingly titled "The Languishing Giant," referring to Elton's diminishing output. Early on, the album consisted of ten strong tracks left over from the *21 at 33* sessions. Geffen rejected six songs, and Elton returned to the studio to write and record new material. The new tracks were produced by Chris Thomas, who had worked with George Martin and known Elton since the late 1960s. "The

Retreat," "Tortured," "Love So Cold," and "The Man Who Never Died" (an instrumental tribute to John Lennon) were among those unwisely axed from the album. In later interviews, Elton said *The Fox* reflected the emotional turmoil that dominated his life at the time. Lyrically, Taupin, Osborne, and Tom Robinson contributed songs related to the star, most obviously "Elton's Song." "Nobody Wins," a painful story about the singer's childhood, charted,

Before MTV: *Visions*, a laser disc and video of *The Fox*, directed by Russell Mulcahy, appeared in 1983. When recorded in 1981, it was the first album-length video by any artist. Unfortunately, poor organization delayed the video's release for two years. Elton expressed disappointment in interviews. *Visions*, with videos fashioned for each song, came before MTV made such projects common. Though Elton had earlier admitted his interest in men, *Visions* marked the first time he had gone public through his music. "Elton's Song" focuses on a boy's crush on an older youth.

but *The Fox* lacked a big hit and got little airplay. The album was a genuine attempt to showcase his maturity as a singer/songwriter. It included two instrumentals, "Carla/ Etude" and "Fanfare." Reviews in industry trade publications proclaimed *The Fox* as Elton's best record since the mid-1970s. That pronouncement would become more common with future albums.

Jump Up!

Released April 1982.
Peaked at #17.
Producer: Chris Thomas.
Studios: Air, France, and Pathe Marconi, France.
Recorded: September-October 1981 and January-February 1982.
Songs: "Dear John" (3:31), "Spiteful Child" (4:15), "Ball & Chain" (3:27), "Legal Boys" (3:05), "I Am Your Robot" (4:43), "Blue Eyes" (3:25), "Empty Garden (Hey, Hey Johnny)" (5:09), "Princess" (4:56), "Where Have All the Good Times Gone?" (4:00), "All Quiet on the Western Front" (5:59).
Outtakes: "Lonely Boy," "Take Me Down to the Ocean," "Hey, Papa Legba," "Choc Ice Goes Mental," "The Ace of Hearts and the Jack of Spades," "Waking up in Europe," "Jerry's Law," "I'm Not Very Well," "Desperation Train," "At This Time in My Life."

Elton's second album for Geffen Records fueled his comeback. *Jump Up!* is a South African phrase denoting a good time, and Elton had one with this release. "A tour de force record," said critic Parke Puterbaugh in *Rolling Stone*. "The sheer stylistic breadth of this record should secure John's reputation as a rare master of pop music." Much praise could be traced to the unconventional ballad "Blue Eyes" and the John Lennon tribute "Empty Garden," which, according to *Billboard* magazine, "more than any other song in recent years comes closest to matching Elton's best work." Those songs combined to give Elton his most successful year on the singles charts since 1976. Like "Empty Garden," most material was written at Pathe Marconi Studios in Paris. Elton was unhappy with the studio and moved the recording sessions. "Ball & Chain," featuring Pete Townshend on guitar, and "Legal Boys," with lyrics by Tim Rice, who co-wrote *Evita* and *Jesus Christ Superstar*, also drew airplay. Elton's band featured familiar faces: James Newton Howard, Dee Murray, Toto's Jeffrey Porcaro, and Ritchie Zito. Lyrics were split between Taupin and Osborne. The album blended the wistfulness of *The Fox* with the guitar edge of *Rock of the Westies*. In all, twelve songs were written, mostly in Paris, France. Producer Chris Thomas recorded tracks three ways, selecting the best sound and tempo for the album. On "Blue Eyes" and "Where Have All the Good Times Gone?," Elton sang in a lower key, as Philadelphia producer Thom Bell had encouraged him three years earlier. Elton would do so more frequently on later recordings. "Desperation Train," a brilliant Taupin song, was omitted from the album. (It later appeared with a different melody on Taupin's 1987 *Tribe* album.) The imagery is vintage Taupin, refreshing in its line-after-line format. "All Quiet on the Western Front" and "Empty Garden" also showed strong lyrical form. Much of Taupin's writing in the 1980s possessed a simpler rhyme scheme. While allowing Elton more ease melodically, it often resulted in typical pop songs. By the late 1980s, Elton began expressing the desire that Taupin stop writing verse-verse-chorus arrangements in favor of a freer format. During the *Jump Up!* sessions, David Geffen pushed Elton to reunite his old band. "It became a big plan," said lyricist Osborne. And Elton followed through with it on his next album.

Too Low for Zero

Released June 1983.
Peaked at #25.
Producer: Chris Thomas.
Studios: Air, France, and Sunset Sound, California.
Recorded: September 1982; mixed March 1983.
Songs: "Cold as Christmas (in the Middle of the Year)" (4:18), "I'm Still Standing" (3:00), "Too Low for Zero" (5:44), "Religion" (4:02), "I Guess That's Why They Call It the Blues" (4:42), "Crystal" (5:04), "Kiss the Bride" (4:20), "Whipping Boy" (3:42), "Saint" (5:18), "One More Arrow" (3:36).
Outtakes: None known.

Elton brought back drummer Nigel Olsson, bassist Dee Murray, and guitarist Davey Johnstone, and he co-wrote all songs with Taupin. The star told the world that he wanted once again to have a number one album. And while *Too Low for Zero* would spend more weeks on the charts than any other Elton John album since *Captain Fantastic*, it would not hit the top spot. But it rightfully drew critical praise. All songs were written in September 1982 at the Air Studio in Montserrat on a rhythm box synthesizer. Only ten songs were written, and they were recorded in a two-week session. Producer Chris Thomas took the tapes to Los Angeles for a week of overdubs. Except for the electric keyboards and synthesizers, the album sounds like vintage Elton, from the solos to the signature backing vocals of his band mates. Furthermore, in June 1982, before recording, Elton and Taupin forged a new bond. Elton spent ten days with Taupin in Los Angeles. "We both realized how much we wanted to do this album," Taupin told *Billboard*. "Before, we'd taken each other for granted and hadn't allowed each other to grow. [This time,] we actually talked about writing songs, which we'd never done before. Elton realized I was far more musically inclined and could objectively criticize what he'd do, and he could do the same for me. We're not as afraid of encroaching on each other's territory." The words and melodies blend nicely. *Rolling Stone*, *Billboard*, and *Cash Box* all hailed the album as a true return to form. Three singles enjoyed great success. "I'm Still Standing" grew to become Elton's anthem, aided by a strong video. "I Guess That's Why They Call It the Blues," recorded with a harmonica solo by Stevie Wonder, evolved into a concert standard. "Kiss the Bride," a rocking single, took on new meaning less than a year later when Elton married the album's engineer, Renate Blauel. Three other songs fall in the company of his best work: the dreamy "Cold as Christmas," the wistful "One More Arrow," and the title cut. Taupin, who has always been less likely to hype an album than Elton, proclaimed it as among their best. He added wryly, "I'm sure a hell of a lot of people don't care."

Breaking Hearts

Released July 1984.
Peaked at #20.
Producer: Chris Thomas.
Studios: Air, France, and 301, Australia.
Recorded: December 1983 through January 1984.
Songs: "Restless" (5:14), "Slow Down, Georgie (She's Poison)" (4:08), "Who Wears These Shoes?" (4:02), "Breaking Hearts (Ain't What It Used to Be)" (3:44), "Li'l 'Frigerator" (3:22), "Passengers" (3:22), "In Neon" (4:16), "Burning Buildings" (4:00), "Did He Shoot Her?" (3:18), "Sad Songs (Say So Much)" (4:46).
Outtakes: "Simple Man," "Here Comes Miss Hurt Again."

Originally titled *Restless*, for the Stones-inspired rocker, the album was the last to feature Nigel Olsson, Dee Murray, and Davey Johnstone as a band. Only 1988's *Reg Strikes Back* would later reunite all three, relegating Murray and Olsson to backing vocals. (Murray died in 1992.) For *Breaking Hearts*, so named in recognition of Elton's marriage, most songs were written in Montserrat during a five-week period around Christmas 1983. Elton and Taupin would begin writing separately in the morning. By mid-day, the band was ready to rehearse and demo several new songs. Elton wrote most melodies in fifteen minutes. Four or five single-take songs appear on the album. Elton came close to walking away from the session, feeling immense pressure after the worldwide success of *Too Low for Zero*. He also felt that the reunited band had begun to stagnate, a view magnified by the subsequent tour, his longest ever. With his resurgence on the charts the year prior, American radio gave the new album good exposure. "Sad Songs (Say So Much)" quickly established itself as a focal point of Elton's concert repertoire. In Europe, the quirky

"Passengers" enjoyed great fanfare. The R&B-tinged "Restless" followed in the tradition of "Saturday Night's Alright (for Fighting)," showcasing the band's rougher side and Johnstone's scorching guitar work. Taupin offered polished lyrics and meticulously sculpted portraits. Fans had often hoped the songwriting duo would recapture the mood of their early work. But ten to fifteen years on, well into their thirties, neither would return — neither could return — to that moment. Where Taupin's lyrics were once esoteric, youthful and filled with mythical and biblical references, his work on *Breaking Hearts* — equally riveting — exhibited maturity and vividness. Though it did not succeed commercially in the same way as his best-known albums, *Breaking Hearts* offered stunning songs like "In Neon," "Burning Buildings," and the title track. With this release and the prior one, Elton had returned to form. It wouldn't last long.

Ice on Fire

Released November 1985.
Peaked at #48.
Producer: Gus Dudgeon.
Studio: The Mill, England.
Recorded: January 1985.
Songs: "This Town" (3:54), "Cry to Heaven" (4:14), "Soul Glove" (3:27), "Nikita" (5:42), "Too Young" (5:10), "Wrap Her Up" (6:04), "Satellite" (3:56), "Tell Me What the Papers Say" (3:40), "Candy by the Pound" (3:54), "Shoot Down the Moon" (4:53), "Act of War" (4:42).
Outtakes: "Angeline," "Leather Jackets," "Hoop of Fire," "Slow Rivers," "Gypsy Heart," "Highlander," "Go It Alone."

By July 1984, the groundwork had been laid for two projects. In February, while touring Australia, the Melbourne Symphony Orchestra approached Elton about doing a group of special concerts (which would not materialize for a few years). And on June 25, guitarist and European star Nik Kershaw, appearing at Elton's Mid-Summer Festival at London's Wembley Arena, struck up a friendship with the host. They worked on several tracks that would later appear on *Ice on Fire*. Twenty-two songs were written and recorded in January 1985. Kershaw played on three songs (one remains unreleased). Originally, the album was to be named *Hoop of Fire*, but the backing vocals on the would-be title track disappointed him. (The song showed up on *Leather Jackets*.) Perhaps seeking inspiration, Elton tapped the talents of many musicians. Following Tina Turner's lead on a 1984 release, Elton used several rhythm sections, including Roger Taylor and John Deacon of Queen. With no tour pressures, Elton intended to work with as many musicians and friends as he could. Duets were rumored to have been recorded during these sessions, and talk abounded that Elton would release an album of them. *Ice on Fire* sold poorly, producing only one U.S. hit: "Nikita." "Wrap Her Up," the first single, surfaced briefly on the American charts but struck gold in England. Both songs featured George Michael on backing vocals. A longtime fan, Michael wanted to lend support after hearing the rough mixes of the songs. He especially liked "Shoot Down the Moon," which Elton submitted without invitation for a James Bond movie. It was rejected. But Michael persuaded him to keep it on the album. "Act of War," a duet with Millie Jackson, failed as a single. (The song was not included on the original LP versions.) Artistically, where the pressure to create a successful follow-up to 1983's *Too Low for Zero* brought great results with 1984's *Breaking Hearts*, *Ice on Fire* represented a drastic slide into mediocrity. Except for "Shoot Down the Moon" and "Cry to Heaven," the album proved weak, cold, and inconsistent. Synthesizers and heavy bass lines dominated the sound. Still, the album could have performed better on the charts. Even at his worst, Elton writes marketable pop songs. This was not the first time, nor would it be the last, that poor judgment and lackluster promotion would affect a release. With the exception of an occasional magazine ad, Geffen did little to sell *Ice on Fire*. The relationship with label chief David Geffen had begun to sour. Elton would complete one more album for Geffen. "I'm sure that Geffen Records will be as glad to get rid of me as I will be to go," said the singer.

Leather Jackets

Released November 1986.
Peaked at #91.
Producer: Gus Dudgeon.
Studio: Wisseloord, The Netherlands.
Recorded: January, June-July, September 1986.
Songs: "Leather Jackets" (4:10), "Hoop of Fire" (4:14), "Don't Trust That Woman" (4:58), "Go It Alone" (4:26), "Gypsy Heart" (4:46), "Slow Rivers" (3:06), "Heartache All Over the World" (3:52), "Angeline" (3:24), "Memory of Love" (4:08), "Paris" (3:58), "I Fall Apart" (4:00).
Outtakes: "Lonely Heart," "Wild Love," "Love Rusts," "Crimes of Passion," "Billy and the Kids," "Lord of the Flies," "Rope Around a Fool," "Love Is a Cannibal," "Let It Shine," "Is It You?," "Love Adventure," "Heavy Traffic," "Timothy."

Signing a new record deal with MCA Records in the summer of 1986 ensured that Geffen would let Elton's final album languish. And if an album deserved such treatment, it was this one. Though *Leather Jackets* has some nice songs — "Paris," "Hoop of Fire," "Slow Rivers" — it rates with his most forgettable efforts. Gus Dudgeon and Elton chose twelve previously demoed songs for the album. Most were remnants from the *Ice on Fire* sessions, written in Hamburg, Germany, in April 1985. They were remixed and re-recorded. Elton reportedly wrote seventeen more songs in three days: ten with Taupin and seven with Osborne. Taupin and Elton even attempted to collaborate in a new fashion, working in the same room. But the arrangement fizzled. Elton had hoped his efforts with Osborne would produce tunes for other artists. Guitarist Davey Johnstone shared songwriting credits on six songs, including "Love Is a Cannibal" and "Heavy Traffic." Several others have yet to be released. Geffen chose "Heartache All Over the World," an up-tempo pop number, as the first single. Different studio mixes of this song are on various singles. On tour in America, Elton played only "Paris" from the album. The song was expected to be a worldwide single but was released only in parts of Europe. Producing no hits, *Leather Jackets* faded quickly, charting lower than any other album of new material in Elton's recording history. He could only go up.

Live in Australia with the Melbourne Symphony Orchestra
Released June 1987.
Peaked at #24.
Producer: Gus Dudgeon.
Recorded: Live at Sydney Entertainment Centre over several nights in December 1986.
Conductor: James Newton Howard.
Songs: "Sixty Years On" (5:06), "I Need You to Turn To" (2:34), "The Greatest Discovery" (3:48), "Tonight" (7:26), "Sorry Seems to Be the Hardest Word" (3:30), "The King Must Die" (4:58), "Take Me to the Pilot" (3:54), "Tiny Dancer" (6:06), "Have Mercy on the Criminal" (5:28), "Madman Across the Water" (5:20), "Candle in the Wind" (3:46), "Burn Down the Mission" (5:26), "Your Song" (3:48), "Don't Let the Sun Go Down on Me" (5:28).
Outtakes: "One Horse Town," "Rocket Man," "The Bitch Is Back," "Daniel," "Song for You," "Blue Eyes," "I Guess That's Why They Call It the Blues," "Bennie and the Jets," "Heartache All Over the World," "Sad Songs (Say So Much)," "This Town," "I'm Still Standing," "Cold as Christmas," "Slow Rivers," "Carla/Etude," "Saturday Night's Alright (for Fighting)."

       With Elton suffering severe voice problems, recording occurred throughout the Australian tour to capture the best vocals. Ironically, the final concert, in Sydney, offered the top performance. Initially, American radio stations were cold to the project. Most critics hailed the musicianship but pointed to Elton's strained vocals as a detriment. Critic Brian Chin's review in the *New York Post* was typical: "The idea of recording this live album was a strange one. Elton's voice is stretched to a painful breaking point, recorded just before his throat operation. But the quality of the songs — some not performed live in a decade — is undiminished." Good promotion on the part of MCA Records loosened the radio play lists enough to break the live "Candle in the Wind." The song's success did more for Elton's image and record sales than any single since 1983's "I'm Still Standing." Few young radio listeners remembered Elton's *Goodbye Yellow Brick Road*, on which the song earlier appeared. They viewed "Candle in the Wind" as a new song. It became so popular in concert that it surpassed the near immortal 1970 classic "Your Song" as an encore favorite. Older fans welcomed the return of obscure

The star and symphony: In the early 1970s, Elton performed at occasional concerts with British orchestras. But he generally found the experience lacking and the musicians uninspired by his work. With the Melbourne Symphony Orchestra, it was different. Orchestra members were enthused and respectful. As a show of thanks, he presented each of the eighty-eight members with a Rolex watch. The symphony, in turn, named him as its first honorary member.

early 1970s songs, such as "Sixty Years On." After the Australian concerts, Elton underwent throat surgery to remove nonmalignant lesions from his vocal chords. The operation improved his voice. Meanwhile, Taupin was involved in separate projects, including a solo album and songs for Heart and Starship. Elton, by seeking to do a live, symphony-backed album, tested his relationship with his new label. MCA passed. Elton would repay the label with his next releases.

Greatest Hits Volume III, 1979-87

Peaked at #84.
Released September 1987.
Songs: "I Guess That's Why They Call It the Blues" (4:42), "Mama Can't Buy You Love" (4:03), "Little Jeannie" (5:16), "Sad Songs (Say So Much)" (4:46), "I'm Still Standing" (3:02), "Empty Garden (Hey, Hey Johnny)" (5:11), "Heartache All Over the World" (4:02), "Too Low for Zero" (5:46), "Kiss the Bride" (4:22), "Blue Eyes" (3:26), "Nikita" (5:43), "Wrap Her Up" (6:07).

This compilation fulfilled Elton's contract with Geffen Records.

Reg Strikes Back

Released June 1988.
Peaked at #16.
Producer: Chris Thomas.
Studios: Air, England; Westside, California; and The Record Plant, California.
Songs: "Town of Plenty" (3:38), "A Word in Spanish" (4:38), "Mona Lisas and Mad Hatters, Part Two" (4:10), "I Don't Wanna Go on with You Like That" (4:32), "Japanese Hands" (4:38), "Goodbye Marlon Brando" (3:27), "The Camera Never Lies" (4:34), "Heavy Traffic" (3:26), "Poor Cow" (3:48), "Since God Invented Girls" (4:38). Outtakes: "Welcome to My Haunted Heart," "Give Peace a Chance," "Dancing in the End Zone."

Musically, 1987 treated Elton well. But the troubles in his personal life overshadowed the successes: Throat surgery, a separation from his wife, ongoing drug and alcohol abuse, and, in a British tabloid, nasty reports — proven erroneous in court — alleging Elton had sex with rent boys. By early fall, Elton had decided to battle the difficulties by returning to the studio. He produced a cheerful, spirited album that defied his depression. *Reg Strikes Back* was Elton's tongue-in-cheek way of fighting the bad press. But it symbolized more. As a shy boy, chubby Reg Dwight lived in fear of his domineering father. He rebelled as the outrageous Elton John. After the album's release, Elton auctioned off most of his belongings, including the gaudy costumes of Captain Fantastic. He shed the trappings of his glitter-rock status. It marked a new start that would be fulfilled two years later when he faced his multiple addictions. Elton wrote five new songs to go with older material already selected for the album. "Town of Plenty" and "Mona Lisas and Mad Hatters, Part Two" were written as extra tracks in the studio. "A Word in Spanish" and "The Camera Never Lies" were originally recorded early in 1988 at James Newton

Howard's house in Los Angeles. Twenty-two songs were recorded during the album session. *Reg Strikes Back* garnered great reviews, with the now-common media proclamations of a "comeback." The album went gold five days after release and spent nearly five months on the charts. "I Don't Wanna Go on with You Like That," a lively dance number, dominated Top 40 stations in late summer. Other songs charted as well. In time Elton came to view *Reg Strikes Back* as weak and inconsistent. "The LP was mostly a good reason to get me back in the studio and get my mind off my personal problems," he said. "It has two or three really nice things on it. But when you're an artist, you

Ready to promote: MCA Records prepared a tremendous promotional campaign for *Reg Strikes Back*. Six-foot-long cover displays, posters, coffee mugs, pins, matchbooks and baseball-bat pens were produced. Elton went all out, too. In June 1988 he made eight brief concert appearances in America, performing new material in 30-minute solo sets. He appeared at several small clubs, such as The Axis Club in Boston, to promote the album and tour. Taupin accompanied him. (In October 1970 The Axis Club was known as the Boston Tea Party, where Elton opened his first American tour.) The 1988 PR effort recalled his September 1970 promotional gigs at the Playboy clubs in New York and Philadelphia.

know that you can't afford to come out with mediocre stuff all the time." Throughout promotional interviews in 1988, Elton said he and Taupin had found a renewed creativity as songwriters and, on their next album, wanted freedom to write without commercial considerations.

The Complete Thom Bell Sessions
Released March 1989.
Did not chart.
Producer: Thom Bell.
Studios: Sigma Sound, Pennsylvania, and Kay Smith,
Washington.
Recorded: October 1977.
Songs: "Nice and Slow" (4:40), "Country Love Song" (5:02), "Shine on Through" (7:45), "Mama Can't Buy You Love" (4:05), "Are You Ready for Love?" (8:15), "Three Way Love Affair" (4:59).

Throughout the 1970s, Elton praised the Philadelphia R&B sound of The Spinners, O'Jays, and Stylistics, whose 1973 *Rockin' Roll Baby* album became a favorite. After the success of "Philadelphia Freedom," Elton talked of recording an R&B album. In the fall of 1977, he found time for the project and sought out producer, arranger, and songwriter Thom Bell, who helped mold the Philadelphia sound. Though proud that he and Bell had recaptured the mood, Elton admitted disappointment in the final product. Another problem developed. The sessions had nearly been completed when The Spinners were brought in for backing vocals. Elton was later discouraged to learn that The Spinners and Thom Bell scrapped almost half of his vocals on "Are You Ready for Love?" and replaced parts with their own. A rare bootleg video of the earlier sessions contains the original mixes. Interestingly, the MFSB Strings and Horns appeared on the sessions — a year after using John's "Philadelphia Freedom" as the title cut on a 1976 album. John contributed two songs to *The Complete Thom Bell Sessions*, Bell contributed three, and Joseph B. Jefferson one. For all of the remixing and the worry over the material, the single "Mama Can't Buy You Love" was a huge success in America in 1979, earning Elton a Grammy nomination. The full session was released a decade later. The work is significant because Bell convinced Elton to sing in a lower register, advice he acted on for such songs as "Blue Eyes."

Sleeping with the Past

Released August 1989.
Peaked at #23.
Producer: Chris Thomas.
Studios: Air, England, and Puk, Denmark.
Recorded: November-December 1988.
Songs: "Durban Deep" (5:32), "Healing Hands" (4:23), "Whispers" (5:29), "Club at the End of the Street" (4:49), "Sleeping with the Past" (4:58), "Stone's Throw from Hurtin' " (4:55), "Sacrifice" (5:07), "I Never Knew Her Name" (3:31), "Amazes Me" (4:39), "Blue Avenue" (4:21).
Outtakes: "Love Is Worth Waiting For."

Sleeping with the Past was far from noncommercial, but it allowed John and Taupin to collaborate to a greater degree than on any album since *Captain Fantastic*. The songs, written while in the Puk Studio in Denmark, paid tribute to specific soul artists who inspired both men: Sam Cooke, Jackie Wilson, The Drifters, Aretha Franklin, James Carr and Betty Everette (of England), Marvin Gaye, Otis Redding, Stevie Wonder, Percy Sledge, Ray Charles, and others. Eighteen songs were written in four days and recorded over several weeks. "Whispers," "Sleeping with the Past," and "Amazes Me" were the first three songs, written and recorded in order. Taupin listened to R&B songs for inspiration, writing lyrical ideas and even lifting bits of lines. For example, "Club at the End of the Street" plainly borrowed from a Percy Sledge song with similar meter and a reference to "the dark end of the street." Elton recorded with his *Reg Strikes Back* touring band. It included his only black rhythm section, drummer Jonathan Moffett and bassist Romeo Williams, with Davey Johnstone and others. The album was released late in Elton's 1989 American tour with little support from MCA Records. The release date had been pushed back, and the promotional campaign that swirled around 1988's *Reg Strikes Back* deteriorated. Questions surrounded the handling of the release. Elton canceled tour shows and interviews. In New Haven, Connecticut, on October 18, 1989, he rushed through his performance rarely talking to the audience. Midway through the concert, he announced he would not perform material from the new album because MCA wasn't promoting it. Later, his quirky tour behavior would be attributed to drug use and alcoholism. The album, on the strength of the singles "Healing Hands," "Sacrifice," and "Club at the End of the Street," became his best selling of the 1980s. In England, it hit number one. *Sleeping with the Past* could have produced more hits. "Blue Avenue" and the title cut are exceptional. After the release, Elton confronted his multiple addictions and retired briefly to get his personal life in order. With the help of his huge catalog, albums kept coming.

To be continued...
Peaked at #84.
Released October 1990.
Songs: "Come Back Baby" (2:44), "Lady Samantha" (3:02), "It's Me That You Need" (4:00), "Your Song" (demo) (3:32), "Rock and Roll Madonna" (4:17), "Bad Side of the Moon" (3:11), "Your Song" (3:59), "Take Me to the Pilot" (3:45), "Border Song" (3:19), "Sixty Years On" (unedited original master) (4:55), "Country Comfort" (5:06), "Grey Seal" (3:34), "Friends" (2:22), "Levon" (5:21), "Tiny Dancer" (6:13), "Madman Across the Water" (5:56), "Honky Cat" (5:11), "Mona Lisas and Mad Hatters" (4:58), "Rocket Man" (4:41), "Daniel" (3:52), "Crocodile Rock" (3:55), "Bennie and the Jets" (5:19), "Goodbye Yellow Brick Road" (3:13), "All the Girls Love Alice" (5:07), "Funeral for a Friend/Love Lies Bleeding" (11:06), "Whenever You're Ready (We'll Go Steady Again)" (2:52), "Saturday Night's Alright (for Fighting)" (4:53), "Jack Rabbit" (1:50), "Harmony" (2:44), "Young Man's Blues" (4:42), "Step into Christmas" (4:29), "The Bitch Is Back" (3:43), "Pinball Wizard" (5:14), "Someone Saved My Life Tonight" (6:44), "Philadelphia Freedom" (5:37), "One Day at a Time" (3:47), "Lucy in the Sky with Diamonds" (6:15), "I Saw Her Standing There" live (3:41), "Island Girl" (3:43), "Sorry Seems to Be the Hardest Word" (3:46), "Don't Go Breaking My Heart" (4:30), "I Feel Like a Bullet (in the Gun of Robert Ford)" live (3:33), "Ego" (3:57), "Song for Guy" (6:38), "Mama Can't Buy You Love" (4:03), "Cartier" (0:52), "Little Jeannie" (5:11), "Donner Pour Donner" (4:25), "Fanfare" (1:26), "Chloe" (4:39), "The Retreat" (4:44), "Blue Eyes" (3:26), "Empty Garden" (5:10), "I Guess That's Why They Call It the Blues" (4:41), "I'm Still Standing" (3:01), "Sad Songs (Say So Much)" (4:08), "Act of War" (4:42), "Nikita" (5:42), "Candle in the Wind" live (3:57), "Carla/Etude" live (4:46), "Don't Let the Sun Go Down on Me" live (5:37), "I Don't Wanna Go on with You Like That" (7:20), "Give Peace a Chance" (3:46), "Sacrifice" (5:07), "Made for Me" (4:21), "You Gotta Love Someone" (4:57), "I Swear I Heard the Night Talking" (4:30), "Easier to Walk Away" (4:23).

As early as January 1989, reports circulated that MCA was planning a box set covering Elton John's career. To the disappointment of many die-hard fans who wanted a package of rarities, MCA developed the four-CD set as a "greatest hits-plus" package. To the casual listener, the box set offered a good overview. For the set (and other projects), Elton recorded twelve new John-Taupin songs with producer Don Was, who was amazed by Elton's speed in the studio. Elton did all vocals in three hours, including overdubs. Four songs required just one take. Most musicians on these new tracks were prominent L.A. session artists who had worked with Bonnie Raitt, Delaney and Bonnie, Joe Cocker, Bob Dylan, The Band, and Toto,

Pulled from the shelves: A dispute over the design of the box set led to its removal from store shelves. Artist David Costa said Elton hated the colorful U.S. package, with its montage cover, because it reminded him of his earlier excesses. His treatment for multiple addictions had changed him, and he had hoped for a more distinguished look. In November 1991, a limited edition version of *To be continued...* was released in Britain. The U.K. set, which substituted a few new songs, offered a more subtle design, with large, beautiful photos and a lyric booklet, lacking in the U.S. release. CD versions of both sets are in demand among collectors.

artists Elton has long admired. The highlights of *To be continued...* included a demo of "Your Song," the 1965 Bluesology single "Come Back Baby," "The Retreat" (an obscure B-side), and live versions of "Carla/Etude" and "I Feel Like a Bullet (in the Gun of Robert Ford)." Song selection aside, another disappointment focused on the poorly researched liner notes, which cited inaccurate dates and misspelled musicians' names. Of the four new songs on the U.S. release, the strongest were a "Healing Hands"-type rocker, "I Swear I Heard the Night Talking," and the ballad "You Gotta Love Someone." The box set marked an effort to recognize the contributions of Elton and would continue with *Two Rooms*, a tribute to the John-Taupin collaboration, and his eventual induction into the Rock and Roll Hall of Fame. The title, *To be continued...*, would prove most accurate.

The One

Released July 1992.
Peaked at #8.
Producer: Chris Thomas.
Studios: Guillaume Tell, France; Air, England; and Townshouse, England.
Recorded: November 1991 through March 1992.
Songs: "Simple Life" (6:22), "The One" (5:52), "Sweat It Out" (6:37), "Runaway Train" (5:22), "Whitewash County" (5:26), "The North" (5:14), "When a Woman Doesn't Want You" (4:52), "Emily" (4:55), "On Dark Street" (4:42), "Understanding Women" (5:01), "The Last Song" (3:18).
Outtakes: "Fat Boys and Ugly Girls," "Suit of Wolves."

By the summer of 1990, Elton's treadmill lifestyle had stopped. Through his own admission, he had become bitter, withdrawn, self-abusive, and deeply troubled. Alcoholism, a cocaine addiction, and bulimia had overtaken his life. "I was tired of running," he said later. "I had to ask for help. It was either that or I was going to be dead." Two things — the death of Ryan White and the insistence of a lover — helped him face his troubles. He sought treatment, came clean, and began a recovery that continues today. He also took a year off from recording and touring. *The One* celebrated his sober return. But in the studio, he faced a mental obstacle: recording while clean. He had not done so since the early 1970s. On the first day, the pressure overcame him and he left frustrated after twenty minutes. He returned a day later and began to write and work. The result: a touching, introspective album about rebirth and pain. Taupin's lyrics, mostly supplied by fax, are stunning, from the penetrating beauty of "The Last Song," about a father's reunion with a son who has AIDS, to "Simple Life," alluding to Elton's new, less complicated lifestyle. "The One," an ethereal love song, has spiritual undertones. All three songs became hits. "Emily" evokes images of "Sixty Years On" from his 1970 album. Others deal with date rape, the disintegration of a family, and overcoming adversity. And the music inspires. It features some of Elton's finest electric-keyboard work, demonstrated in solos on songs like "Sweat It Out," "Whitewash County," and "Runaway Train," a duet with Eric Clapton, highlighted by Elton's only organ solo. Driven by keyboard programming and drum machines, the music offers an airy, unrushed, and peaceful sound. "There were two or three songs that just did not fit in with the serious mood of this record, so they were cut," he said. "I didn't want the songs to be very poppy." Elton and Taupin had forged a stronger relationship, which would become apparent in 1995 on their next studio album, *Made in England*.

Rare Masters

Released October 1992.

Did not chart.

Songs: "I've Been Loving You" (3:16), "Here's to the Next Time" (2:58), "Lady Samantha" (3:02), "All Across the Havens" (2:51), "It's Me That You Need" (4:00), "Just Like Strange Rain" (3:44), "Bad Side of the Moon" (3:12), "Rock and Roll Madonna" (4:16), "Grey Seal" (3:34), the *Friends* sound track, "Madman Across the Water" (alternate version) (8:50), "Into the Old Man's Shoes" (4:01), "Rock Me When He's Gone" (5:01), "Slave" (alternate version) (2:48), "Skyline Pigeon" (3:51), "Jack Rabbit" (1:51), "Whenever You're Ready (We'll Go Steady Again)" (2:51), "Let Me Be Your Car" (4:52), "Screw You (Young Man's Blues)" (4:41), "Step into Christmas" (4:30), "Ho! Ho! Ho! Who'd Be a Turkey at Christmas" (4:03), "Sick City" (5:23), "Cold Highway" (3:26), "One Day at a Time" (3:47), "I Saw Her Standing There" (3:51), "House of Cards" (3:09), "Planes" (4:14), "Sugar on the Floor" (4:33).

For collectors of obscure Elton John recordings, *Rare Masters* exceeded the *To be continued...* box set. PolyGram purchased the rights to a large chunk of Elton's early catalog. The singer's manager, John Reid, wanted to draw attention to the re-release of thirteen albums on CD. Bill Levenson of PolyGram hatched the idea of a rarities package. In London, he scoured master tapes at Decca, Dick James Music, and PolyGram. The result: a collection of classic B-sides to singles, the *Friends* sound track (not previously available on CD) and alternate song versions. The highlights: a demo of "Let Me Be Your Car," written for Rod Stewart, an accelerated version of "Slave," and Mick Ronson playing lead guitar on "Madman Across the Water." Levenson said he uncovered enough material to guarantee another package of rarities.

Greatest Hits 1976-1986
Did not chart.
Released 1992.
Songs: Same as Greatest Hits Volume III, except "Too Low for Zero" and "Heartache All Over the World" were replaced by "Sorry Seems to Be the Hardest Word," "Who Wears These Shoes?," and "Don't Go Breaking My Heart."

      MCA obtained the rights to the Geffen recordings and promptly released its own compilation. The timing was questionable, with Elton promoting a new album, *The One*. Earlier, it had been announced that Elton would be jumping from MCA to PolyGram in the mid-1990s. This album helped fulfill his contract.

Duets
Released November 1993.
Peaked at #25.
Multiple producers and studios.
Recorded: August-October 1993.
Songs: "Teardrops" with k. d. lang (4:52), "When I Think About Love (I Think About You)" with P.M. Dawn (4:34), "The Power" with Little Richard (6:24), "Shakey Ground" with Don Henley (3:50), "True Love" with Kiki Dee (3:32), "If You Were Me" with Chris Rea (4:23), "A Woman's Needs" with Tammy Wynette (5:16), "Old Friend" with Nik Kershaw (4:15), "Go On and On" with Gladys Knight (5:49), "Don't Go Breaking My Heart" with RuPaul (4:58), "Ain't Nothing Like the Real Thing" with Marcella Detroit (3:34), "I'm Your Puppet" with Paul Young (3:34), "Love Letters" with Bonnie Raitt (4:00), "Born to Lose" with Leonard Cohen (4:31), "Don't Let the Sun Go Down on Me" live with George Michael (5:46), "Duets for One" with himself (4:51).

The sighing game: Elton's insistence that his RuPaul duet be a single brought nightmares for longtime fans who remembered his disastrous disco album, *Victim of Love*. With their work together, Elton and cross-dresser RuPaul struck up a friendship. Both spend considerable time in Atlanta, Georgia, and have appeared together often — partly to hype their single. RuPaul was among Elton's guests at his induction into the Rock and Roll Hall of Fame. On Valentine's Day 1994, they co-presented an award at a British music event. Later, they appeared on a German TV show similar to "The Newlywed Game." Their video features the two men dressed as famous couples. Elton had proposed that they record "It Takes Two," but RuPaul preferred to remake Elton's 1976 hit. Over a half dozen mixes of the dance song have been released.

In late summer 1993, Elton's record company worked to compile a small package of old duets for a Christmas release. Elton insisted that a few new songs be included, so he recorded with Bonnie Raitt, Tammy Wynette, and k. d. lang. The project expanded quickly. After Chris Rea offered "If You Were Me," Elton was convinced to pursue an album. Within eight weeks, he had recorded

The sales duds: Elton's poorest-selling albums:
- ❖ *Empty Sky.*
- ❖ *11-17-70.*
- ❖ *Victim of Love.*
- ❖ *The Fox.*
- ❖ *Leather Jackets.*
- ❖ *The Complete Thom Bell Sessions.*

with a wide range of artists, including three European stars (Rea, Paul Young, and Nik Kershaw), two idols (Little Richard and Leonard Cohen), a country queen, several friends, and a few singers on the rise. At the same time, Frank Sinatra released an identically titled album. Unlike Sinatra, Elton recorded in person with all but one of his guests (Paul Young) — rather than electronically by long distance. Sinatra and Elton were to record together, but those plans evaporated. Though Sinatra's release sold better in America, Elton's effort drew more praise. "It's the chairman of the board vs. Captain Fantastic, and the Captain — who at least sang with his guests — is the winner," wrote Gary Graff of the *Detroit Free Press*. Two songs — "The Power" and "A Woman's Needs" — are John-Taupin compositions. Other entries, like P.M. Dawn's, were written by the guests. Most were remakes of earlier hits. In England, the Kiki Dee duet, Cole Porter's "True Love," rocketed to number two on the charts and the album enjoyed a stay in the top 10. In America, though, it performed dismally. To the consternation of many fans — and some advisers — Elton insisted that the dance single with transvestite RuPaul be the second release. Remixed and extended, "Don't Go Breaking My Heart" flew up the dance charts in February 1994, competing in the top 10 with Hammer, Shabba Ranks, and Snoop Doggy Dogg. It surpassed his 1988 dance mix of "I Don't Wanna to Go on with You Like That." Many strong songs appear on the album, the most unique being the Elton-Cohen remake of Ray Charles's "Born to Lose." Elton hoped to record with Sting, Neil Young, and James Taylor, but could not work out the scheduling. The album introduced producer Greg Penny, who did three tracks, supervised the project, and was asked to handle Elton's next album.

The Lion King
Released June 1994.
Peaked at #1.
Several producers.
Recorded at several studios throughout 1993 and 1994.
Songs: "Circle of Life" (3:53), "I Just Can't Wait to Be King" (2:49), "Be Prepared" (3:38), "Hakuna Matata" (3:31), "Can You Feel the Love Tonight?" (2:56), "This Land" (2:53), "...To Die For" (4:16), "Under the Stars" (3:42), "King of Pride Rock" (5:56), "Circle of Life" (4:49), "I Just Can't Wait to Be King" (3:35), "Can You Feel the Love Tonight?" (3:59).
Outtakes: "Warthog Rhapsody."

    This is not a true Elton John album, but it requires mention given its success as the sound track for the animated feature by Disney. Elton wrote the first five songs with lyricist Tim Rice, and he performed three of them on the album. Four instrumentals were composed by Hans Zimmer. Elton's version of "Can You Feel the Love Tonight?" put him back in the top 10. The album rocketed to number one, staying there nine weeks, and selling over seven million copies, tops for 1994. Rice, who had contributed to *Aladdin*, told Disney that he wanted to work with Elton John. Rice found him to be an exceptionally quick writer, reeling off melodies in 20-30 minutes. Elton wrote and re-wrote "Circle of Life," but Zimmer gave the movie version its distinctive African feel. Three of the songs were nominated for Oscars. "Can You Feel the Love Tonight?" won a Grammy and an Oscar.

Made in England

Released March 1995.
Peaked at #13.
Producers: Greg Penny and Elton John.
Studio: AIR Lyndhurst, England.
Recorded: February-April 1994, with additional work continuing sporadically through the rest of the year.
Songs: "Believe" (4:55), "Made in England" (5:09), "House" (4:27), "Cold" (5:37), "Pain" (3:49), "Belfast" (6:29), "Latitude" (3:34), "Please" (3:52), "Man" (5:16), "Lies" (4:25), "Blessed" (5:01).
Outtakes: "Hell," "Leaves," "Live Like Horses."

Bolstered by an intensive promotional campaign, the enormous success of *The Lion King* sound track, and publicity surrounding Elton's Oscar and Grammy awards, *Made in England* entered the American charts at number thirteen. It was Elton's highest debut since 1976's *Blue Moves* — an honor fitting this organic, back-to-his-roots album. *Made in England* is significant for many reasons. It qualifies as a "band" album, with members — especially guitarist Davey Johnstone — contributing significantly to the sound. The recording marked the return of arranger Paul Buckmaster, known for his wild work on early classics like "Madman Across the Water" and "Have Mercy on the Criminal." Further, Elton composed on piano without the aid of a drum machine and Taupin wrote his terse, poetic lyrics while at the studio. Co-producer Greg Penny encouraged and embellished some of Elton's best work on such songs as "Belfast"

Go figure: Elton splits time between England and America. But his albums occasionally play quite differently with the buying public. *Madman Across the Water* spent twenty-five weeks on the U.S. charts and hit number eight. In England, it stayed for just two weeks, never exceeding the forty-first position. Similarly, *Sleeping with the Past* topped the charts in Britain, but stalled at number twenty-three in America. The success is hard to predict. For example, 1975's *Blue Moves* was his first number one album in France. Fortunately for the artist, when one country has been less than responsive to a record, another has sent it flying up the charts. In the early to mid-1970s, the United States led the way. Europe followed in the late 1970s and early 1980s. His native land, England, has given him some of his greatest success in the late 1980s and early 1990s — with studio albums and a two-CD compilation, *The Very Best of Elton John*, which was not released in America.

and "Blessed." Several compositions were rejected before Elton wrote "Believe." The song set the tone for the album. It was to be the title track. At the last moment, Elton changed the name. He felt *Believe* sounded too mystic. The title track, "Made in England," is autobiographical, alluding to Elvis and Little Richard, Elton's early influences. Lyrically and musically, the album pays tribute to The Beatles without ever mentioning them by name. Many of Taupin's verses, particularly in "House," "Pain" and "Believe," are obviously inspired by John Lennon and songs like "God." An astute listener can detect The Beatles on almost every song, especially "Please." For "Latitude," Penny called on the talents of The Beatles' legendary producer, George Martin, who arranged the song. Elton's greater-than-usual role in the studio earned him the title of co-producer. The hard work paid off. Rock critics received the album kindly, writing again that it harkened to Elton's best mid-1970s work. Even *Rolling Stone* magazine — rarely a fan of Elton — offered kind words, proclaiming it "a startlingly fine album." The publicity machine was running at full strength, with Elton landing on the cover of several American and British magazines. He and Taupin even went so far as to hold a public autograph session at Tower Records in Los Angeles after midnight on the day of the release. The album was to appear on MCA, but PolyGram negotiated for the rights to it and released it on the Rocket-Island label.

The authors rate Elton John's albums

1. *Goodbye Yellow Brick Road*: A masterpiece. Brilliant and consistent.
2. *Captain Fantastic and the Brown Dirt Cowboy*: The John-Taupin autobiographical version of *Sgt. Pepper's Lonely Hearts Club Band*.
3. *Tumbleweed Connection*: The best Band album never recorded by Robbie Robertson and company.
4. *Madman Across the Water*: Elton's finest piano album.
5. *Elton John*: A poignant, impeccably arranged American debut.
6. *Honky Chateau*: Light, airy, and drunk.
7. *Made in England*: A covert Beatles tribute, equal to some of his best 1970s work.
8. *Blue Moves*: Dark, moody, and improving with age.
9. *Sleeping with the Past*: A tasteful tribute to R&B giants.
10. *The One*: Inspired and intelligent songwriting. Sober, too.
11. *Don't Shoot Me, I'm Only the Piano Player*: A Beach Boy wanna-be plays to teenage fantasies.
12. *Rock of the Westies*: This number-one-album routine is getting old.
13. *Caribou*: Even his lesser albums contain classics.
14. *Too Low for Zero*: It proved he's still standing.
15. *The Fox*: Mature European pop — and instrumentals.
16. *Breaking Hearts*: Taupin certainly didn't with his cinematic lyrics.
17. *Reg Strikes Back*: After his preceding studio album, he desperately needed to.
18. *A Single Man*: Quirky, campy, and erratic.
19. *Jump Up!*: Bursts of brilliance amid bubbles of banality.
20. *Live in Australia*: Swooping strings, romantic, and dramatic.
21. *11-17-70*: A testament to his live playing.
22. *21 at 33*: Whatever happened to "Little Jeannie"?
23. *Ice on Fire*: The ice won.

24. *Empty Sky*: Glimpses of the struggling young artist (yes, officially, it was a 1960s release).
25. *Friends* and *The Lion King*: Some great work, but not Elton albums in the true sense.
26. *Duets*: Mostly fine songs, but it's only half Elton.
27. *Leather Jackets*: Old outtakes with new overdubs. Better off dead.
28. *The Complete Thom Bell Sessions*: Leon Redbone meets the Stylistics.
29. *Here and There*: And in need of one more album to finish out a contract.
30. *Victim of Love*: Do the hustle!

Performances

Unlike Pink Floyd and the Rolling Stones, who tour a few times a decade, Elton has rarely played the laws of supply and demand to his benefit. He has toured in twenty of the past twenty-six years. He thrives on live performance and believes it contributes immensely to his consistent record sales. As Reg Dwight, he toured with the band Bluesology. This section, however, focuses on his live performances as Elton John.

1968
❖ **November 3:** Played solo on BBC radio, performing "Skyline Pigeon" and "All Across the Havens."

1969
❖ **July 20:** Backed by Hookfoot, he performed "Lady Samantha" and "Sails" live on BBC radio.

1970
❖ **April-August:** Though Elton had earlier released singles, he and his boosters realized he would have to tour to promote his self-titled album. Elton put together his first band: bass player Dee Murray and drummer Nigel Olsson. Their debut took place April 20 on BBC in England. Elton undertook a broad European tour, including concerts that paid just $119 per appearance. He captured top honors in a music contest at the Knokke Festival in Belgium. On June 21, he played The Pop Proms at Roundhouse Chalk Farm, London, England. BBC's John Peel hosted the affair, which featured T. Rex, Pretty Things, Heavy Jelly, and Elton. He

A 1971 concert ad.

also played the August 14 Yorkshire Jazz, Folk and Blues Festival in Krumlin, England, with Pretty Things, Juicy Lucy, and The Groundhogs.

❖ **August-December:** American debut. Though Elton had been struggling for years in England, his first U.S. performance at the Troubadour literally turned him into an industry celebrity overnight. After his August 25 debut (check the Troubadour entry for details), he performed a series of music industry luncheons and concerts. Work permit problems forced him back to England. Around Halloween, on October 29, he returned, opening his first actual tour at the Boston Tea Party. On November 17, Elton appeared on radio in a live studio concert, captured on the *11-17-70* album. A day later, he duetted with singer Odetta on "Take Me to the Pilot" at a party hyping her latest release. His big east coast break came November 20-21 at the Fillmore East when he shared the bill with Leon Russell, whose work he admired. Backstage, Elton arranged for Bernie Taupin to meet his idol, Bob Dylan. On December 4, Elton played Anaheim Convention Center at Disneyland and donned a set of Mickey Mouse ears. A typical 1970 concert would have included "Amoreena," "Bad Side of the Moon," "Ballad of a Well-Known Gun," "Border Song," "Burn Down the Mission," "Can I Put You On?," "Country Comfort," "Honey Roll," "I Need You to Turn To," "Indian Sunset," "The King Must Die," "My Father's Gun," "Sixty Years On," "Take Me to the Pilot," and "Your Song." Occasionally, the rising star threw in songs by The Beatles, Stones and American artists.

❖ **December 20:** Elton played a charity show at the Roundhouse in London. The Who headlined with Pete Townshend dedicating "Tommy, Can You Hear Me?" to Elton — years before he played a part in the movie.

1971

❖ **January-March:** Hawaii and Britain. Taupin married and honeymooned on the U.S. island. A March 3 concert with the Royal Philharmonic was filmed for TV.

❖ **April-June:** American tour. Less than six months after they declared him "rock's new superstar," critics scathed Elton. His inclination toward unusual stage dress had emerged, and he continued to develop his piano gymnastics routine. One reviewer described his performance as "the death of a clown." With just Dee Murray and Nigel Olsson, Elton played primarily to college-age audiences. His June 10-11 Carnegie Hall concerts were typical two-hour affairs, with the first half featuring Elton solo. Aside from songs from his first three albums, he occasionally threw in "Mercedes Benz," "Get Back," and "Whole Lot of Shakin' Going On."

❖ **June-September:** A few dates in America and Europe. He headlined the Garden Party Show at the Crystal Palace in London on July 31. But critics slammed him for performing the entire unreleased *Madman Across the Water* album. Also on the bill: Tir Na Nog, Hookfoot, Fairport Convention, Rory Gallagher, and Yes.

❖ **October-December:** Japan, Britain, and Australia. Exhausted, Elton declined a dinner engagement with the Dean of Perth, prompting headlines of a snub. Marc Bolan of T. Rex did an encore with Elton in England.

1972

❖ **February:** Dates in England.

❖ **March:** A few concerts in Germany.

❖ **April-May:** Brief North American tour. First leg opened April 26 in Waco, Texas, and ended May 10 in Urbana, Illinois, after ten shows.

❖ **June 3:** Elton and Keith Moon joined the Beach Boys for an encore.

❖ **September-November:** Second leg of North American tour. It opened September 26 in Ithica, New York, and ended November 26 in St. Petersburg, Florida, after forty-eight shows. The clown criticism did not deter Elton. His concerts became more

> **Royal Festival Hall, February 5, 1972:** Guitarist Davey Johnstone debuted as a band member. Elton took the stage in a silver top hat and silver "EJ" boots. He opened solo, was joined by his band and, during the second half, the Royal Philharmonic Orchestra, conducted by Paul Buckmaster. Rounding out the band were Nigel Olsson, Dee Murray, guest guitarist Alan Parker of Blue Mink, and backup singers Madeline Bell, Lesley Duncan, and Caroline Attard. The performance was televised. Songs: "Rocket Man," "Honky Cat," "Mona Lisas and Mad Hatters," "Holiday Inn," "Can I Put You On?," "Sixty Years On," "The Greatest Discovery," "Tiny Dancer," "Love Song," "Border Song," "Burn Down the Mission," "Take Me to the Pilot," "Mellow," "Suzie (Dramas)," "I Think I'm Gonna Kill Myself," "Amy," "Salvation," "Hercules," "Madman Across the Water," "Your Song," and "I Need You to Turn To."

of a circus, with, among other features, "Legs" Larry Smith tap dancing to "I Think I'm Gonna Kill Myself."

❖ **October 30:** Elton, Liberace, and Jack Jones played a command performance for the queen.

1973

❖ **January:** Elton joined Dusty Springfield onstage.

❖ **February-March:** Britain. English fans mobbed Elton at venues. In Glasgow, after-concert crowds kept the band barricaded in the building for an hour. Rod Stewart appeared onstage March 23 to give Elton a bouquet of flowers for his upcoming birthday.

❖ **April:** Italy. Kiki Dee sang backup in preparation for her opening role in 1974.

❖ **August-October:** American tour. Began August 15 in Mobile, Alabama, and

ended October 21 in Gainesville, Florida, after forty-three shows. Elton shattered stadium attendance records set by Elvis Presley. It was an extravagant tour with a fake wedding and a Mr. Universe look-alike carrying Elton onstage atop his shoulders. On September 25, Stevie Wonder joined Elton for an encore, performing "Superstition," "Higher Ground," "Honky Tonk Women," and "You Are the Sunshine of My Life" in Wonder's first appearance since a serious car accident put him in a coma. In Baltimore, Maryland, on September 30, Elton became

---

The Hollywood Bowl, September 7, 1973: Elton took his flamboyance to a new plateau. The stage backdrop, spotlighting the Hollywood Hills, lowered to reveal five multicolored grand pianos, an illuminated staircase, and palm trees. Porn star Linda Lovelace hosted the affair, with look-alikes for Queen Elizabeth II, Elvis Presley, Batman, Frankenstein, Groucho Marx, Mae West, The Beatles, the Pope, Marilyn Monroe, and John Wayne parading across the stage. When lifted, the tops on the pianos spelled ELTON and unleashed hundreds of white doves. During "Crocodile Rock," sound engineer Clive Franks played electric piano dressed as the celebrated reptile. Meanwhile, a live crocodile crawled across the stage. Songs: "Elderberry Wine," "High-Flying Bird," "Honky Cat," "Goodbye Yellow Brick Road," "Hercules," "Rocket Man," "Madman Across the Water," "Teacher I Need You," "Have Mercy on the Criminal," "All the Girls Love Alice," "Daniel," "Funeral for a Friend/ Love Lies Bleeding," "Crocodile Rock," "Saturday Night's Alright (for Fighting)," "Honky Tonk Women," and "Your Song."

---

angry over a fan's treatment by a security force. Mid-concert, he dismissed the guards. Five hundred fans stormed the stage. As a result, officials barred Elton from performing in Maryland for seven years. In Atlanta, Elton and Iggy Pop made an impromptu appearance at Richard's, a local club.

❖ **December:** Christmas shows in England.

1974

❖ **February-March:** Japan, Australia, and New Zealand.

❖ **April-May:** Canceled European dates. Briefly toured Japan. Headlined three benefits for his Watford Football Club, including a May 5 concert with Nazareth and Rod Stewart. Elton and Stewart duetted on "Country Comfort," "Angel," and "Sweet Little Rock 'n' Roller."

❖ **June 14:** Joined the Beach Boys for an encore.

❖ **September-December:** North American tour. Opened September 25 in Dallas, Texas, and closed December 2 in Philadelphia, Pennsylvania, after 49 shows. Stardom exploded. With *Goodbye Yellow Brick Road* still on the charts, *Caribou* rocketed to number one and "The Bitch Is Back" cracked the top 5 — his fourth song to do so in a year. Every show was a sellout, and police escorts were mandatory. The band included Davey Johnstone, Nigel Olsson, Dee Murray, Ray Cooper, and the Muscle Shoals Horns.

❖ **December:** Performed Christmas shows at Hammersmith Odeon in London, England. Stewart and Gary Glitter took the stage on Christmas Eve.

1975

❖ **January:** Jammed with the Average White Band and the Doobie Brothers in separate concerts.

❖ **June 19:** Joined the Rolling Stones onstage.

❖ **June 21:** His new band debuted at the Mid-Summer Music Festival at Wembley.

Madison Square Garden, November 28, 1974: This Thanksgiving performance in New York would leave thousands of rock fans grateful. Earlier in the year, Elton and John Lennon had appeared on each other's albums. They struck a deal: If Lennon's *Walls and Bridges* topped the charts, the ex-Beatle would join Elton in concert. Near the concert's finale, Elton, wearing a red boa, confirmed the rumors that had swept the city: "Seeing it's Thanksgiving and Thanksgiving is a joyous occasion, we thought we'd invite someone up with us onstage. It's our great privilege to see and hear John Lennon." The crowd thundered its approval, and Lennon — who had been suffering so greatly from stage fright that Davey Johnstone had to tune his guitar — joined Elton's band. They performed "Whatever Gets You Thru the Night," "Lucy in the Sky with Diamonds," and "I Saw Her Standing There." Later, Lennon reappeared for the final song, "The Bitch Is Back." But the evening had not ended. Elton had arranged for Yoko Ono to meet Lennon backstage. Within days, John and Yoko had ended their separation. Lennon, of course, was murdered in 1980. The Thanksgiving concert was his final stage appearance. Songs: "All the Girls Love Alice," "Bennie and the Jets," "The Bitch Is Back," "Burn Down the Mission," "Candle in the Wind," "Crocodile Rock," "Daniel," "Don't Let the Sun Go Down on Me," "Funeral for a Friend/Love Lies Bleeding," "Goodbye Yellow Brick Road," "Grey Seal," "Grimsby," "Honky Cat," "I Saw Her Standing There," "Lucy in the Sky with Diamonds," "Rocket Man," "Saturday Night's Alright (for Fighting)," "Take Me to the Pilot," "Whatever Gets You Thru the Night," "You're So Static," and "Your Song."

The group played the *Captain Fantastic and the Brown Dirt Cowboy* album in running order. Also on the bill: the Beach Boys, Rufus, The Eagles, Joe Walsh, and Stackridge.

❖ **June 29:** Elton played with the Doobie Brothers and The Eagles at Oakland Coliseum.

❖ **August-October:** North American tour. Elton celebrated the fifth anniversary of his American debut by returning to the Troubadour Club August 25-27. His tour opened two days later in San Diego with the new *Rock of the Westies* band. It ended October 25-26 at the Dodger Stadium spectacular, where Elton played to 55,000 fans each day. Emmylou Harris and Joe Walsh preceded Elton's three-hour and forty-five-minute set, which included appearances by Bernie Taupin, Billie Jean King, Kiki Dee, and the forty-five-member Rev. James Cleveland Choir. To the audience's delight, Elton removed his overalls to reveal a sequined Los Angeles Dodgers uniform. Though the concert is considered one of his most memorable, the star was dealing with a deep depression that two weeks earlier had prompted him to try to end his life with sleeping pills. His song mix included "Street Kids," "Let It Be," "Curtains," and "Dixie Lily."

1976

❖ **April-May:** Britain.
❖ **June-August:** North Ameri-

can tour. Opened June 29 in Washington, D.C., and closed August 17 in New York after twenty-nine shows. The "Louder Than a Concorde (But Not Quite as Pretty)" tour played to rowdy stadium crowds. In Detroit, Elton ranted onstage after nearly being hit by a bottle. Though he was growing tired after years of touring, the shows were still energetic and enthusiastic. His fame reached such heights that Elton John Day became a common celebration and mayors, like Frank Rizzo in Philadelphia, presented the star with the keys to their cities. Police escorts were essential. During a week at Madison Square Garden, he dressed as the Statue of Liberty and performed encores with Alice Cooper, transvestite Divine, Billie Jean King, Kiki Dee, and the New York Community Choir.

> **Only Elton could...**
> ❖ Fall off the stage while performing "I'm Still Standing."
> ❖ Collapse from exhaustion and illness while singing "Better Off Dead" in 1979 at the Universal Amphitheatre.
> ❖ Set the mood at a 1973 Christmas show by having artificial snow fall on stage — and render his piano useless by wedging between the keys.
> ❖ Perform the same song twice in one show. Two times. In 1992 at Dodger Stadium, he sang "Don't Let the Sun Go Down on Me" — once solo and once with George Michael. In Philadelphia in 1988, he offered a double dose of "Philadelphia Freedom," claiming that he had no other songs rehearsed for encores.

❖ **September 17:** Solo at the Festival of Popular Music in Scotland.

1977

❖ **May 2-7:** Acoustic charity concerts at the Rainbow Theatre in London with percussionist Ray Cooper.

❖ **September:** Joined Bonnie Raitt and Kiki Dee onstage at the Dr. Pepper Festival in New York's Central Park.

❖ **November 3:** Announced his retirement from touring at a Wembley Stadium show and then, with the crowd screaming "no," performed "Sorry Seems to Be the Hardest Word." Premiered "Shine on Through." Jammed with Stevie Wonder on "Bite Your Lip (Get up and Dance)."

1978

❖ **June:** Performed at a British sports charity.

❖ **October 14:** A solo concert at an MCA convention to promote *A Single Man*.

❖ **October 20:** A solo show in Paris, France, at a small radio station. It was a warm-up for the forthcoming tour.

1979

❖ **February-April:** Europe with Cooper. His first tour in two years. He planned the two-man tour to force him to concentrate on his vocals and piano work. In France, as a thank you for the nation's warm embrace of the *Blue Moves* album, Elton sang

"Iles Amore" in French and "I Love Paris in the Springtime."

❖ **May:** Grabbed headlines with Elton-Cooper shows in Russia, Ireland, and Israel.

❖ **September-November:** American tour. Opened September 19 in Tempe, Arizona, and closed November 11 in Houston, Texas, after forty-one shows. The "Back in the USSA" concerts featured Elton with percussionist Ray Cooper. Widely regarded as his best tour, it allowed Elton to showcase his musicianship at intimate venues — a decade before the word "unplugged" grew popular.

❖ **November-December:** Australia with Cooper.

1980

❖ **September-November:** North American tour. Opened September 4 in Madison, Wisconsin, and ended November 16 in Honolulu, Hawaii, after forty-four shows. Elton launched his first large-venue tour in four years. Though his popularity had waned, the shows drew large crowds. Symbolic of his desire to return to the top of the charts, he relied on songs from his best-known album, *Goodbye Yellow Brick Road*. Out of respect to Nigel Olsson's solo career, Elton allowed his drummer to perform two of his own songs in the middle of the set. The September 16 show marked the first time since 1973 that he had performed in

Rossya Concert Hall, Russia, May 28, 1979: Despite the hype, Elton was not the first entertainer from the West to tour Russia. (Cliff Richard, B.B. King, and The Nitty Gritty Dirt Band all proceeded him.) But Elton's eight-show tour was a much bigger event than any of the others — and not without controversy, given the Cold War sentiments of the day. The entertainer viewed it as his greatest accomplishment to that point. The groundwork was laid two years earlier when he performed at the Rainbow Theatre in London. Russian diplomats made two requests: Do not kick over the piano stool during "Bennie and the Jets" and do not perform "Back in the U.S.S.R." Elton obliged on the first. The concert was filmed for a TV documentary and broadcast live on BBC radio. Though his records had not been legally available in the country, many in the audience sang to the tunes, having purchased black market albums. The audience's response was unprecedented, according to journalists who covered the event. The event reignited Elton's enthusiasm. Songs: "Your Song," "Sixty Years On," "Daniel," "Skyline Pigeon," "Take Me to the Pilot," "Rocket Man," "Don't Let the Sun Go Down on Me," "Goodbye Yellow Brick Road," "Roy Rogers," "Candle in the Wind," "Ego," "Where to Now, St. Peter?," Jim Reeves's "He'll Have to Go," "I Heard It Through the Grapevine," "Funeral for a Friend," "Tonight," "Better Off Dead," "Idol," "I Think I'm Gonna Kill Myself," "I Feel Like a Bullet (in the Gun of Robert Ford)," "Bennie and the Jets," "Sorry Seems to Be the Hardest Word," "Part-Time Love," "Crazy Water," "Song for Guy," a medley of "Saturday Night's Alright (for Fighting)" and "Pinball Wizard," and a medley of "Crocodile Rock," "Get Back," and "Back in the U.S.S.R."

Central Park, New York, September 13, 1980: A mammoth crowd of 450,000 gathered to see Elton John's history-making free concert to benefit New York city parks. Some fans camped out two days in advance to secure a good spot on the lawn. The pianist was in a mood to celebrate. Hundreds of red, white, and blue balloons were released into sunny skies on the opening notes of "Funeral for a Friend." Among the highlights were his sweet performance of friend John Lennon's "Imagine," a short distance from the Dakota, and his rendition of "Your Song" while dressed as Donald Duck. Song list: "Funeral for a Friend/Love Lies Bleeding," "Tiny Dancer," "Goodbye Yellow Brick Road," "All the Girls Love Alice," Nigel Olsson singing lead on "All I Want Is You," "Rocket Man," "Sartorial Eloquence," "Philadelphia Freedom," "Sorry Seems to Be the Hardest Word," Olsson singing lead on "Saturday Night," "Saturday Night's Alright (for Fighting)," "Harmony," "White Lady, White Powder," "Little Jeannie," "Bennie and the Jets," "Imagine," "Ego," "Have Mercy on the Criminal," "Someone Saved My Life Tonight," "Your Song," and "Bite Your Lip (Get up and Dance)."

Maryland, where he had been banned for an earlier incident.

1981
❖ **June:** Played a private concert for Prince Andrew's twenty-first birthday. Danced with Princess Anne to "Hound Dog" and with Queen Elizabeth II to "Rock Around the Clock."

1982
❖ **June-August:** North American tour. Opened June 12 in Denver, Colorado, and closed August 7 in New York, after forty-one shows. Elton reunited with his heyday band of Nigel Olsson, Dee Murray, and Davey Johnstone — the first time since 1975 that all four had played together. Among the songs they performed were several that fans rarely hear in current concerts: "Blue Eyes," "Dear John," "Where Have All the Good Times Gone?," "Ticking," "Teacher I Need You," and "Ball & Chain." The July 7 show in Kansas City was broadcast over radio, becoming the most successful carried by the NBC network. The broadcast took a 15.9 share among adult listeners 18 to 24.
❖ **November-December:** Britain.

1983
❖ **May 26-June 10:** While vacationing in China, he made a few solo appearances.

1984
❖ **February-March:** New Zealand, Australia, and Hong Kong. In Australia, ticket sales were phenomenal, breaking all previous records.
❖ **April-June:** Europe, including Yugoslavia, Hungary, Czechoslovakia, and Poland, where Solidarity leader Lech Walesa attended a concert. A June 30 show at

Wembley Stadium included Nik Kershaw.

❖ **August-November:** North American *Breaking Hearts* tour. Began August 17 in Tempe, Arizona, and ended November 4 in Worcester, Massachusetts, after fifty-three shows. They were similar to the 1982 concerts, but with Alice Cooper's ex-music director, Fred Mandel, as part of the band. Aside from drawing on his usual greatest hits, he played a few less-familiar songs like "Hercules," "Teacher I Need You," and the rocker "Restless."

1985

❖ **June-July:** Several special performances highlighted his summer tour. In early June, he and Millie Jackson performed "Act of War" live at the Montreaux Rock Festival. On June 28, dressed as Ronald McDonald, he performed at Wham!'s fare-well concert. At Live Aid on July 13, he debuted his new band, performing "Rocket Man," "I'm Still Standing," "Bennie and the Jets," "Can I Get a Witness?," "Don't Go Breaking My Heart" (with Kiki Dee), and "Don't Let the Sun Go Down on Me" (backing George Michael).

A 1985 concert bill.

❖ **November-December:** Launching a world-wide tour in Britain in November, Elton showed off a new wardrobe of outrageous stage costumes, including an Eiffel Tower hat and pink mohawk wig. When it hit the U.S. shore in 1986, the tour broke house records by the Rolling Stones and Grateful Dead. Designer Bob Mackie produced many memorable costumes, including one of Mozart. This was Elton's glitziest tour since 1973-74. Elton was planning to do his largest world tour, but throat problems cut it short. His ten-piece band included a horn section. Energized musically, Elton gave a new slant to several standards like "Rocket Man," "Daniel," "Candle in the Wind," and "Your Song," with a taste-ful sax accompaniment.

1986

❖ **March-April:** Europe. The tour continued from 1985.

❖ **August-October:** North American tour. Opened August 17 in Clarkston, Michigan, and closed October 12 in Los Angeles, California, after thirty-eight shows. He was hampered by what was thought then to be laryngitis. By mid-September, he was reduced to a whisper during many encores. In an unusual move, Elton played "Love Song" on acoustic guitar with other guitarists backing him. (He had done something similar in 1976.) Ex-band member Caleb Quaye joined him for "Satur-day Night's Alright (for Fighting)" at his final concert of the tour. The show was broadcast on American radio.

❖ **November-December:** He played Australia with the Melbourne Symphony

Orchestra. In all, one hundred musicians took the stage.

1987

❖ **January 5:** Plans for a return tour of America had to be dropped when he underwent a brief surgery in Australia to remove nodules from his vocal cords. Though British tabloids portrayed it as a career-threatening ailment, it proved to be a mundane procedure that sidelined the performer for a few months.

❖ **April 1:** In his first post-surgery show, Elton appeared at the "Stand by Me" AIDS benefit. He performed Carole King's "Will You Still Love Me Tomorrow?" and "I Guess That's Why They Call It the Blues."

1988

❖ **April:** He joined George Michael onstage in New Zealand.

❖ **June 24:** Performed a half hour solo set at The Axis Club in Boston for a media crowd. Among the songs: "I Heard It Through the Grapevine," "Get Back," and "Whole Lotta Shakin' Going On."

❖ **July 8:** At a Los Angeles benefit for children with AIDS, he produced a fourteen-song set

Sydney Entertainment Center, Australia, December 14, 1986: No rock star had ever undertaken a major tour with a world-renown orchestra. After two years of discussion and intense rehearsals, this ambitious project materialized. Save for Elton's troubled voice, the show was a resounding success. Conductor James Newton Howard had spent several months adapting Paul Buckmaster's cello-oriented arrangements for the eighty-eight-piece orchestra. The concert was recorded and released as an album and video. One of the visual highlights occurred during "Candle in the Wind," when Elton played against a backdrop of orchestra members holding lit candles. Always the stage clown, Elton chose to lighten the evening when a stage light exploded. He grabbed his chest as if being shot and fell to the floor with a smile. Songs: With his band, "Funeral for a Friend," "One Horse Town," "Rocket Man," "The Bitch Is Back," "Daniel," Leon Russell's "Song for You," "Blue Eyes," "I Guess That's Why They Call It the Blues," "Bennie and the Jets," "Heartache All Over the World," "Sad Songs (Say So Much)," "This Town," "I'm Still Standing." With the band and orchestra, "Sixty Years On," "I Need You to Turn To," "The Greatest Discovery," "Tonight," "Sorry Seems to Be the Hardest Word," "The King Must Die," "Cold as Christmas," "Take Me to the Pilot," "Carla/Etude," "Tiny Dancer," "Have Mercy on the Criminal," "Slow Rivers," "Madman Across the Water," "Don't Let the Sun Go Down on Me," "Candle in the Wind," "Burn Down the Mission," "Your Song," and "Saturday Night's Alright (for Fighting)."

that featured the never-to-be-released "Love Is Worth Waiting For" and the only live performance of "Town of Plenty." The "For the Love of Children" show also introduced his new band: Davey Johnstone, Jonathan Moffett, Romeo Williams, Guy Babylon, Fred Mandel, and backup singers Marlena Jeter, Natalie Jackson, and Alex Brown.

❖ **September-October:** North American tour. Began September 9 in Miami, Florida, and ended October 22 in New York after thirty-one shows. Elton wanted to test his throat on a short, six-week tour before going worldwide. For the *Reg Strikes Back* tour, he abandoned the costumes of old in favor of hat/suit combinations. Concerts opened with a string of early songs — "Sixty Years On," "I Need You to Turn To," "The King Must Die," and "Burn Down the Mission," which had been featured on the *Live in Australia* album. A synthesizer supplied the orchestral arrangements. A large stage screen provided close-ups of Elton's keyboard work. Elton offered a greatest hits package, as well as rarer tunes like "The Ballad of Danny Bailey" and "A Word in Spanish," the latter off his then-current album. It marked his first tour without a piano. He played electric keyboards. Numerous artists made guest appearances at his concerts, including Eric Clapton, Toto's Steve Lukather, Bruce Hornsby, Jon Bon Jovi, Billy Joel, and Debbie Gibson.

❖ **November 2:** Elton and Mark Knopfler joined Eric Clapton in Japan.

> **No rehearsals:** The only songs Elton John says he can play without practicing.
> ❖ "Your Song."
> ❖ "Daniel."
> ❖ "Candle in the Wind."
> ❖ "Song for Guy."
> ❖ "Rocket Man."

1989

❖ **March-June:** Europe. In Paris, Elton collapsed onstage during a dance number, took a brief break to receive medical treatment, and finished the show.

❖ **Summer:** Did a surprise forty-minute set at the China Club in Los Angeles, joined by Michael Bolton on "Lucille." Michael J. Fox played guitar.

❖ **July-October:** North American tour. Opened July 28 in Hartford, Connecticut, and closed October 22 in New Haven, Connecticut, after forty-five dates. Having tested his voice in 1988, Elton took a similar show on a longer *Sleeping with the Past* tour. The song set featured many new songs. For some shows, he even dusted off "Come Down in Time." A pay-per-view concert was canceled as were radio interviews. Rumors abounded about Elton's health. With Elton physically and mentally drained, several shows were canceled. Clapton joined Elton on "Rocket Man" October 7. Eleven days later, Elton threw a fit on stage, declaring it to be his last concert. Alcoholism and a cocaine addiction gripped his life. He had become the bloated and distant Elvis Presley that he had met in 1976.

❖ **August 24:** At the Los Angeles Amphitheater, he appeared as the Pinball Wizard during a live staging of The Who's *Tommy*.

1990

❖ **January:** Australia, New Zealand, and Tasmania. The non-American leg of his tour continued. Elton performed a few special dates in America. But his performance was visibly off. His piano playing had slowed and he continously forgot lyrics.

❖ **April:** He played Farm Aid IV, dedicating the effort to friend Ryan White. Days later, he sang at the teen's funeral.

❖ **May:** Performed at a series of special events, including a Lupus Foundation fund-raiser with Little Richard in Beverly Hills on May 8, an MTV unplugged concert on May 16, and the opening of Donald Trump's Taj Mahal on May 18-20 in

Atlantic City, where he premiered the song "Made for Me."

❖ **June 30:** Participated in the Knebworth benefit in England, with Paul McCartney, Phil Collins, Cliff Richard, and many others. The performances were released on a double CD and video. In July, he admitted himself into a hospital for treatment of multiple addictions.

❖ **November 11:** He played his first show since emerging from treatment for multiple addictions. A London benefit at Grosvenor House with Ray Cooper.

1991

❖ **March 10:** He lent support to Sting's rainforest benefit at Carnegie Hall, singing "Your Song," "Sacrifice," "Come Down in Time," and "The Girl from Ipanema." The last two were duets with Sting. As part of his therapy, Elton devoted most of the year to his personal life. Performances were rare.

❖ **March 25:** Elton celebrated his own birthday by joining George Michael onstage.

❖ **April 1:** Surprised Rod Stewart on April Fool's Day at Wembley Stadium. Dressed in blond wig, high heels, and a strapless gown, Elton duetted with Stewart on "You're in My Heart." Stewart was expecting his wife to appear.

> **Grand Ole Opry, March 15, 1992:** Dee Murray, the bass player in Elton's first band, had died in January 1992 after a battle with cancer. These solo concerts (two in one day) paid tribute to Murray and raised money for his wife and children. It was a somber, emotional affair, witnessed by longtime associates, numerous stars and fans who traveled from other nations. "When Dee passed away..., he left a big hole in my life," said Elton. "I'm here to say thanks to him." The concert closed with Elton singing "That's What Friends Are For" as photos of Murray flashed on a screen behind him. Few eyes were dry. Songs: "Sixty Years On," "Sorry Seems to Be the Hardest Word," "Tiny Dancer," "Philadelphia Freedom," "Blue Eyes," "Daniel," "The North," "I Guess That's Why They Call It the Blues," "Sad Songs," "Sacrifice," Jim Reeves's "He'll Have to Go" (in honor of the venue), "Burn Down the Mission," "Don't Let the Sun Go Down on Me," "Your Song," "Bennie and the Jets," "Candle in the Wind," and "That's What Friends Are For."

1992

❖ **March 12:** Performed at another Sting rainforest benefit with Natalie Cole, Don Henley, and James Taylor.

❖ **April 20:** Appeared at England's Concert for Life, honoring Freddie Mercury. Sang "The Show Must Go On" and duetted with Axl Rose on "Bohemian Rhapsody."

❖ **May-July:** European tour. Played the June 5-7 Rock Am Ring, an open-air music festival in Germany, with Bryan Adams, Michelle Shocked, Pearl Jam, Lisa Stansfield, Glen Frey, Tori Amos, and Crowded House.

❖ **August-November:** North American tour. Opened August 11 in Atlanta, Georgia, and closed November 14 in Mexico City after fifty shows. Looking trim, renewed, and years younger (thanks partly to a hair weave), Elton launched his first sober tour in more than fifteen years. Between songs, he talked about his recovery and thanked his fans for being the one constant in an often tumultuous public life. He spoke of losing many loved ones to AIDS and performed "The Last Song" and Queen's "The Show Must Go On," in honor of friend Freddie Mercury. Newspaper critics praised the enthu-

> **Big events**: Some of the multi-act events that have included Elton.
> ❖ Live Aid, 1985.
> ❖ Prince's Trust, 1986 and 1987.
> ❖ Stand by Me AIDS benefit, 1987.
> ❖ Farm Aid IV, 1990.
> ❖ Knebworth, 1990.
> ❖ Concert for Life, 1992.

siasm and sincerity of his performances. The U.S. portion of the tour included four stadium concerts with Eric Clapton. The New York and Los Angeles shows featured little interaction between the stars, who flipped coins to see who would go on first. They had done several dates together in Europe as well. At some concerts, Clapton joined Elton to duet on "Runaway Train." The tour, without Clapton, ended with rare appearances in Mexico City, November 13-14, at Azteca Stadium. The South American tour was canceled.

1993

❖ **February-March:** Australia.

❖ **April-May:** North American tour. Featuring a full band, the tour opened April 8 in Washington, D.C., and closed May 8 in Atlanta, Georgia, after twenty shows. The concerts resembled the 1992 shows, with a few changes. He opened with "Pinball Wizard," dusted off "Come Down in Time" and "Captain Fantastic and the Brown Dirt Cowboy," and offered the Stones' "Jumpin' Jack Flash" as an encore.

❖ **June:** Europe and Israel.

❖ **September-October:** Elton's tour with percussionist Ray Cooper began September 30 in Ft. Lauderdale, Florida, and ended October 24 in Portland, Maine, after sixteen shows. The brief Cooper tour featured Elton solo at a grand piano for half of the concert, before the percussionist joined him. Rich in his 1970s compositions, the shows spotlighted such obscurities as "Talking Old Soldiers," "Idol," and "Indian Sunset." Concerned about his ability to remember the lyrics to older songs, he often performed with an inconspicuous

---

The authors' top ten Elton concerts

1. Troubadour Club, August 25, 1970. Ignited his career.

2. Dodger Stadium, October 25, 1975. The first act since The Beatles to play the venue.

3. Dee Murray benefit, March 15, 1992. A touching solo tribute.

4. Hollywood Bowl, September 7, 1973. His biggest extravaganza.

5. Madison Square Garden, November 28, 1974. With John Lennon.

6. Central Park, September 13, 1980. A comeback of sorts.

7. Russia, May 28, 1979. Rattling the iron curtain.

8. Atlanta, August 19, 1994. With Billy Joel in Elton's adopted hometown.

9. *11-17-70*: Live on radio.

10. Sydney, Australia, December 14, 1986. The star and the symphony.

teleprompter that flashed the words.
❖ **December:** Four dates in South Africa with Ray Cooper.

1994

❖ **April 9:** Rainforest benefit with Sting in New York.
❖ **July-August:** American tour with Billy Joel. Opened July 8 in Philadelphia, Pennsylvania, and closed August 21 in Orlando, Florida, after twenty-one dates. Joel hatched the idea and approached Elton. The two men offered a festive celebration of piano rock. Titled "Face to Face," the tour succeeded beyond expectations. Despite the hefty competition — the Rolling Stones, The Eagles, and Pink Floyd — the Joel-John stadium toured grossed $47 million. At $224,157 per show, they were second only to Barbra Streisand. The concert opened with the two men playing together, center stage, at baby grand pianos. Each performer did a set with his own band. Elton offered a version of Joel's "New York State of Mind." Joel did "Goodbye Yellow Brick Road." The two bands jammed late in the concert, storming through songs by rockers who had inspired John and Joel: The Beatles' "A Hard Day's Night," Little Richard's "Lucille," and Jerry Lee Lewis's "Great Balls of Fire." The event concluded with Elton on his Yamaha, Joel on his Steinway, and the audience singing "Piano Man" — as "Piano Men."
❖ **September:** With percussionist Ray Cooper on West Coast.
❖ **November-December:** With Ray Cooper in Paris, London and Italy. Similar to 1993 dates. At some shows, he performed "Believe" and "Live Like Horses." A special AIDS foundation benefit on December 1 included Boy George, Kiki Dee, Lisa Stansfield, and George Michael.

Warming up: Though he performed on the bill with other entertainers in 1970 and 1971 (Leon Russell, The Byrds, and The Kinks were among them), this list notes artists who did not co-headline events but opened for him on tours.
❖ 1971: England Dan and John Ford Coley in Britain. Redeye and Mark Almond in America.
❖ 1972: Family on some dates, Linda Lewis and Sunshine on others.
❖ 1973: Longdancer (with Dave Stewart) in Britain. The Sutherland Brothers and Quiver in America.
❖ 1974: Kiki Dee.
❖ 1976: Murray Head in England. Billy Connolly in America. John Miles in Boston.
❖ 1980: Judie Tzuke.
❖ 1982: Quarterflash.
❖ 1984: Mental as Anything in New Zealand. Mondo Rock in Australia.
❖ 1988: Wet, Wet, Wet in America.
❖ 1989: Nik Kershaw at Wembley in England.
❖ 1992: Andrew Strong of The Commitments on May 5 in Sweden. Steve Forbert in Germany. Curtis Steiger and Bonnie Raitt for the joint London concerts of Elton and Eric Clapton.

Forgotten hits: Smash singles Elton rarely performs.
❖ "Honky Cat."
❖ "Island Girl."
❖ "Crocodile Rock."
❖ "Lucy in the Sky with Diamonds."
❖ "Little Jeannie."
❖ "Mama Can't Buy You Love."
❖ "Nikita."
❖ "Goodbye Yellow Brick Road."

An ad for a 1972 concert.

1995

❖ **January 19:** An all-star performance at the Commitment to Life AIDS benefit concert in Los Angeles. Bernie Taupin co-produced the affair.

❖ **February:** Japan with Ray Cooper.

❖ **March 27:** Academy Awards performance of "Can You Feel the Love Tonight?"

❖ **March-April:** North American tour with Billy Joel. Opened March 22 in San Diego, California, and closed April 14 in Miami, Florida, after a dozen dates. Nearly identical to the 1994 tour. Elton added "Believe" to his set. In Las Vegas, the audience helped him celebrate his birthday by singing to him. On April 12, Elton and Joel joined Bruce Springsteen, Paul Simon, Jon Bon Jovi, James Taylor, and Jessye Norman at Sting's rainforest benefit.

❖ **May-July:** Europe (including Russia) and Australia with his band.

❖ **August-October:** North American tour.

Tell me what the papers say...

❖ "Elton John, a British singer-songwriter who is the current 'most talked-about' pop music arrival, made his New York concert debut at the Fillmore East this weekend, and proved the rumors were true. ... With lyricist Bernie Taupin, John has created some songs of grand brilliance. 'Sixty Years On' and 'Burn Down the Mission' are at once sensitive and powerful." Mike Jahn, *New York Times*, November 22, 1970.

❖ "The crowd was happy to stomp and clap where stomping and clapping were called for. But in the middle of 'Sixty Years On,' when Dee Murray's dramatic bass stopped echoing and the piano took an abrupt decrescendo, there was, in Carnegie Hall, from parquet to last balcony, absolute silence." Nancy Erlich, *Billboard*, April 26, 1971.

❖ "The audience was spared no expense as a chorus line of young women rocketed its ways across the stage. 'Legs' Larry Smith broke into a manic tap dance, clicking away to Mr. John's percussive piano playing." Ian Dover, *New York Times*, November 22, 1972.

❖ "With his Liberace style, ever funky piano and a sackful of new songs to deliver, Elton has entered a new phase of his career, which has brought a vast surge in popularity. It has also made him a better entertainer..." Chris Charlesworth, *Melody Maker*, March 31, 1973.

Medley fodder: Fifteen standards that Elton has weaved into live medleys.

❖ "Boogie Woogie Bugle Boy," 1979.

❖ "The Yellow Rose of Texas," 1971.

❖ "Oh, Suzanna," 1974.

❖ "Don't Be Cruel," 1979.

❖ "Hound Dog," 1979, 1982, 1988.

❖ "Strolling Through the Park," 1979.

❖ "Twist and Shout," 1979, 1982, 1984, 1989.

❖ "Great Balls of Fire," 1980.

❖ "Good Golly Miss Molly," 1980.

❖ "Be Bop-a-Lula," 1979.

❖ "In the Mood," 1982, 1984.

❖ "Chattanooga Choo Choo," 1984, 1986.

❖ "Back in the U.S.S.R.," 1979.

❖ "I Love Paris in the Springtime," 1979.

❖ "Brown Sugar," 1989-90.

Wish list: Five songs he has never performed in concert, but should.
- ❖ "Seasons."
- ❖ "Blues for Baby and Me."
- ❖ "Sugar on the Floor."
- ❖ "Billy Bones and the White Bird."
- ❖ "Sick City."

You can count on it: Songs Elton nearly always performs live.
- ❖ "Your Song."
- ❖ "Sad Songs (Say So Much)."
- ❖ "Rocket Man."
- ❖ "Candle in the Wind."
- ❖ "Bennie and the Jets."

One song he should not perform nearly every time.
- ❖ "Sad Songs (Say So Much)."

Still waiting: Five songs Elton has not performed in concert, though pledging to do so.
- ❖ "What Becomes of the Brokenhearted" by Jimmy Ruffin.
- ❖ "Dream Baby" by Roy Orbison.
- ❖ "Moon on the Rain" by Fairground Attraction.
- ❖ "No Woman, No Cry" by Bob Marley and the Whalers.
- ❖ "Subterranean Homesick Blues" by Bob Dylan.

❖ "John's Saturday and Sunday appearances at Dodger Stadium were indeed akin to a World Series for rock music fans. ... The 55,000 fans Saturday reacted to the key moments of John's show with ... enthusiastic abandon." Robert Hilburn, *Los Angeles Times*, October 27, 1975.

❖ "Elton's opening night at Universal Amphitheatre in California was probably the single most dynamic performance this reviewer has ever seen. ... (It) was a three-hour, 25-song non-stop extravaganza that recapped his career from the beginning to its present." Ed Harrison, *Billboard*, October 1979.

❖ "John showed with his July 3rd performance at Municipal Auditorium in Nashville that time's passage has done little to diminish his showmanship. His band proved that it could still double the sound of bands twice its size, while John demonstrated his strength of timing and proved his music still weaves magic." Kip Kirby, *Billboard*, July 1982.

❖ "The Elton of the '80s is a hit-maker again. And 'Sad Songs' and 'Who Wears These Shoes?' find him at the top of his form, emitting campy cries of love and deploying piano riffs that linger in your memory long after the songs have ended." Ken Tucker, *Philadelphia Inquirer*, October 21, 1984.

❖ "Elton John makes the fusing of classical music and pop rock and roll look easy. While he's best known for pop songs, he turned the show's first 40 minutes into a suite of brilliant symphonic rock." Thor Christensen, *Milwaukee Journal*, September 19, 1988.

❖ "Everyone always raves on about Elton John live, about how the British pop superstar gives you better value for your concert buck than anyone else in the biz. And, for once, the hype is all too accurate. He's the ultimate showman." Brandan Kelly, *Montreal Daily News*, September 26, 1989.

❖ "The good news is he's healthy. The bad news is his show should see a doctor. ... His flowing locks look like he has taken to wearing one of Less Nessman's old wigs and taken grooming tips from Captain Kangaroo." Cliff Radel, *Cincinnati Enquirer*, August 25, 1992.

❖ "I came away most awestruck by the new material. ... Elton's working at the peak of his powers after 22 years in the limelight and he's getting better and better with each passing season." Robert Oermann, *Nashville Tennessean*, September 7, 1992.

❖ "The elder statesman of rock isn't resting on his laurels... John played his instrument ... with passion and agility." Sarah Rodman, *Boston Herald*, October 25, 1993.

Though troubled, Elton could still put on a passionate performance in 1988.

Photo by Nannette M. Bac

The *Sleeping with the Past* tour was the last before Elton sought treatment for multiple addictions. At the Detroit show (right), he brought songwriting partner Bernie Taupin onstage.

Photo by Sharon Kalinoski

Photo by Nannette M. Bac

Photo by Belinda Bogan

A difference of three years: Between 1990 and 1993, Elton changed his ways.

Photo by Melissa Delgado

The Elton John AIDS Foundation has contributed millions toward care and education. The annual Smash Hits tennis benefit (above) raises money for the organization. Other fundraisers have included the sale of a specially designed Hard Rock T-shirt, for which Elton made a Boston appearance in 1993.

Photo by Sharon Kalinoski

Photo by Tom Stanton

Axl Rose inducted Elton John into the Rock and Roll Hall of Fame in 1994. Elton gave the award to lyricist Bernie Taupin.

Photo by Belinda Bogan

Piano gymnastics have always been part of Elton's band concerts.

Photo by George Matlock, Hercules UK

In late 1994 Elton opened a temporary resale shop to raise money for his AIDS foundation. Shoppers bought items from the star's wardrobe.

Songs

Elton John has been prolific in the music profession for over a quarter century. He has written or recorded more than 500 songs. What follows is the most complete list ever offered, including songs he has written himself, with Bernie Taupin and other lyricists, as well as songs he has recorded, dozens of which have never been officially released.

The Ace of Hearts and the Jack of Spades: Unreleased. An outtake from *Jump Up!*

Act of War: On *Ice on Fire*. Single released in July 1985. Failed to chart. Elton hoped to duet with Tina Turner on this hard-rocking number. But she disliked the song's mood, inspired, ironically, by her cover of "The 1984 Song." Instead, Elton teamed up with Millie Jackson, who contributed an energetic, Turner-like performance. Various extended versions of the song appeared on dance releases.

Ain't Nothing Like the Real Thing: On *Duets*. Elton and Marcella Detroit of Shakespear's Sister covered this Motown classic. It was a single in Britain, with several dance/rap mixes available.

All Across the Havens: On *Rare Masters*. A B-side to "Lady Samantha."

All Quiet on the Western Front: On *Jump Up!* A single in England.

All the Girls Love Alice: On *Goodbye Yellow Brick Road*. Album-oriented stations gave strong play to this tale about lesbians. The title may also be a tongue-in-cheek reference to Alice Cooper. Taupin and Elton were friends with Cooper. Elton commented in early interviews about young girls' reactions to Cooper in concert.

All the Nasties: On *Madman Across the Water*. Taupin struck back for unkind press reviews in 1971 when a glut of Elton John music hit the market. Elton named the song in honor of his critics.

All the Way Down to El Paso: Unreleased. Outtake from *Elton John*. Taupin has often credited Marty Robbins's "El Paso" for arousing his interest in lyrics. This song confirmed its impact.

Amazes Me: On *Sleeping with the Past*. Tinged with southern blues, the song honored Ray Charles.

Amen: On *All Men Are Brothers*. Performing with the Sounds of Blackness, Elton's rendition concluded this 1994 star-studded tribute to Curtis Mayfield.

America: Unreleased. From 1971.

Amoreena: On *Tumbleweed Connection*. Taupin suggested that Ray Williams, an early manager, name his future daughter Amoreena. He did, and Taupin wrote the song using her name. He described it as a "bawdy love song." Later, the song opened the movie *Dog Day Afternoon*. Despite the Williams connection, "Amoreena" is an obvious nod to the 1969 Joe Cocker hit "Delta Lady," written by Leon Russell. Both songs paint lyrical images of a lusty country girl in a pastoral setting.

Amy: On *Honky Chateau*. Taupin touched on an early relationship with an older woman, who was involved with another. The same woman inspired "Bennie and the Jets."

And the Clock Goes Round: Unreleased. Late 1960s.

Angel Tree: Recorded in the late 1960s, it was one of many early demos never officially released. It focuses on a favorite tree from Taupin's childhood near his family's Maltkin Farm in Market Rasen, Lincolnshire. The giant tree sat high on a hill overlooking pastures. Taupin went there to dream and write. According to local legend, an angel resided at the tree and passed a message from God to a shepherd. When the shepherd tried to spread the word, the villagers stoned him. He died in poverty with the divine message. The tree receives mention in two other songs, "Curtains" and "Burn Down the Mission."

Angeline: On *Leather Jackets*.

Annabella: The song, written by Elton, appeared as the B-side to Long John Baldry's "Let the Heartaches Begin" in the late 1960s.

Annabella (Who Flies to Me When She's Lonely): Unreleased. Late 1960s.

Are You Ready for Love? On *The Complete Thom Bell Sessions*. Elton covered The Spinners song.

At This Time in My Life: Unreleased. An outtake from *Jump Up!*

Baby, I Miss You: Unreleased. Late 1960s.

Bad Side of the Moon: On *11-17-70* (live) and *Rare Masters*. Covered and released first by the band Toe Fat, "Bad Side of the Moon" was critically acclaimed in Elton's 1970 concert reviews. The overproduced studio recording appeared only as a B-side until its inclusion on *Rare Masters*. It is often confused with the simi-

---

Number one singles in America
- ❖ "Crocodile Rock."
- ❖ "Bennie and the Jets."
- ❖ "Lucy in the Sky with Diamonds."
- ❖ "Philadelphia Freedom."
- ❖ "Island Girl."
- ❖ "Don't Go Breaking My Heart."
- ❖ "Don't Let the Sun Go Down on Me" duet.

Number one in England
- ❖ "Don't Go Breaking My Heart."
- ❖ "Sacrifice."

larly titled Pink Floyd album.

Ball & Chain: On *Jump Up!* Single released in November 1982. Did not chart. Pete Townshend played lead guitar.

Ballad of a Well-Known Gun: On *Tumbleweed Connection*.

The Ballad of Danny Bailey (1909-34): On *Goodbye Yellow Brick Road*.

Basque: Instrumental written by Elton in 1980 but never released by him. It appeared on flutist James Galway's *The Wind Beneath My Wings*, earning Elton a 1992 Grammy for best instrumental composition.

Be Prepared: On *The Lion King* sound track.

Belfast: On *Made in England*. Elton has talked about making an animated film to accompany the song.

Believe: On *Made in England*. Single released in February 1995. Peaked at #13.

Bennie and the Jets: On *Goodbye Yellow Brick Road*. Single released in February 1974. Hit #1. The song carries its own legend. Uncertain that it even merited a spot on the album, Elton initially opposed releasing it as a single. A program director for a black Detroit station convinced Elton by phone that the song should be a single. Enamored with the thought of topping the rhythm and blues charts, Elton reluctantly released "Bennie" in America. But in England, he insisted on his first choice, "Candle in the Wind." "Bennie" tells of a futuristic punk rock group that reaches the top of the charts. It refers subtly to a "hip" early girlfriend of Taupin, Sally Bennington, "Bennie." Though recorded in a studio, the cut included a clap track from a live performance at the Royal Festival Hall in February 1972 — as well as a snippet from a Jimi Hendrix recording. "Bennie" topped the pop and R&B charts and landed Elton a spot on TV's "Soul Train," a first for a white artist.

The Best of Both Worlds: Unreleased. Elton recorded the Don Black-Mark London song in 1968. Dick and Steve James wanted him to release it as a single. Instead, he came out with his own "Lady Samantha." Lulu had a hit with the Black-London song.

Better Off Dead: On *Captain Fantastic and the Brown Dirt Cowboy*. It has been described as John Prine lyrics set to a Gilbert and Sullivan melody.

Between Seventeen and Twenty: On *Blue Moves*.

Big Circle of Stone: Unreleased. Late 1960s.

Big Dipper: On *A Single Man*. The song flaunts a vampish, gay tone with Elton's Watford Football Club singing background.

Billy and the Kids: Outtake from *Leather Jackets*. Released in England as a B-side to "Slow Rivers."

Billy Bones and the White Bird: On *Rock of the Westies*.

Billy's Bag: Unreleased. A cover version of Billy Preston's song, recorded by the Bread and Beer Band, which included Elton.

The Bitch Is Back: On *Caribou*. Single released in September 1974. Peaked at #4. Taupin's first wife, Maxine, hatched the phrase "the bitch is back" in reference to Elton and his mood swings. Initially, MCA Records was concerned about the track's potentially offensive title. Some radio stations, especially in the South, were cold to the single and bleeped out the word "bitch." MCA's concern prompted a confusing initial push to promote "Cold Highway," the B-side, as the single.

Bite Your Lip (Get up and Dance): On *Blue Moves*. Single released in January 1977. Peaked at #28. Against the wishes of his record company and producer, Elton insisted that the song be a single. He felt certain it would be a massive hit. The charts proved him wrong. Three mixes of the song were released.

Bitter Fingers: On *Captain Fantastic and the Brown Dirt Cowboy*. The autobiographical song deals with Elton and Taupin and their unhappiness trying to write formula tunes for Dick James Music in the late 1960s.

Blessed: On *Made in England*.

Blue Avenue: On *Sleeping with the Past*. Taupin described Elton's failed marriage to Renate Blauel. The song may also be a subtle tribute to Roy Orbison, who died a few months before the session. His 1963 hit, "Blue Bayou," has similar bass lines, and all songs on the *Sleeping with the Past* album served as tributes to artists who inspired Elton and Taupin. During interviews promoting the album, Elton described the song as a "sort of Billy Joel thing," perhaps "Innocent Man." Though not released as a single in America, "Blue Avenue" charted throughout Europe. It is regarded as one of his strongest 1980s ballads.

Blue Bottle Blues: Unreleased. Late 1960s.

Blue Eyes: On *Jump Up!* Single released in July 1982. Peaked at #12. This Elton-Gary Osborne composition topped adult contemporary charts and cracked the top 10 in England, Australia, Belgium, Canada, Italy, Israel, and the Netherlands. Written with Frank Sinatra in mind, the track earned a Grammy nomination. The last song recorded for the album (on February 9, 1982), it was nearly abandoned after six takes because of difficulty getting acceptable vocals. Elton sang in a lower-than-usual key and even contributed a phrase to the lyrics.

Blues for Baby and Me: On *Don't Shoot Me, I'm Only the Piano Player*.

Bobby Goes Electric: Unreleased. An outtake from *21 at 33*. A Bob Dylan tribute.

Bonnie's Gone Away: Unreleased. Late 1960s.

Boogie Pilgrim: On *Blue Moves*.

Border Song: On *Elton John*. Released in March 1970. His first official American single, it hit #92. The last verse was written by Elton. He felt the song was too short and tried to summarize it at the end. Composed in a classical vein, "Border Song" also shows gospel roots. Several artists have covered it, including Eric Clapton and Aretha Franklin, whose version also charted in 1970. It remains one of Elton's favorites.

Born Bad: On *Victim of Love*.

Born to Lose: On *Duets*. Canadian poet-singer Leonard Cohen lent his deep lingering voice to this recording. Ray Charles scored a country hit with the song in the 1960s.

Breakdown Blues: Co-written by Elton and released in 1969 by the Bread and Beer Band. A British B-side to "The Dick Barton Theme (The Devil's Gallop)."

Breaking Down the Barriers: On *The Fox*. Originally called "Free the People."

Breaking Hearts (Ain't What It Used to Be): On *Breaking Hearts*. A not-so-subtle reference to Elton's marriage, released in Britain on Valentine's Day 1985, his and wife Renate's first anniversary.

Burn Down the Mission: On *Tumbleweed Connection*. It deals with English folklore, as well as America's Civil War. The desperation in the lyrics has the feel of "King Harvest (Has Surely Come)" by The Band, which influenced early John-Taupin work.

Burning Buildings: On *Breaking Hearts*.

But Not for Me: On the soundtrack of *Four Weddings and a Funeral*. Elton recorded the Gershwin song for the 1994 film.

Cadillac: Unreleased. The song, written by Bo Diddley, was intended as a non-album single in the fall of 1975, featuring backing vocals by the Beach Boys.

The Cage: On *Elton John*.

Cage the Songbird: On *Blue Moves*. Guitarist Davey Johnstone co-wrote the ballad. Graham Nash and David Crosby did backing vocals. Country star Crystal Gayle also released a version.

The Camera Never Lies: On *Reg Strikes Back*.

Can I Put You On? On *Friends*.

Can You Feel the Love Tonight? On *The Lion King* sound track. Single released in May 1994. Peaked at #4. His version played over the credits at the end of the movie. The lyrics differed from the cast rendition because of late changes in the story line. The song became Elton's fourteenth gold single and spent several weeks at #1 on the adult contemporary charts.

Candle in the Wind: On *Goodbye Yellow Brick Road* and on *Live in Australia*. Live single released in America in September 1987. It peaked at #6. It has become synonymous with Marilyn Monroe. But Taupin has said the song focuses on media abuse of stars, and, with the change of a few words, could just as easily have been about another icon, James Dean. The songwriters view it as perhaps their most perfect blend of lyric and melody.

Candy by the Pound: On *Ice on Fire*. Inspired by Smokey Robinson and the Miracles.

Can't Get Over Getting Over Losing You: Unreleased. *A Single Man* outtake flavored with honky-tonk piano.

Can't You See It? Unreleased. Late 1960s.

Captain Fantastic and the Brown Dirt Cowboy: The title cut from the album. Elton is the Captain and Taupin the Cowboy.

Carla/Etude: On *The Fox*. The short instrumental blended with "Fanfare to provide a lush introduction to "Chloe."

Cartier: On *To be continued...* A whimsical ditty paying homage to a favorite jeweler, this B-side to "Sartorial Eloquence" also surfaced as a commercial. John-Taupin wrote it under an appropriate alias: Dinah Card/Carte Blanche.

Chameleon: On *Blue Moves*. Elton wrote the song over six months in 1974 for the Beach Boys. But they rejected it. He released it two years later.

Chapel of Love: On the sound track of *Four Weddings and a Funeral*. He rocked to the Dixie Cups' hit.

Chasing the Crown: On *21 at 33*.

Child: Unreleased. Late 1960s.

Chloe: On *The Fox*. Single released in July 1981. Hit #34.

Choc Ice Goes Mental: An outtake from *Jump Up!* Released as a B-side to "Kiss the Bride."

Circle of Life: On *The Lion King* sound track. Single released in August 1994. Peaked at #18.

City of Blue: Unreleased. An outtake from *Blue Moves*.

Club at the End of the Street: On *Sleeping with the Past*. Single released in April 1990. Peaked at #28. Inspired by The Drifters's 1972 hit "Down at the Club" and Percy Sledge's "At the Dark End of the Street."

Cold: On *Made in England*.

Cold as Christmas (in the Middle of the Year): On *Too Low for Zero*. It originally featured a James Newton Howard arrangement, which was scrapped. As a British single, it charted. It was intended for American release, too, but withdrawn. The song rates as one of Taupin's favorites from the early 1980s.

Cold Highway: On *Rare Masters*. Taupin writes about a friend killed in an auto accident. A B-side to "The Bitch Is Back."

Color Slide City: Unreleased. Late 1960s. One of the few Elton songs to reveal a strong Beatles influence.

Come Back Baby: Written by Reg Dwight and released in Britain in July 1965, it was Bluesology's first single. He composed it while an errand boy at Mills Music. The song title is similar to that of one by an early idol, Ray Charles.

Come Down in Time: On *Tumbleweed Connection*. Recorded first during the sessions for the *Elton John* album, it originally featured Elton on piano with a simple rhythm section. Later, Paul Buckmaster arranged the song for orchestra.

Conquer the Sun: An outtake from *21 at 33*. The B-side to "Little Jeannie."

Country Comfort: On *Tumbleweed Connection*. The first version, never released, was recorded without Elton on piano. It featured Pete Robinson, a member of the group Quartermass and a student at the Royal Academy of Music with Elton and arranger Paul Buckmaster. Elton was on tour in the Netherlands. Later, he recorded the piano part. Rod Stewart released "Country Comfort" on *Gasoline Alley*, a version Elton prefers to his own. Incidentally, though the lyrics paint a portrait of earlier American times, several references — one to a hedgehog in clay, for example — allude to the countryside of Taupin's childhood in Lincolnshire, England. The song also reflects the impact on Taupin of The Band lyricist Robbie Robertson and his song "Rocking Chairs."

Country Love Song: On *The Complete Thom Bell Sessions*. The arrangement resembles a 1973 Jefferson/Hawes track, "There's No Reason."

Countryside Love Affair: Unreleased. Late 1960s.

Crazy Water: On *Blue Moves*. Viewed by producer Gus Dudgeon as one of Elton's greatest songs, it might have been released as a single in America had Elton not insisted on "Bite Your Lip (Get up and Dance)."

Crimes of Passion: Unreleased. An outtake from *Leather Jackets*. He performed it at an October 1986 concert in Los Angeles.

Crocodile Rock: On *Don't Shoot Me, I'm Only the Piano Player*. Single released in November 1972. His first number one hit. Elton lost a lawsuit because of the song's similarity to "Speedy Gonzales." The song borrowed from other recordings — Eddie Cochran's "Come on Everybody" and Neil Sedaka's "Oh, Carol" — to give it a nostalgic flavor.

Cry to Heaven: On *Ice on Fire*. Elton initially picked the song as the album's first single, but it was not released. "Cry to Heaven" shares its name with an earlier work by author Anne Rice, whom both Taupin and John admire. Instrumentally, the song also honored Sting's "Russians."

Cry, Willow, Cry: Unreleased. Late 1960s.

Crystal: On *Too Low for Zero*. In an Australian book, Gary Clarke (confirmed by Elton to be an ex-lover) contends that Taupin wrote the song for Clarke at Elton's request.

Curtains: On *Captain Fantastic and the Brown Dirt Cowboy*. The lyric alludes to several early John-Taupin compositions: "Scarecrow," "Angel Tree," and "A Dandelion Dies in the Wind." The tune's long ending is reminiscent of The Eagles' "Desperado Reprise" from 1973.

Dan Dare (Pilot of the Future): On *Rock of the Westies*. A tribute to the cartoon hero.

Dancing in the End Zone: An outtake from *Reg Strikes Back*. A B-side to "Healing Hands."

A Dandelion Dies in the Wind: Unreleased. Late 1960s. Inspired by the era's psychedelic sound, including "Dandelion" on the 1967 Rolling Stones' album.

Daniel: On *Don't Shoot Me, I'm Only the Piano Player*. Single released in March 1973. Peaked at #2. The Grammy-nominated ballad has been misinterpreted as a gay love song. While composing it, Elton edited lyrics that, according to Taupin, identified Daniel as a blind Vietnam veteran. Inspired by a story in *Newsweek* about the second-rate treatment of returning soldiers, "Daniel" is told from the perspective of the veteran's younger brother. Elton and Dick James argued over the prospect of it being a single. James and MCA felt it would be a marketing disaster as the album's first release. Elton insisted and James relented, with Elton vowing to pay promotional costs if the song flopped. It was the first song written for the album.

Dark Side of the Moon: Unreleased. From late 1960s. Though identical in title, it has nothing to do with the Pink Floyd song.

Dear God: On *21 at 33*.

Dear John: On *Jump Up!*

Desperation: Unreleased. An outtake from *Rock of the Westies*. Possibly intended for another artist, the song was composed while Elton toured America in October 1974.

Desperation Train: Unreleased. An outtake from *Jump Up!* Martin Page later wrote a melody to it and the song appeared on Taupin's 1987 album, *Tribe*.

The Dick Barton Theme (The Devil's Gallop): Released in February 1969 and November 1972 by the Bread and Beer Band, a studio group including Elton John.

Did He Shoot Her? On *Breaking Hearts*.

Digging My Grave: Unreleased. Late 1960s.

Dirty Little Girl: On *Goodbye Yellow Brick Road*. Inspired by the Rolling Stones.

Dixie Lily: On *Caribou*.

Dogs in the Kitchen: Unreleased. An outtake from *Captain Fantastic*. The lyrics are included in the album's scrapbook, but may not have been set to music.

Donner Pour Donner: On *To be continued...* A duet with French star France Gall. Written by Taupin and Michel Berger, Gall's husband.

Don't Go Breaking My Heart: On *Greatest Hits Vol. II*. Single released in June 1976. Hit #1. Never intended for an album, this duet with Kiki Dee was recorded during the *Rock of the Westies* sessions. It was written on electric piano in the studio during technical difficulties with "Between Seventeen and Twenty." Contrary to their usual writing technique, Elton composed the melody first and hummed it over the phone to Taupin (vacationing in Barbados), who then created the lyrics. Elton wrote the title. Though Dee and Elton recorded a version together in London, the final release merged her London vocals with his from a Canadian session. Elton hoped to call the duo "Reg and Pauley." John and Taupin used pseudonyms on the songwriting credits: Ann Orson/Carte Blanche. The single became the year's most popular in radio play and sales. It remained Elton's only number one hit in England until "Sacrifice" in 1990. The song also appeared on *Duets* with transvestite RuPaul and Elton giving it a satirical, dance hall interpretation. Released as a single, the later version peaked at #92 in March 1994 but fared better on the dance charts.

Single-minded: Five songs that shouldn't have been singles.

❖ "Bite Your Lip." He should have taken his own advice.

❖ "Johnny B. Goode." Roll over, Chuck Berry.

❖ "Don't Go Breaking My Heart" with RuPaul. Once was enough.

❖ "Sartorial Eloquence." Hardly.

❖ "Ball & Chain." A waste of Pete Townshend's talent.

Five songs that should have been U.S. singles:

❖ "High-Flying Bird."

❖ "Harmony."

❖ "Where Have All the Good Times Gone?"

❖ "Blue Avenue."

❖ "Sleeping with the Past."

Don't Let the Sun Go Down on Me: On *Caribou*. Single released in May 1974. Peaked at #2. Elton hated his vocals and didn't want the song on the album. Time proved him wrong: The song earned him a Grammy nomination. For backing vocals, he brought together an all-star cast, including Cat Stevens, Billy Preston, Dusty Springfield, Brian Wilson, and Danny Hutton of Three Dog Night. But the talents and egos did not blend. In the final version, Carl and Brian Wilson, Toni Tennille, Daryl Dragon, and others sang backup, with Bruce Johnston arranging. Re-recorded live in March

1991 in London as a duet with George Michael and released in December, the song hit #1. That version appeared on *Duets*. In addition, a live version by Elton appears on an "unplugged" collection released by MTV in 1994.

Don't Trust That Woman: On *Leather Jackets*. Co-written by Cher and Lady Choc Ice (Elton).

Don't You Wanna Play This Game No More? See Sartorial Eloquence.

Dreamboat: An outtake from *A Single Man*. Released in England as a B-side to "Kiss the Bride."

Ducktail Jiver: Unreleased. An up-tempo pop outtake from *Caribou*. It showed Elton's breezy pop style. With no piano, the recording featured Davey Johnstone on acoustic guitar. The song resembles 1988's "Heavy Traffic" in structure.

Duets for One: On *Duets*. Elton sings with himself. He co-wrote it with Chris Difford of Squeeze.

Durban Deep: On *Sleeping with the Past*. Patterned after Leo Dorsey's "Working in a Coal Mine," it uses diamond mines in South Africa to make a political statement.

Earn While You Learn: An outtake from *A Single Man*. Released in England as a B-side to "I'm Still Standing."

Easier to Walk Away: On *To be continued...* The R&B-flavored tune was one of four new songs produced by Don Was and included on the American box set.

Ego: On *To be continued...* Single released in March 1978. Peaked at #34. Written originally as an instrumental during the *Blue Moves* session and later embellished with lyrics, the song became a nonalbum single, as Elton's popularity waned. To hype its release, MCA and Elton's management prepared an involved promotional campaign, featuring pins, watches and videos shown at movie theaters. But U.S. radio stations in America had little interest in the song, which deserved better treatment. In one interview, Elton dedicated it to Mick Jagger, David Bowie and Paul McCartney — hardly a compliment, given the song's critical view of rock and roll egos.

Elderberry Wine: On *Don't Shoot Me, I'm Only the Piano Player*.

Elton's Song: On *The Fox*. Written with British activist Tom Robinson ("Glad to Be Gay"), the song is about Elton. The video casts it from the eyes of a boy who has a crush on an older youth. At the time, Elton referred to it as one of his finest compositions.

Emily: On *The One*. Lyrically, it evokes comparisons to "Sixty Years On." The song may refer subtly to an ill girl Elton met visiting Ryan White in the hospital.

Empty Garden (Hey, Hey Johnny): On *Jump Up!* Single released in March 1982. Peaked at #13. Taupin wrote the lyrics the day after John Lennon's December 1980 murder. He said he locked himself in his office, refusing to watch the news or read the papers. "I knew in the back of my mind that everybody would be doing the same thing, and I thought, 'God, am I cashing in? Am I being cold and calculating?' But then I realized it was the only thing I could do. I couldn't cry because that comes later." Taupin borrowed a line — "can't you come out to play" — from The

Beatles' "Dear Prudence."

Empty Hands: Unreleased. Late 1960s. Songwriter unknown.

Empty Sky: The title track from Elton's first solo album. Written on Jan. 7, 1969, it hints at his early musical respect for Mick Jagger and "Going Home" by the Stones.

Fanfare: On *The Fox*. The song, written by James Newton Howard, connects "Carla/Etude" and "Chloe."

Fascist Faces: On *The Fox*. The Rev. James Cleveland and his choir sing backup, as Elton lashes out at media coverage critical of his 1979 concerts in the Soviet Union, at a time when the nation was embroiled in international controversy for its actions in Afghanistan.

Fat Boys and Ugly Girls: An outtake from *The One*. A B-side to "Runaway Train" (though the title was accidently reversed).

Feed Me: On *Rock of the Westies*. Taupin ponders drug addiction.

First Episode at Hienton: On *Elton John*. Lyrics touch on Taupin's coming of age.

Flames of Paradise: On Jennifer Rush's *Heart over Mine*. This duet was released in July 1987. It peaked at #36. Elton did not write it.

Flinstone Boy: An outtake from *Blue Moves*. Released as the B-side to "Ego." The song — with words by Elton — illustrates why he needs lyricist Taupin.

The Flowers Will Never Die: Unreleased by Elton. Recorded in the late 1960s. A cover version was released by Ayshea in 1976.

Fools in Fashion: An outtake from *The Fox*. Released as a B-side to "Nobody Wins."

The Fox: On *The Fox*. It is about Elton.

Friends: Title track from the movie sound track. Single released in March 1971. Peaked at #34.

From Denver to LA: From the movie *The Games*. Single released against the artist's wishes in January 1970 and credited to "Elton Johns." It failed to chart. He did not write the song.

Funeral for a Friend/Love Lies Bleeding: On *Goodbye Yellow Brick Road*. The song has become a staple on classic rock stations. Engineer David Hentschel wrote and recorded the beginning organ part. He used chords from "Candle in the Wind" and producer Gus Dudgeon fused the piece with "Love Lies Bleeding," which was to be a separate song. Knocked out by what he heard, Elton kept the tunes together and added an instrumental segue. Taupin has described the lyrics as "a statement of what touring and rock and roll does to the family life." Elton's instrumental recalls the 1970 Procol Harum song "Piggy, Pig, Pig," produced, ironically, by Chris Thomas.

Georgia: On *A Single Man*. Elton's Watford Football Club sang backup.

Get Back: On *11-17-70*. A cover of The Beatles' song.

Get Out (of This Town): An instrumental written by Elton and released by the band Mr. Bloe in 1971, with Elton on piano.

Giles J. Burke: Unreleased. Late 1960s.

The Girl on Angel Pavement: Unreleased. Late 1960s.

Give Me the Love: On *21 at 33*. Co-written with British singer Judy Tzuke.

Give Me Your Smile: Unreleased. From 1973-74.

Give Peace a Chance: On *To be continued...* This remake of the John Lennon classic gave voice to one of Elton's most-used aliases, Lady Choc Ice.

Go It Alone: On *Leather Jackets*. A musical bow to Tina Turner.

Go On and On: On *Duets*. Gladys Knight and Elton sang it. Stevie Wonder wrote, produced, and played all instruments on the song.

The Goaldigger Song: Only 500 copies were released in March 1977 of this charity song by soccer boosters Jimmy Hill, Brian Moore, Eric Morecombe, and Elton.

God Knows (a Bit of Freedom): Unreleased. Recorded by the Bread and Beer Band.

Going Home: Unreleased. Late 1960s.

Good Morning: Unreleased. A 1972 ballad.

Goodbye: On *Madman Across the Water*. Recorded on February 27, 1971.

Goodbye Marlon Brando: On *Reg Strikes Back*. It deals with tabloids and gossip.

Goodbye Yellow Brick Road: Title track from the album. Single released in October 1973. Peaked at #2. Many lines refer to Taupin's struggles with career decisions and images of his family farm in Market Rasen, Lincolnshire.

(Gotta Get a) Meal Ticket: On *Captain Fantastic and the Brown Dirt Cowboy*.

Gotta Get Back to England: Unreleased. An outtake from *Goodbye Yellow Brick Road*.

The Greatest Discovery: On *Elton John*. Taupin wrote about the birth of a younger brother.

Grey Seal: On *Goodbye Yellow Brick Road*. The song was re-recorded. The original version, written for but not included on the *Elton John* album, appeared on *Rare Masters*.

Grimsby: On *Caribou*. Elton wanted Taupin to write a "tribute town" song, a la Randy Newman's "Cleveland." The result: "Grimsby," about a small seaport near Taupin's childhood home.

Grow Some Funk of Your Own: On *Rock of the Westies*. Single released in January 1976. Peaked at #14, sharing that honor with the B-side tune "I Feel Like a Bullet (in the Gun of Robert Ford)." Radio stations were divided over which song should get airplay.

Gulliver: On *Empty Sky*. A lyrical ode to Taupin's childhood dog.

Gypsy Heart: On *Leather Jackets*.

Hakuna Matata (No Worries): On *The Lion King* sound track.

Hard Luck Story: On *Rock of the Westies*. On piano and vocals, Elton sounds much like one of his idols, Leon Russell on "Roll Away the Stone." The song was intended for *Caribou* but bumped to a later album. Kiki Dee released it first.

Harmony: On *Goodbye Yellow Brick Road*. Featuring Beach Boys-like vocals, the song, though never a single, rated as one of his most-requested, non-hits in mid-1970s concerts. In 1973, Paul Drew, as vice president of programming for RKO AM radio in New York, was among the most influential men in radio. He recalled the popularity of "Harmony" on the program "Battle of the Hits," where listeners voted for favorite songs. The tune "remained champion, beating out legitimate single releases, for an unheard of thirty-three straight weeks. That has never, ever happened in the history of radio programming, especially for an album track," he said.

Have Mercy on the Criminal: On *Don't Shoot Me, I'm Only the Piano Player*.

Hay Chewed: On *Empty Sky*. The title plays off The Beatles' "Hey Jude."

Healing Hands: On *Sleeping with the Past*. Single released in August 1989. Peaked at #13; topped the adult contemporary charts. It paid tribute to The Four Tops and "Reach Out, I'll Be There."

Heart in the Right Place: On *The Fox*. Lyricist Gary Osborne takes a slap at journalists.

Heartache All Over the World: On *Leather Jackets*. Single released in October 1986. Peaked at #55. It was the first song completed for *Leather Jackets*.

Heaven Help Us: Unreleased. Written by Reg Dwight and recorded in 1968 by Bluesology with Long John Baldry.

Heavy Traffic: On *Reg Strikes Back*.

Heels of the Wind: On *The Fox*.

Hell: Unreleased. An outtake from *Made in England*.

Hercules: On *Honky Chateau*. Elton chose Hercules as his middle name a year earlier, in 1971. Musically, the song captures a Jerry Lee Lewis style. But with Ray Cooper's rhino whistle and Davey Johnstone's sliding guitar, "Hercules" offers shades of Dylan's 1965 "Highway 61 Revisited," the title cut to an early, favorite album of John and Taupin.

Here Comes Miss Hurt Again: Unreleased. An outtake from *Breaking Hearts*, this country-western song may date back to *Caribou*. Elton reworked it, but label chief David Geffen disliked the song and kept it off *Breaking Hearts*.

Here's to the Next Time: On *Rare Masters*. Late 1960s. The song was written as a message to Marsha Hunt, who left Bluesology to play in *Hair*.

Hero on Parade: Elton never released it, but Albert Hammond did, after altering the lyrics of the John-Osborne composition "Sweetheart on Parade."

Hey Lord, You Made the Night Too Long: Written by Elton, Long John Baldry, and Tony Macaulay. The B-side to Baldry's "Let the Heartaches Begin."

Hey, Papa Legba: An outtake from *Jump Up!* A B-side to "Blue Eyes." It was first recorded in the fall of 1979 while Elton and Ray Cooper were touring America.

Hi-Heel Sneakers: Unreleased. Elton covered this 1964 Tommy Tucker hit at the *Honky Chateau* sessions.

High-Flying Bird: On *Don't Shoot Me, I'm Only the Piano Player*. A musical bow to Van Morrison.

Highlander: An outtake from *Ice on Fire*. This instrumental emerged as a B-side to "Heartache All over the World." It might have been written for the movie, which was directed by Russell Mulcahy, who did several Elton videos.

Treasures on demo: Elton John has two distinctive sides musically: the flashy rocker and the shy balladeer. The duality permeates some of his best work. But no where is it more apparent than on demo recordings and alternate studio versions, which surface on bootleg releases and, occasionally, official compilations. Solo demos are usually recorded immediately after Elton puts music to Taupin's lyrics. They offer his early, unembellished vision for the song. The songs are usually re-recorded, with other instrumental parts layered in. Experimentation at this stage can lead to alternate versions of the track. For example, "Slave" appears on *Honky Chateau* as a slow ballad. A different take on the song, released on *Rare Masters*, features a rapid beat and Elton singing frantically. A few other cases illustrate why collectors find such out-takes intriguing:

❖ "Lady What's Tomorrow?" Elton's voice is much more expressive on the demo. Too often complete studio versions cannot recapture the mood of a demo, and the sound quality of the demo recording often keeps it from being used.

❖ "Come Down in Time." An early version features a rhythm section, later replaced with an orchestral arrangement.

❖ "Your Song." Compare the 1969 demo (on *To be continued...*) with the official release. One year made a world of difference in the maturity of his voice.

Ho! Ho! Ho! (Who'd Be a Turkey at Christmas?): On *Rare Masters*. B-side to "Step into Christmas." A verse was omitted from the recording but appeared on the picture sleeve of the Japanese single.

Holiday Inn: On *Madman Across the Water*. The song originally included another verse, which was edited from the release but performed in a few concerts. The lyrics complained about cold French fries and poor room service. Elton also drop the phrase "motel prison" from the song. Recorded on August 9, 1971.

Honey Man: Unreleased. Cat Stevens and Elton recorded this duet in 1970. A dispute between record labels kept the song, written by Stevens, from being released, though a bootleg copy escaped.

Honey Roll: On *Friends*.

Honky Cat: On *Honky Chateau*. Single released July 1972. Peaked at #8.

Honky Tonk Women: On *11-17-70*. A live rendition of the Stones' number.

Hoop of Fire: On *Leather Jackets*.

Hour Glass: Unreleased. Late 1960s. Not written by Elton.

House: On *Made in England*.

House of Cards: On *Rare Masters*. A B-side to "Someone Saved My Life Tonight."

H.R.H.: Unreleased. An instrumental written in the mid-1980s as a wedding gift for Prince Andrew and Sarah Ferguson.

Hymn 2000: On *Empty Sky*. In later years, Elton tried to disown the song, calling the lyrics "psychedelic rubbish" and the melody a "painful Dylan-type thing."

I Am Your Robot: On *Jump Up!* The original title was "Robot Man." Presumably, it was changed because of the similarity to "Rocket Man." Elton wrote the serial numbers featured in the song.

I Can't Go on Living Without You: Unreleased by Elton. The song made it to number six in the English qualifying round for the 1968 Eurovision Song Festival. Lulu performed it, and the young songwriters were acknowledged briefly on her show — their first television appearance.

I Could Never Fall in Love with Anybody Else: Unreleased. Late 1960s.

I Cry at Night: An outtake from *21 at 33*. Released as the B-side to "Part-Time Love." Taupin shares his pain over a crumbling marriage.

I Don't Care: On *A Single Man*.

I Don't Wanna Go on with You Like That: On *Reg Strikes Back*. Single released in June 1988. Peaked at #2. A remixed and extended version became a dancehall hit. Shep Pettibone also did a mix of the song.

I Fall Apart: On *Leather Jackets*.

I Feel Like a Bullet (in the Gun of Robert Ford): On *Rock of the Westies*. Single released in January 1976. Peaked at #14, sharing the honor with the reverse side, "Grow Some Funk of Your Own."

I Get a Little Bit Lonely: Unreleased. Late 1960s.

I Guess That's Why They Call It the Blues: On *Too Low for Zero*. Single released in October 1983. Peaked at #4. A letter Taupin wrote to his second wife, model Toni Russo, resulted in the lyrics. Stevie Wonder plays harmonica. It became the first John-Taupin song to hit the top 10 since 1976. The song also fared well in Europe. Elton's vocal were recorded in one take.

I Heard It Through the Grapevine: Live version released in 1984 as a B-side to "Who Wears These Shoes?" Recorded at his 1977 Wembley concert.

I Just Can't Wait to Be King: On *The Lion King* sound track.

I Love You and That's All That Matters: Unreleased. Late 1960s.

I Loved a Man: Bonnie Tyler recorded this 1988 song, with Dylan Thomas lyrics put to music by Elton.

I Need You to Turn To: On *Elton John*.

I Never Knew Her Name: On *Sleeping with the Past*. Elton subtly honors Aretha Franklin and her song "I Never Loved a Man."

I Saw Her Standing There: On *Rare Masters*. John Lennon joined Elton onstage for this live version.

I Swear I Heard the Night Talking: On *To be continued...* Recorded for the box set.

I Think I'm Gonna Kill Myself: On *Honky Chateau*. Larry "Legs" Smith of The Bonzo Dog Doo-Dah Band tap-danced on the song. Originally, Elton's stepfather was to play the spoons.

I Want to See You Smile: Unreleased. Late 1960s. Written by Reg Dwight and Caleb Quaye.

Idol: On *Blue Moves*. Taupin responded to critics who dismissed Elton and his music in 1976. He said he wrote the song from their standpoint, viewing Elton ten years on. The song is also thought to be about Elvis Presley.

If I Asked You: Unreleased. Late 1960s.

If I Were a Carpenter: Unreleased. The Bread and Beer Band covered it.

If There's a God in Heaven: On *Blue Moves*. The song was meant to evoke the Chi-Lites' "There Will Never Be Any Peace on Earth Till God Is Seated at the Conference Table."

If You Could See Me Now: Unreleased. Late 1960s.

If You Were Me: On *Duets*. Elton and Chris Rea, who charted in the United States in 1978 with "Fool (If You Think It's Over)," performed the Rea composition.

I'll Be There Tomorrow: Unreleased. An outtake from *Honky Chateau*.

I'll Make You Smile: Unreleased. Late 1960s.

I'll Never Let You Go: Unreleased. Late 1960s.

I'll Stop Living When You Stop Loving Me: Unreleased. Late 1960s.

I'll Try: Unreleased. Outtake from *A Single Man*.

I'm Going Home: Unreleased. Outtake from *Elton John*.

I'm Going to Be a Teenage Idol: On *Don't Shoot Me, I'm Only the Piano Player*. The song is about Marc Bolan of T. Rex, a friend of Elton. A few years later, Bolan died in a car accident.

I'm Not Very Well: Unreleased. An outtake from *Jump Up!*

I'm Ready: On *Rock, Rhythm & Blues*. Elton covered the Fats Domino song on this 1989 U.S. release.

I'm Still Standing: On *Too Low for Zero*. Single released in April 1983. Peaked at #12. It became Elton's anthem, though its commercial success surprised him. Taupin said he wrote it as a testament to his partner's staying power.

I'm Your Man: On *Tower of Songs*. Elton covered the song on this 1995 homage to Canadian singer, songwriter, and poet Leonard Cohen.

I'm Your Puppet: On *Duets*. Paul Young and Elton remade the 1966 hit.

In Neon: On *Breaking Hearts*. Single released in November 1984. Peaked at #38.

In the Morning: Late 1960s. John-Taupin composition performed by Rowena Cortez at a song festival in Japan.

Indian Maiden: Unreleased. An outtake from the 1970s.

Indian Sunset: On *Madman Across the Water*. While in America in 1970, Taupin visited the western towns and scenic landscapes that he had dreamed and read about as a boy. His romantic view of legendary cowboys and western folklore was dealt a cold blow at an Indian reservation. He expressed his disillusionment in the song, released first by Mary Travers. The song was written in October 1970.

Into the Old Man's Shoes: On *Rare Masters*. An outtake from *Elton John* and a British B-side. The ballad tells of a Western boy who moves from Tombstone, Arizona, to escape comparisons with his heroic father.

Is It You? Unreleased. An outtake from *Leather Jackets*.

Island Girl: On *Rock of the Westies*. Single released in September 1975. Hit #1. Taupin said he knew he had written a hit before hearing the melody.

It Ain't Gonna Be Easy: On *A Single Man*.

It's Me That You Need: On *Rare Masters*. Single released in May 1969 in England.

I've Been Loving You: On *Rare Masters*. Released in England in March 1968, it carries the distinction of being Elton's first solo single.

I've Seen That Movie Too: On *Goodbye Yellow Brick Road*.

I've Seen the Saucers: On *Caribou*.

Jack Rabbit: On *Rare Masters*. An outtake from *Goodbye Yellow Brick Road*. Appeared as a B-side.

Jamaica Jerk-Off: On *Goodbye Yellow Brick Road*.

Japanese Hands: On *Reg Strikes Back*.

Jerry's Law: Unreleased. An outtake from *Jump Up!*

Johnny B. Goode: On *Victim of Love*. Single released in December 1979. This disco interpretation of Chuck Berry's classic did not chart.

Just a Little Bit: An English B-side to "Since I Found You Baby" released in 1967 by Bluesology. A non-Elton composition.

Just an Ordinary Man: Unreleased. Late 1960s.

Just Like Belgium: On *The Fox*.

Just Like Strange Rain: On *Rare Masters*. An English B-side to 1969's "It's Me That You Need."

J'Veux d'la Tendresse: Released in Europe. Elton recorded the French-language version of "Nobody Wins" — with the original French lyrics by Jean-Paul Dreau, not Gary Osborne.

The King Must Die: On *Elton John*. Lyrically, it plays off the title of a book by English author Mary Renault.

Kiss the Bride: On *Too Low for Zero*. Single released in August 1983. Peaked at #25. Fans played it outside the church during his wedding.

La Vie En Rose: In 1994, Elton recorded the Edith Piaf classic for a French TV commercial promoting Cartier.

Lady Samantha: On *Rare Masters*. Released first as a single in England in January 1969. It originally had a more esoteric verse that set the scene of autumn evolving into winter, songbirds growing silent and a cloak of mist spreading across the ground. The song expanded Elton's reputation beyond that of a songwriter. It gained him attention as a solo artist. Lyrically, it has strong similarities to "Long Black Veil" by The Band.

Lady, What's Tomorrow? On *Empty Sky*.

The Last Good Man in My Life: An outtake from *Goodbye Yellow Brick Road*. Released by Kiki Dee in 1973.

Last Night: Unreleased. An instrumental cover recorded by the Bread and Beer Band.

The Last Song: On *The One*. Released in October 1992. Peaked at #23. It marked the first of his American singles to benefit his AIDS foundation. Taupin faxed the lyrics to Elton in Paris, shortly after Freddie Mercury died. "I was crying all the time as I wrote the music," Elton told *The Advocate*, "and it was very hard for me to sing it." The song tells of an estranged father coming to terms with the sexuality of his gay son, who is dying of an AIDS-related illness. Gus Van Sant was not the first choice to direct the video. David Hockney and Madonna declined the offer. Originally titled "Song for 1992," it was renamed to avoid dating it.

The Last to Arrive: Unreleased. An outtake from *Empty Sky*. This country/western ballad resembles "Lady, What's Tomorrow?," with Elton singing in a southern drawl.

Latitude: On *Made in England*. The Beatles' George Martin, who owns AIR Studio Lyndhurst where the album was recorded, arranged the song.

Leather Jackets: Title cut from the album. A jaunty tribute to the golden age of rock music, 1955-58.

Leaves: Unreleased. An outtake from *Made in England*.

Legal Boys: On *Jump Up!* Tim Rice, who co-wrote *Jesus Christ Superstar*, contributed the lyrics. Elton composed a melody — even recorded a harpsichord instrumental version of the song — and then received Rice's lyrics in the mail. Fittingly, the words have a theatrical feel.

Lemonade Lake: Unreleased. Late 1960s.

Les Aveux: Duet with French singer France Gall. Originally titled "Reach Out to Me," it was recorded around the time of *21 at 33* and released in Europe. Elton wrote it with Michel Berger, Gall's husband. In France, the duet hit number one.

Let It Shine: Unreleased. An outtake from *Leather Jackets*.

Let Me Be Your Car: On *Rare Masters*. Elton wrote it for Rod Stewart around the time of *Goodbye Yellow Brick Road* and described it then as the "best rock and roll song" he had ever composed. Stewart released it in 1974.

The Letter: Unreleased. A remake recorded by the Bread and Beer Band.

Levon: On *Madman Across the Water.* Single released in November 1971. Peaked at #24. Written in October 1970. The first song recorded for the album.

Lies: On *Made in England*.

Li'l 'Frigerator: On *Breaking Hearts*.

Little Jeannie: On *21 at 33*. Single released in May 1980. Peaked at #3. His first hit of the 1980s.

A Little Love Goes a Long, Long Way: Unreleased. Late 1960s.

Live Like Horses: Unreleased. An outtake from *Made in England*. Ironically, Elton played the song in several European concert appearances in 1994.

Lonely Boy: An outtake from *The Fox*. Released as a B-side to "Who Wears These Shoes?" It has a heavy bass beat. An early demo of the song reveals that it was originally titled "Lonely Man."

Lonely Heart: An outtake from *Leather Jackets*. Elton's version remains unreleased. Sylvia Griffin, formerly of Kissing the Pink, covered the song in 1988.

Lonnie and Josie: An outtake from *Goodbye Yellow Brick Road*. Kiki Dee issued it as a single in 1973.

Loosen Up: An Elton instrumental recorded by Mr. Bloe.

Lord of the Flies: An outtake from *Leather Jackets*. A Dixie-flavored English B-side to "Slow Rivers."

Love Is a Cannibal: On *Ghostbusters II* soundtrack. An outtake from *Leather Jackets*. A B-side to "Sacrifice."

Love Is Worth Waiting For: Unreleased. This gospel-tinged ballad was meant to be a star-studded AIDS charity song. Cher and Madonna were to be involved. The project never took off. The song was performed live in July 1988 in Los Angeles. It was re-recorded for *Reg Strikes Back* but not released. In structure, the song resembles "That's What Friends Are For" and "Sartorial Eloquence."

Love Letters: On *Duets*. John sung the 1940s hit with Bonnie Raitt, whose work he has long admired.

Love Lies Bleeding: See "Funeral for a Friend."

Love Rusts: Unreleased. An outtake from *Leather Jackets*. Elton wrote a melody to an old set of Taupin lyrics, not realizing that Martin Page had already set the words to music for Starship.

Love So Cold: An outtake from *21 at 33*. A B-side to "I'm Still Standing." After trying for three hours to record a steel drum solo, Elton laid down the piano track in ten minutes. He has cited it as among his best piano solos.

Love Song: On *Tumbleweed Connection*. For many years, the song was wrongly introduced as a John-Taupin creation. Lesley Duncan, a friend who helped Elton survive lean times in the late 1960s, wrote it and joined Elton in singing it. She tapped her foot throughout the recording and it can be heard.

Lovesick: An outtake from *A Single Man*. A B-side to "Song for Guy."

Loving You Is Sweeter Than Ever: Following the success of "Don't Go Breaking My Heart," Elton and Kiki Dee teamed up again on this 1981 duet released on her label, Ariola. Stevie Wonder wrote the song.

Lucy in the Sky with Diamonds: On *Greatest Hits II*. Single released in November 1974. Hit #1. John Lennon, as Dr. Winston O'Boogie, played on this Beatles' remake. While watching *Yellow Submarine*, Taupin wondered why The Beatles never released the song as a single. Elton decided to do it.

Made for Me: On *To be continued...* The version of "Made for Me" recorded for the box set offered a much slower pace than the R&B-charged tune that Elton previewed months earlier in concert. He wrote the song on Mother's Day 1990, while visiting his mom. Ironically, in the 1950s, a group called the Eltonites recorded a song with a similar title.

Made in England: On *Made in England*. Single released in June 1995. Peaked at #52. The song is about Elton, with references to his parents, childhood and early idols Little Richard and Elvis.

Madman Across the Water: Title cut from the album. An alternative version, included on *Rare Masters*, featured guitarist Mick Ronson of David Bowie's Spiders. Taupin dismissed lyrical interpretations that labeled the "madman" as Richard Nixon.

Madness: On *A Single Man*. Lyricist Gary Osborne captured Elton's sentiments about the strife in Northern Ireland. Elton contributed the title and a few lines.

Mama Can't Buy You Love: On *The Complete Thom Bell Sessions*. Single released in June 1979. Peaked at #9. It hit the top spot on the adult contemporary chart. Elton earned a Grammy nomination for this Spinners song.

Man: On *Made in England*.

The Man Who Loved to Dance: An outtake from *Blue Moves*. Released by Kiki Dee in 1977, the song was credited to Tripe and Onions, another John-Taupin pseudonym.

The Man Who Never Died: Released as a B-side to "Wrap Her Up." The instrumental tribute to John Lennon was written soon after he died. But with Taupin having separately written "Empty Garden," this song, strongly resembling "Song for Guy," remained unreleased for five years.

The Measure of a Man: On *Rocky V* sound track. Written by Alan Menken of *Beauty and the Beast* fame, the song featured Elton on vocals.

Medicine Man: On *Nobody's Child: The Romanian Angel Appeal*, a 1990 album.

Medley (Yell Help, Wednesday Night, Ugly): On *Rock of the Westies*. The song sounds inspired by the 1974 Little Feat release, "Tripe Face Boogie," which appeared on *Feets Don't Fail Me Now*, one of Elton's favorite albums at the time.

Mellow: On *Honky Chateau*. Jean Luc Ponty contributed electric violin. His solo was recorded on the first take.

Hits in Britain, but not in America
- ❖ "Pinball Wizard," 1976, #7.
- ❖ "Song for Guy," 1978, #4.
- ❖ "Crazy Water," 1977, #27.
- ❖ "Passengers," 1984, #5.
- ❖ "True Love," 1993, #2.

Mellow Yellow: Unreleased. The Bread and Beer Band covered Donovan's hit.

Memory of Love: On *Leather Jackets*. According to lyricist Gary Osborne, Elton wrote the title and most of the chorus. "The song wasn't my finest work," said Osborne.

Michelle's Song: On *Friends*.

Midnight Creeper: On *Don't Shoot Me, I'm Only the Piano Player*.

Mirrors of My Mind: Unreleased. Late 1960s.

Mr. Frantic: Bluesology single released in February 1966 and penned by Reg Dwight. It did not chart. Elton said the band's singles failed because of bad timing.

Mr. Lightning Strikerman: Unreleased. Late 1960s.

Mona Lisas and Mad Hatters: On *Honky Chateau*. Tragedy inspired the song. While Taupin was staying at a hotel in midtown Manhattan in September 1970, a man was shot in the street below his hotel room.

Mona Lisas and Mad Hatters, Part Two: On *Reg Strikes Back*. This follow-up, produced over fifteen years later, contrasts the mood of the original. It is an upbeat, dance number. Jazz artist Freddie Hubbard contributed a hot sax solo. Though it was not a single, Elton often performs an extended, jazzy rendition of it in concert, which sounds inspired by Kenny Kirkland's piano work on Sting's live "When the World Is Running Down." He is a fan of both artists.

Moral Majority: Unreleased. From 1982.

My Baby Left Me: On *11-17-70*.

My Bonnie's Gone Away: Unreleased. Late 1960s.

My Father's Gun: On *Tumbleweed Connection*. Robbie Robertson and The Band inspired the album and this song in particular. Musically, the song resembles "The Weight." Lyrically, it compares to Robertson's "The Night They Drove Old Dixie Down."

Needles and Pins: Unreleased. This instrumental remake of the 1964 Searchers' hit was recorded by the Bread and Beer Band.

Never Gonna Fall in Love Again: On *21 at 33*. Written by Elton and Tom Robinson. Recorded separately and released by both artists.

Nice and Slow: On *The Complete Thom Bell Sessions*. The song's arrangement is closely patterned after Bell's own "Rock 'n Roll Baby." Bell co-wrote "Nice and Slow" with Elton and Taupin.

Nikita: On *Ice on Fire*. Single released in January 1986. Peaked at #7. Charted throughout Europe. Taupin has admitted that some songs are intentionally sexually ambiguous, due to differences in his and Elton's preferences. Contrary to the song's video, featuring a European-looking woman, Nikita is a masculine name in Russia. George Michael and Nik Kershaw appeared on the song.

Nina: Unreleased. Late 1960s.

No Shoe Strings on Louise: On *Elton John*. He tried to impersonate Mick Jagger. The song is about loose women.

> **"I'd like to thank":** Instrumentals that have won Ivor Novello awards (Britain's Grammy).
> ❖ 1977: "Theme from a Non-Existent TV Show."
> ❖ 1979: "Song for Guy."

Nobody Wins: On *The Fox*. Single released in May 1981. Hit #21. While driving through St. Tropez, France, Elton heard Janic Prevost's version of "Nobody Wins" ("I Want Tenderness" or "J'Veux d'la Tendresse") on a car radio. He was so overcome that he pulled to the side of the road to listen. He asked Gary Osborne to write an English verse to Prevost's haunting melody. Osborne wrote about Elton's unloving relationship with his father. "When a mild man says to you, 'My father never liked me,' you can't be unmoved," said Osborne, who considers the song among his best.

The North: On *The One*. The piano introduction is reminiscent of Bruce Hornsby's "Lost Soul," a recording of which Elton admits to having "worn out." He and Hornsby performed "Lost Soul" together at an AIDS benefit.

Not the Man I Used to Be: Unreleased. Late 1960s.

Old Friend: On *Duets*. Nik Kershaw penned the tune and sang it with Elton.

On Dark Street: On *The One*. The song deals with poverty, unemployment, and a man's efforts to keep his family together. Elton removed a Taupin reference to President Ronald Reagan. Lyrically, it captures the flavor of a similarly titled Percy Sledge song.

The One: On *The One*. Released in June 1992. Peaked at #9. "The One" can be interpreted on many levels, from romantic to religious. Elton has identified it as a spiritual song, referring perhaps to the "higher power" mentioned in the dedication of the *To be continued...* box set.

One Day at a Time: On *Rare Masters*. John Lennon lent a hand, as Elton covered his song. A B-side to "Lucy in the Sky with Diamonds."

One Horse Town: On *Blue Moves*.

One More Arrow: On *Too Low for Zero*. It rates among Elton's own favorites from the early 1980s.

One Time, Sometime or Never: Late 1960s. A John-Taupin composition recorded by Spencer Davis.

Open Your Eyes to the Sun: Unreleased. Late 1960s. Songwriters unknown.

Our Love Is Here to Stay: On Larry Adler's 1994 *The Glory of Gershwin* tribute album.

Out of the Blue: On *Blue Moves*.

The Pacifier: On *For Our Children*. Featured on this Disney benefit for the Pediatric AIDS Foundation, the song appeared as an instrumental, though it was recorded with Taupin lyrics. A careful listen reveals backup singers throughout the song. Taupin expressed disappointment with Disney executives when told they preferred the track as a jazzy instrumental.

Pain: On *Made in England*. Written by Taupin as his father, Robert, was dying of cancer.

Paris: On *Leather Jackets*. "Paris" was written at the Mayfair Hotel in London in the fall of 1985. A demo was made in Amsterdam in January 1986 with just Elton at the piano. The song was a single in France.

Part-Time Love: On *A Single Man*. Single released in November 1978. Hit #22. The Four Tops' influence is obvious.

Passengers: On *Breaking Hearts*. A single cracked the top 5 in England.

Philadelphia Freedom: On *Greatest Hits Vol. II*. Single released in February 1975. Hit #1. Elton and Taupin wrote the song for friend and tennis star Billie Jean King, founder of an American tennis league and leader of the Philadelphia Freedoms team. With help from arranger Gene Page, who sweetened Barry White's tunes, the non-album single captured the feel of the mid-1970s Philly sound.

Pinball Wizard: On *Greatest Hits Vol. II*. Released only as a promotional single in the United States, it cracked the top 10 in England in 1976. In April 1974 Elton and his band went to The Who's Rampart Studio to record Pete Townshend's "Pinball Wizard." The session took one day. The track marked the last recording for nine years by the band featuring Davey Johnstone, Nigel Olsson, and Dee Murray. According to producer Gus Dudgeon, the song's arrangement — eight bars of guitar work — was formatted to fit the movie *Tommy*, which was already finished. For good measure, Elton threw in a little of The Who's "I Can't Explain."

Pinky: On *Caribou*.

Planes: On *Rare Masters*. A *Captain Fantastic* outtake. It contains references to John-Taupin songs from the 1967-68 era, including "Watching the Planes (Go By)" and "Skyline Pigeon," and to a mid-1960s teen night spot, The Casbah Club in West Derby, England. The club, owned by the mother of ex-Beatle Pete Best, showcased such young acts as The Who, the Rolling Stones, and Bluesology (with Elton). Melodically, the song resembles an upbeat "Daniel." Elton recorded it twice and shelved it twice. He and producer Gus Dudgeon viewed it as ideal for Rocket artist Colin Blunstone, formerly of the Zombies. Blunstone released his Dudgeon-produced version in November 1976.

Please: On *Made in England*. Another track inspired by The Beatles.

Poor Cow: On *Reg Strikes Back*.

The Power: On *Duets*. Little Richard and Elton performed this John-Taupin composition. Backing vocals were arranged by gospel singer Andrae Crouch.

Princess: On *Jump Up!* A tribute to Princess Diana.

Queen of Diamonds: Unreleased. Late 1960s.

Quick Joey Small (Run Joey Run): Unreleased. An instrumental version of the 1968 hit by the Kasenetz-Katz Singing Orchestral Circus was recorded by the Bread and Beer Band, including Elton.

Razor Face: On *Madman Across the Water*. Recorded on August 9, 1971.

Reach Out to Me: See Les Aveux.

Regimental Sergeant Zippo: Unreleased. Late 1960s. Inspired by The Beatles.

Religion: On *Too Low for Zero*.

Remember (I'm Still in Love with You): Unreleased by Elton. Taupin and John wrote it for Frank Sinatra, who recorded but never issued it. It is likely part of a Reprise Records studio session that Sinatra aborted in 1977 and 1978. Eventually, European singer Donatella Rettore covered the song.

Reminds Me of You: Unreleased. Late 1960s.

Restless: On *Breaking Hearts*. Issued in 1984, the year of George Orwell's prophetic book, it addresses Big Brother issues. The Rolling Stones' influence is obvious. The song, recorded in one take, netted Elton a Grammy nomination for rock vocals.

The Retreat: On *To be continued...* David Geffen rejected the song, relegating it to B-side status. The war theme gives it a *Tumbleweed Connection* flavor. Subtle vocals and expansive piano work leave one wondering why Geffen removed the song from *The Fox*.

> **C'est la vie**: Five Elton songs best left forgotten.
> ❖ "Hey, Papa Legba": Legba? Footba? Baseba?
> ❖ "Flinstone Boy": Elton proved he was not a lyricist.
> ❖ "The Pacifier": It wasn't.
> ❖ "I Am Your Robot": Warning! Warning! Dr. Smith!
> ❖ "Simple Man": Backwoods Man, maybe.

Return to Paradise: On *A Single Man*. It offers a tongue-in-cheek glimpse of British people who go on vacation, hoping not to return. Musically, it resembles Herb Albert's work. It was a single in parts of Europe.

Reverie: On *A Single Man*. An instrumental.

Rock and Roll Madonna: On *Rare Masters*. Single released in June 1970 in England. An unreleased piano demo, just over three minutes long, reveals the song's roots in 1950s rockabilly, Jerry Lee Lewis style. The original single is less steeped in that sound. With its opening applause (taken from a Jimi Hendrix recording), it sounds like an attempt by Dick James to hype Elton John as a dynamic live performer.

Rock Me When He's Gone: On *Rare Masters*. An outtake from *Madman Across the Water*, it was released first by Long John Baldry.

Rocket Man: On *Honky Chateau*. Single released in April 1972. Peaked at #6. Taupin said the song borrowed from an identically titled song by Tom Rapp of the group Pearls Before Swine. Though John and Taupin downplay the connection, the song was arranged by Paul Buckmaster and produced by Gus Dudgeon — whose work on David Bowie's "Space Oddity" first attracted Elton's attention. Taupin was inspired while driving under a star-filled night sky near his hometown of Lincolnshire.

Rollin' On: Unreleased by Elton. This John-Osborne song was issued by Garth Hewitt in 1979.

Rolling Western Union: Unreleased. An outtake from *Tumbleweed Connection*.

Rope Around a Fool: An outtake from *Leather Jackets*. A B-side to "I Don't Wanna Go on with You Like That."

Rotten Peaches: On *Madman Across the Water*.

Roy Rogers: On *Goodbye Yellow Brick Road*. A lyrical tribute to another American icon and, musically, to The Everly Brothers.

The Rumour: Written by John and Taupin for Olivia Newton-John, it appeared on her 1988 album of the same title. Davey Johnstone played on it.

Runaway Train: On *The One*. Released in August 1992. Did not chart. It first appeared on the sound track for the 1992 film *Lethal Weapon 3*. The release of this duet by Eric Clapton and Elton preceded a brief, joint tour they undertook in 1992. The song alludes to the pain each had recently endured — for Clapton, the death of his young son; for Elton, overcoming multiple addictions.

Sacrifice: On *Sleeping with the Past*. Single released in November 1989. Peaked at #18. Inspired by Aretha Franklin and Percy Sledge, it deals with failed relationships from the perspective of a middle-age man. After being re-released, "Sacrifice" became Elton's first solo number one single in England. The song's latent potential was uncovered by BBC DJ Steve Wright, who while vacationing in Florida in May 1990 heard the song on U.S. radio. He decided to push it on his show when he returned to England, unaware that it had been released earlier in Britain. Because of his effort, the song became a hit. To thank Wright, Elton performed "Sacrifice" live on his show on June 26, 1990.

Sad Songs (Say So Much): On *Breaking Hearts*. Single released in May 1984. Peaked at #5. The music was written almost straight through in four minutes, using a synthesizer with a drum machine. The first recorded version took a slower, more gospel approach. It was scrapped, but a similar rendition has surfaced in live shows.

"Sad Songs" appeared as a series of TV commercials taken from Elton's video, with the title line changed to "Sassons say so much." The clothes company sponsored Elton's 1984 American tour after he and Taupin approached Sasson with the idea for the ad.

Sails: On *Empty Sky*. The song appears to have vague origins in the 1968 Leonard Cohen ballad "Suzanne." Both refer to China, sailors and imported spices. But the song is also clearly borne of Taupin's teenage adventures in northern English seaports.

Saint: On *Too Low for Zero*. It was considered as the follow-up single to "I'm Still Standing" but was never released.

Salvation: On *Honky Chateau*. Elton wanted "Salvation" to be a single, but it was not released as one.

Sartorial Eloquence (Don't You Wanna Play This Game No More?): On *21 at 33*. Single released in August 1980, against Elton's wishes. Hit #39. Written with Tom Robinson. The U.S. release was titled "Don't You Wanna Play This Game No More?" The British issue was called "Sartorial Eloquence."

> **Offensiveness, 1970s style:** Songs that made would-be censors cringe.
> ❖ "The Bitch Is Back," for its language.
> ❖ "Screw You," for its sexual language.
> ❖ "Rocket Man," for drug references.
> ❖ "Sweet Painted Lady," for its unsafe sex.
> ❖ "All the Girls Love Alice," same-sex sex.

Satellite: On *Ice on Fire*. Written with James Brown in mind.

Saturday Night's Alright (for Fighting): On *Goodbye Yellow Brick Road*. Single released July 1973. Peaked at #12. To get the raucous, rocking sound he wanted, Elton leaped around the studio taunting his band members. Later, he added his piano part. Drummer Nigel Olsson dislikes the tempo: "If I could go back and change something that I recorded on an Elton John song, it would have to be that track."

The Scaffold: On *Empty Sky*.

Scales: Unreleased. This short instrumental from 1971 appeared in the movie *Friends*, but not on the sound track.

Scarecrow: Unreleased. The first song Elton and Taupin wrote and demoed as a team.

Screw You (Young Man's Blues): On *Rare Masters*. Taupin touches on his early personal struggles working in a dingy print shop. MCA objected to the title of the song (which appeared first as the B-side of "Goodbye Yellow Brick Road") and forced it to be renamed "Young Man's Blues." The backing vocal reference to "Jean, Jeannie" was a musical bow to David Bowie.

Season of the Rain: Written by Elton and released in 1970 by Nite People.

Seasons: On *Friends*.

71-75 New Oxford: The instrumental was released as a single in Britain in August 1970 by Mr. Bloe, with Elton on piano. The title named the address of Dick James Music, where Elton worked in the late 1960s. A few years earlier, the Rolling Stones, a major influence on Elton, recorded "2120 S. Michigan Ave." in honor of the famed Chicago-blues Chess Studio.

Shakey Ground: On *Duets*. Ex-Eagle Don Henley and Elton covered this former Temptations hit.

She Sings Rock and Roll: Unreleased. An outtake from *Elton John*.

She's Only Anne: Unreleased. Late 1960s. Songwriter unknown.

Shine on Through: On *A Single Man*. The melody was written during the *Blue Moves* sessions. Though Taupin tried unsuccessfully to write lyrics to it, the words are Gary Osborne's. Another version of the song was included on *The Complete Thom Bell Sessions*. That track's musical arrangement pays homage to the 1973 Stylistics single "You Make Me Feel Brand New."

Shoot Down the Moon: On *Ice on Fire*. Uninvited, Elton submitted the song for use in a James Bond movie. But it was rejected.

Shooting Star: On *A Single Man*. Though not well known, the song has been rated by Elton as a favorite from the era.

Shoulder Holster: On *Blue Moves*.

The Show Must Go On: A live recording of this Queen song surfaced as the B-side to "True Love" in England. Elton performed it first at the Freddie Mercury AIDS benefit and, later, on tour in 1992-93 as a tribute to his friend.

Sick City: On *Rare Masters*. Originally the B-side to "Don't Let the Sun Go Down on Me," the song explores the raunchy side of rock and roll, a favorite Taupin topic.

Simple Life: On *The One*. Single released in February 1993. Peaked at #30. It deals with Elton's new, addiction-free lifestyle.

Simple Man: An outtake from *Breaking Hearts*. A B-side to "Sad Songs."

Since God Invented Girls: On *Reg Strikes Back*. Based on the lyrics, Taupin expected a rock track, not a ballad. The song mentions Brian Wilson and honors the Beach Boys, specifically their song "God Only Knows." It also contains thinly veiled references to female genitalia. Written in September 1987 at Elton's home studio, it was the first song composed for *Reg Strikes Back*. Elton wrote it straight through in 15 minutes.

Since I Found You Baby: English single released in 1967 by Bluesology. Non-Elton composition.

Since the Poet Came: Unreleased. Late 1960s. Songwriter unknown.

Sing Me No Sad Songs: Unreleased by Elton. Late 1960s. Interestingly, the lyrics to this work contained two future song titles: "Don't Go Breaking My Heart" and "Sad Songs."

Sitting Doing Nothing: Unreleased. Late 1960s. Written with Caleb Quaye.

Sixty Years On: On *Elton John*. Arranger Paul Buckmaster has expressed dissatisfaction with his arrangement. He preferred Elton's 1970 live version over what he referred to as his "1930s horror-movie score." The lyrics were inspired by Taupin's relationship with his grandfather.

Skyline Pigeon: On *Empty Sky*. It refers to a twelfth century bell tower that Taupin climbed as a kid. There he spent many hours watching sunsets fade. Elton remade the song and released it as the B-side of "Daniel." He played it at Ryan White's funeral. The hymn-like lyrics remain a favorite of the singer.

Slave: On *Honky Chateau*. A faster version appeared on *Rare Masters*.

Sleeping with the Past: Title cut from the album.

Slow Down Georgie (She's Poison): On *Breaking Hearts*.

A Slow Fade to Blue: Unreleased. Late 1960s. Songwriter unknown.

Slow Rivers: On *Leather Jackets*. A duet with Cliff Richard, whose record sales in England put him in the company of Elvis Presley.

Smile That Smile: Unreleased by Elton, it was the first song on which Gary Osborne and Elton collaborated.

Smokestack Children: Unreleased. Late 1960s.

Snakes and Ladders: Unreleased. Late 1960s.

Snookeroo: Composed by Elton and Taupin for Ringo Starr's 1974 album, *Goodnight Vienna*, the song, featuring simple lyrics and a pop melody, is about Starr. Elton played piano on the song. Taupin said he had "Yellow Submarine" in mind when writing it. A rare solo demo by Elton has surfaced on bootleg recordings.

Snow Queen: An outtake from *Blue Moves*. As the B-side to "Don't Go Breaking My Heart," this drug song paints a nasty portrait of Cher, compliments of Taupin, and features Elton with Kiki Dee.

Social Disease: On *Goodbye Yellow Brick Road*.

Solar Prestige a Gammon: On *Caribou*. He has performed live at only one series of concerts (in London May 2-7, 1977). The song is nonsensical — to frustrate listeners who over-analyzed their songs. It was Elton's idea to write a song equivalent to John Lennon's "The Sun King."

Some Other World: On 1992's *Ferngully* sound track. Performed by Elton, who wrote the melody. Bruce Roberts wrote the lyrics.

Someone Saved My Life Tonight: On *Captain Fantastic and the Brown Dirt Cowboy*. Single released in June 1975. Peaked at #4. Before becoming famous, Elton was engaged to Linda Woodrow. Despondent over his upcoming marriage, he made a half-hearted attempt to end his life by inhaling gas from an oven in his flat. The song explores the experience. It was the first song Elton wrote for the album.

Someone to Watch over Me: On *The Glory of Gershwin* tribute album. Elton recorded the tune in 1994.

Someone's Final Song: On *Blue Moves*.

Son of Your Father: On *Tumbleweed Connection*. The released version, a runaway rocker, differed from the demo, a slow, gospel-flavored ballad.

Song for Guy: On *A Single Man*. Single released in March 1979. The instrumental did not chart in America. Elton wrote the dirge on Sunday, August 18, 1978, and found out the next day that a Rocket Records messenger boy, 17-year-old Guy Burchett, had been killed on Sunday. At the song's conclusion, Elton mumbles the line "Life isn't everything." MCA opposed putting the song out as a single. "Music Box Dancer" was a hit at the time, and label officials believed the public wouldn't embrace another instrumental. Elton won the struggle, and the song charted in England. But the artistic battle frustrated Elton. Soon after, he left MCA for Geffen Records.

Song for You: A live version of this Leon Russell hit appeared on a European release. Elton performed it in 1986 with the Melbourne Symphony Orchestra.

Sorry Seems to Be the Hardest Word: On *Blue Moves*. Single released in November 1976. Peaked at #6. Recorded on March 22, 1976, this John-Taupin composition differed from the vast majority in that the music came first. Elton said he could envision Frank Sinatra singing the song. (Indeed, Sinatra did perform it in 1976 at Albert Hall.) "I remember Elton had a house on Tower Grove Drive in Los Angeles, and I stopped by one afternoon," recalled Taupin. "He was tinkling on the piano and I just listened for awhile. Finally, I thought of the title line and went home and completed the song. It's probably our best song from that period."

S.O.S: Unreleased. Late 1960s.

Soul Glove: On *Ice on Fire*. It was originally recorded with a string section.

Spiteful Child: On *Jump Up!* The title was changed from "Slice of Life."

Spotlight: On *Victim of Love*.

Steal Away Child: An outtake from *21 at 33*. Released as a B-side in England.

Step into Christmas: On *Rare Masters*. Released in November 1973, nine days after its Nov. 18 recording. Hit #1 on that year's Christmas charts.

Stinker: On *Caribou*. Lyrically, the song may play off of Loudon Wainwright's 1973 hit, "Dead Skunk in the Middle of the Road."

Stone's Throw from Hurtin': On *Sleeping with the Past*. Influenced by Marvin Gaye's "I Heard It Through the Grapevine."

Strangers: An outtake from *A Single Man*. Released as a B-side to "Victim of Love." Later recorded by ex-Eagle Randy Meisner and Heart's Ann Wilson.

Street Boogie: On *Victim of Love*.

Street Kids: On *Rock of the Westies*. Taupin explores his rebellious teen years.

Sugar on the Floor: On *Rare Masters*. Released as the B-side to "Island Girl." Kiki Dee wrote and recorded the song. Elton loved it. The song offered a platform for his more introspective side. His vocal performance was arguably the best of the entire *Westies* sessions.

Suit of Wolves: An outtake from *The One*. A B-side to "The One."

Supercool: Unreleased by Elton. An outtake from *Goodbye Yellow Brick Road*. Kiki Dee released it in 1973 on *Loving and Free*.

Suzie (Dramas): On *Honky Chateau*.

Swan Queen of the Laughing Lake: Unreleased. Late 1960s.

Sweat It Out: On *The One*.

Sweet Painted Lady: On *Goodbye Yellow Brick Road*. A tale of sailors and prostitutes. Lyrically, its style honors performer Noel Coward.

Sweetheart on Parade: Unreleased by Elton. A song demo reveals strong vocals by Elton. It rates among the best of the John-Osborne ballads. It appeared first as "Hero on Parade" on a 1982 Albert Hammond album. Hammond adapted the song, which was written from a woman's viewpoint. The song may have been intended for Kiki Dee. Her 1981 album, *Perfect Timing*, featured other John-Osborne songs. Judy Collins later released it.

Sylvania Flasher, King of the Casbah, Polaroid Swinger and Older Than Bill: Unreleased. From 1979-80. A frivolous, just-for-fun song.

Tactics: An instrumental outtake from *21 at 33*. A B-side to "In Neon," it was written as background music for BBC-TV soccer coverage.

Take Me Back: On *21 at 33*.

Take Me Down to the Ocean: An outtake from *Jump Up!* A B-side to "Empty Garden."

Take Me to the Pilot: On *Elton John*. Though often analyzed, the lyrics make no sense, according to Taupin. MCA executives wanted to release it as an American single in 1970, with "Your Song" as the B-side. The singer's representatives, however, convinced company executives to mark neither song as the A-side on the promotional copy. The initial response favored "Your Song." "Take Me to the Pilot" became the B-side on the official release. Eighteen years later, a live version of the song was distributed as a single but failed to chart.

Taking the Sun from My Eyes: Unreleased by Elton. From late 1960s. It reflected an effort to duplicate the Burt Bacharach-Dionne Warwick sound.

Talking Old Soldiers: On *Tumbleweed Connection*. It was dedicated to folk singer David Ackles, who shared the bill with Elton at his August 25, 1970, debut at the Troubadour. (Taupin produced Ackles's 1971 album, *American Gothic*.) "Talking Old Soldiers" was recorded in one take, with vocals and piano together.

Tartan Colored Lady: Unreleased. Late 1960s.

Teacher I Need You: On *Don't Shoot Me, I'm Only the Piano Player*. A tribute to Bobby Vee.

Teardrops: On *Duets*. Elton and k. d. lang joined forces on this R&B tune.

Tell Me What the Doctor Said. Unreleased. An outtake from *Don't Shoot Me, I'm Only the Piano Player*.

Tell Me What the Papers Say: On *Ice on Fire*.

Tell Me When the Whistle Blows: On *Captain Fantastic and the Brown Dirt Cowboy*. The song focuses on Taupin's anticipation after leaving his rural home as a teenager to meet his songwriting partner at Dick James Studio in London. One line — about his cheap suitcase — harkens to Elton's remembrance of their first meeting and Taupin's cardboard luggage.

Texan Love Song: On *Don't Shoot Me, I'm Only the Piano Player*.

Thank You for Your Loving: Unreleased by Elton. Written in the late 1960s with Caleb Quaye. Recorded by Dukes Nobleman.

Thank You, Mama: Unreleased. Late 1960s. The Happenings, supplied with an Elton demo, considered recording the song but did not.

That's What Friends Are For: Elton joined Dionne Warwick, Stevie Wonder, and Gladys Knight on this AIDS benefit, which hit number one in 1985. Elton was third in line for the part, behind George Michael and Rod Stewart. He performed the song solo once, at a 1992 tribute to bass player Dee Murray in Nashville, Tennessee.

Theme from a Non-Existent TV Series: On *Blue Moves*. In 1977, the instrumental won an Ivor Novello Award, England's Grammy equivalent.

There Is Still a Little Love: Unreleased. Late 1960s.

There's Still Time for Me: Unreleased. Late 1960s.

This Song Has No Title: On *Goodbye Yellow Brick Road*. It deals with Taupin's early discovery of his poetic talent, as well as his doubts.

This Town: On *Ice on Fire*.

Three Way Love Affair: On *The Complete Thom Bell Sessions*.

Through the Storm: The duet was the title track to an Aretha Franklin album. Single released in April 1989. Peaked at #16. Elton and Franklin recorded their parts separately.

Thunder in the Night: On *Victim of Love*.

> **The other Elton:** Elton masterpieces that were too long to be hit singles.
> ❖ "Ticking."
> ❖ "Indian Sunset."
> ❖ "Madman Across the Water."
> ❖ "Belfast."

Ticking: On *Caribou*. This epic tale of a young man who goes on a murderous rampage rates with "Indian Sunset" and "Song for Guy" as obscure fan favorites. Elton originally laid down the piano while listening to a whisper track of his vocal. In the end, the only way he could do the vocals and piano right was to record them at the same time. Because of the intricate piano playing, it remains a remarkable testament to his musicianship.

The Tide Will Turn for Rebecca: Unreleased. Late 1960s. Two versions were fully recorded, including one that featured an orchestra.

Times Getting Tougher Than Tough: A B-side to "Come Back Baby" released in 1965 by Bluesology in England. It is a non-Elton composition.

Timothy: Unreleased. An outtake from *Leather Jackets*.

Tiny Dancer: On *Madman Across the Water*. Released in February 1972. Peaked at #41. Taupin wrote it about his first wife, Maxine Feilbelman, and it alludes to Elton's early tours of America. Though not a big hit, partly because of its six-minute running time, the song has become a concert standard. Recorded on August 9, 1971.

Tonight: On *Blue Moves*. It relates to Taupin's marital problems.

Too Low for Zero: Title cut off the album.

Too Young: On *Ice on Fire*.

Tortured: An outtake from *21 at 33*. Released as a B-side to "Chloe."

Tower of Babel: On *Captain Fantastic and the Brown Dirt Cowboy*.

Town of Plenty: On *Reg Strikes Back*. The song was written and recorded in two hours. Pete Townshend later added guitar work.

True Love: On *Duets*. Released in October 1993. Peaked at #56. Sung with Kiki Dee. This Cole Porter tune, featured in the Grace Kelly-Bing Crosby movie *High Society,* was the first single off the album. It became a number two hit in England, 17 years after the duo topped the charts with "Don't Go Breaking My Heart."

Trying to Hold on to a Love That's Dying: Unreleased. Late 1960s.

Trying Too: Unreleased. An outtake from *A Single Man*.

Turn to Me: Unreleased by Elton. Recorded in 1969 by Plastic Penny, a group that featured Elton's future drummer, Nigel Olsson.

Two of a Kind: Unreleased. Late 1960s.

Two Rooms at the End of the World: On *21 at 33*. After a two-year break, Taupin and John began collaborating again. The song refers to their writing method, separation, and reunion.

Ugly Girls and Fat Boys: This incorrect title appeared on the U.S. B-side to "Runaway Train." See "Fat Boys and Ugly Girls."

Understanding Women: On *The One*. A longer remix appeared on the "Runaway Train" single. David Gilmour of Pink Floyd plays guitar.

Valhalla: On *Empty Sky*. It was inspired by Leonard Cohen, the Canadian singer-songwriter whose 1968 album rated as a favorite of John and Taupin at the time.

Velvet Fountain: Unreleased. Late 1960s.

Victim of Love: On *Victim of Love*. Single released in September 1979. Hit #31. Like all other songs on the album, it was not written by Elton.

Waking up in Europe: Unreleased. An outtake from *Jump Up!*

Warm Love in a Cold World: On *Victim of Love*.

Warthog Rhapsody: An outtake from *The Lion King*. The song, a cast version of which appears on *Rhythm of the Pride Lands*, was written by Elton and Tim Rice. It was replaced in the movie by "Hakuna Matata."

Watching the Planes (Go By): Unreleased. Late 1960s.

We All Fall in Love Sometimes: On *Captain Fantastic and the Brown Dirt Cowboy*. It describes the early, brotherly relationship between John and Taupin and alludes to the writing of "Your Song." In 1991, Elton said the song meant more to him than any other he and Taupin had written.

Welcome to My Haunted Heart: Unreleased. An outtake from *Reg Strikes Back*. It didn't fit the mood of the album, so it was cut. Elton gave Nigel Olsson a copy to record. Olsson describes it as a ballad, similar in structure to "Levon."

Western Ford Gateway: On *Empty Sky*.

When a Woman Doesn't Want You: On *The One*. Its date-rape admonition gets lost in the pop melody. Taupin admits he modeled it after Percy Sledge's "When a Man Loves a Woman."

When I Think About Love (I Think About You): On *Duets*. P.M. Dawn wrote the song and recorded it with Elton.

When I Was Tealby Abbey: Unreleased. Late 1960s.

When the First Tear Shows: Unreleased. Late 1960s.

Whenever You're Ready (We'll Go Steady Again): On *Rare Masters*. An outtake from *Goodbye Yellow Brick Road*, it emerged as the B-side to "Saturday Night's Alright (for Fighting)." The song, among the strongest of B-side tunes, showcases his piano-pounding talent.

Where Have All the Good Times Gone?: On *Jump Up!*

Where It's At: Unreleased. Late 1960s. Written by Elton and Nicky James.

Where to Now, St. Peter?: On *Tumbleweed Connection*.

Where's the Shoorah?: On *Blue Moves*.

Whipping Boy: On *Too Low for Zero*. It resembles a 1973 John-Taupin song, "Supercool," with similar guitar riffs by Davey Johnstone.

Whispers: On *Sleeping with the Past*. Like the entire album, it served as a tribute to favorite rock-soul artists, in this case Jackie Wilson and his 1966 hit "Whispers (Getting Louder)."

White Lady, White Powder: On *21 at 33*. The song is about cocaine.

White Man Danger: An outtake from *21 at 33*. Released as a B-side to "Sartorial Eloquence."

Whitewash County: On *The One*.

Who Wears These Shoes?: On *Breaking Hearts*. Single released in September 1984. Peaked at #16.

Whole Lotta Shakin' Going On: A live version of the Jerry Lee Lewis classic appeared as part of a medley on the B-side of "Cry to Heaven."

Who's Gonna Love You?: Unreleased. Written with Kirk Duncan.

The Wide Eyed and Laughing: On *Blue Moves*.

Wild Love: Unreleased. An outtake from *Leather Jackets*.

Wintergreen: Unreleased. Elton recorded a version of this Yoko Ono composition for her 1981 album, which never materialized.

The Witch's House: Unreleased. Late 1960s.

A Woman's Needs: On *Duets*. Elton and Taupin wrote the song for a duets collection by country star Tammy Wynette. Elton liked the blend of his and Wynette's voices so much that he released it first on his own album. The success of *The Lion King* scuttled this song's release as a single.

Wooly Bully: Unreleased. The Bread and Beer Band recorded an instrumental version of the 1960s classic.

A Word in Spanish: On *Reg Strikes Back*. Single released in September 1988. Peaked at #19.

Wrap Her Up: On *Ice on Fire*. Single released in October 1985. Peaked at #20. The song features George Michael prominently on backing vocals. Elton planned to use Roy Orbison's "Dream Baby" as the backing track, but Michael talked Elton into writing his own, similar tune.

Writing: On *Captain Fantastic and the Brown Dirt Cowboy*.

Year of the Teddy Bear: Unreleased. Late 1960s.

You Gotta Love Someone: On *To be continued...* Released in November 1990. Peaked at #43. Reportedly written with Ryan White in mind, it was the only single off the box set. A different mix of the track was featured on the 1990 *Days of Thunder* sound track.

You'll Be Sorry to See Me Go: Unreleased. Late 1960s. Written by Reg Dwight and Caleb Quaye.

Young Man's Blues: See "Screw You."

Your Sister Can't Twist (But She Can Rock 'n Roll): On *Goodbye Yellow Brick Road*. Elton changed "twist" to "surf" in the last chorus — a musical hats-off to the Beach Boys.

Your Song: On *Elton John*. Single released October 1970. Hit #8. Elton composed it in ten minutes. Taupin, then 17, wrote the words at breakfast. The original lyrics sheet is stained with egg and coffee. "Your Song" became their first major hit and has remained, more than any other song, as their standard. Elton wrote the melody on Oct. 27, 1969. An excerpt from his diary noted: "In the end I did nothing today ... wrote a new song called 'Your Song.' "

Your Starter For...: On *Blue Moves*. Instrumental written by Caleb Quaye.

You're So Static: On *Caribou*.

Zorba the Greek: Unreleased. By the Bread and Beer Band.

Section notes

* U.S. chart information refers to *Billboard* rankings.

* "Unreleased" means a song did not appear on an official release. Some "unreleased" songs appear on bootleg issues.

* Duets are listed, but Elton's guest-artist contributions to others' recordings are detailed under "Guest appearances" in the "Elton: A-Z" section.

* Early in his career, Elton, then Reg Dwight, recorded sound-a-like albums for several labels, as well as demos for other artists. These songs can be found in the "Sessions" entry in the "Elton: A-Z" section.

* Songs by Bluesology, a recording and touring group that included Reg Dwight; the Bread and Beer Band, a studio group with which he played; and Mr. Bloe, with which he sometimes recorded; are listed in this "Songs" section.

Appendix I

Elton John Songs Recorded by Other Artists

Bad Side of the Moon: Toe Fat, April Wine.
Ball & Chain: Kathy Mattea.
Ballad of a Well Known Gun: American Eagle, Silver Metre, Kate Taylor.
Basque: James Galway.
Bennie and the Jets: The Beastie Boys and Biz Markie, 101 Strings, King's Road, Tom Draper, Philadelphia, Sonnie Carr, Kenny Blake, London Concert Orchestra, Master Plan.
The Bitch Is Back: Westminster String, Holly String, Benny and the Jets, Hugo Montenegro, Tina Turner (two versions), Bitch.
Bite Your Lip: Evergreen.
Bitter Fingers: Bobby Crush.
Blue Eyes: Twilight Orchestra, Stars Unlimited Orchestra, Paul Mauriat, Richard Clayderman, James Galway, London Starlight Orchestra, Tesca Company, Starsound Orchestra, Royal Philharmonic, Buddy Emmons and Ray Pennington, Paul Keogh, Allegro Milano.
Border Song: Kenny Rogers and The First Edition, Mia Martini, Dorothy Morrison, Aretha Franklin, Jose Feliciano, Geoffrey Love Orchestra, Mike Batt Orchestra, Eric Clapton, London Starlight Orchestra, 5th Dimension, Les Humphries Singers.
Burn Down the Mission: Phil Collins, Mike Batt Orchestra.

The Cage: California License, Brainchild, Mike Batt Orchestra.
Cage the Songbird: Crystal Gayle.
Candle in the Wind: Kate Bush, Paul Windsor Orchestra, Anna Lotta Larsons, Geoffrey Love Orchestra, Twilight Orchestra, Richard Clayderman, Sharon McKnight, London Starlight Orchestra, Sandy Denny, Bobby Crush, Westminster Strings, Holly Strings, The Diamonds, Tesca Company, Udo Lindenberg, Royal Philharmonic Orchestra, Sonnie Carr, The Spectrum, Allegro Milano, Junior English, Brainchild.
Can't Get Over Getting Over Losing You: Bobby Craddock.
Chameleon: Flowers.
Circle of Life: Carmen Twillie, Spagna.
Come Down in Time: Judy Collins, Lani Hall, Mike Batt Orchestra, Sting, Ramsey Lewis.
Country Comfort: Colorado, Benny and the Jets, Rod Stewart, Milton C. Carroll, Juice Newton, Mike Batt Orchestra, Rex Allen Jr., Brook Benton, Kate Taylor, Ace Cannon,

Orange Bicycle, The Chesley Clancy Brothers, Silver Metre.
Crocodile Rock: Beach Boys, Geoffrey Love Orchestra, King's Road, The Chipmunks, London Starlight Orchestra, The Farmers, Bobby Crush, Westminster Strings, Holly Strings Quartet, The Diamonds, Tesca Company, Sir Echoes, Sonnie Carr, Allegro Milano.

Daniel: Benny and the Jets, Hugo Montenegro, Paul Windsor Orchestra, King's Road, Geoffrey Love Orchestra, Dijango and Bonnie, Danny O'Brian, M. Morton, Twilight Orchestra, Terry Baxter, Fastbacks, Bobby Crush, Westminster String, Holly Strings Quartet, The Diamonds, Tesca Company of Singers, John Morrell, Royal Philharmonic Orchestra, Leslie Gore, James Last, Wilson Phillips, Sound of '70s Orchestra, Jimmy Castor Bunch, Junior English, Blue Marvin, Sonnie Carr, Sound Effects, Julio Martini Orchestra, The Chesley Clancey Brothers.
Dixie Lily: Roy Drusky, The Chesley Clancey Brothers.
Don't Go Breaking My Heart: Paul Windsor Orchestra, Midnight String, Living Voices, London Starlight Orchestra, Frank Pourcel, Bobby Crush, James Last, New Seekers, Tesca Company, Miss Piggy, Jon Peterson, Allegro Milano, Olympia System.
Don't Let the Sun Go Down on Me: 101 Strings, Benny and the Jets, Paul Windsor Orchestra, King's Road, Realistics, Roger Daltrey, Geoffrey Love Orchestra, Gloria Estefan, Twilight Orchestra, Oleta Adams, London Starlight Orchestra, Joe Cocker, Westminster String, Holly String, James Last, The Tesca Company, Spectrum, The Three Degrees, Cover Band, The Spectrum, London Concert Orchestra, Maynard Ferguson, George Michael.

Easier to Walk Away: Royal Philharmonic Orchestra.
Elderberry Wine: Mae McKenna.
Elton's Song: Tom Robinson.
Empty Garden: Paul Mauriat.
Empty Sky: Roy Everett.

First Episode at Hienton: Connie Vanderbos.
The Flowers Will Never Die: Ayshea.
Friends: E, Square Set, Frank Pourcel.
Funeral for a Friend: Simon Park.

Get Out (of This Town): Mr. Bloe.
Goodbye Yellow Brick Road: 101 Strings, Benny and the Jets, Hugo Montenegro, Paul Windsor Orchestra, King's Road, Geoffrey Love Orchestra, Roger Williams, King's Singers, John Blackinsell Orchestra, Twilight Orchestra, Living Strings, Young Generation, London Starlight Orchestra, Ray Coniff, Los Tropicalientes, Tom Janathan, Bobby Crush, Westminster Strings, Holly Strings, The Diamonds, James Last, Tesca Company, Royal Philharmonic, Pierced Arrow, Bob Ralston, Billy Joel, Ed Maciel, Sonnie Carr, The Spectrum, London Concert Orchestra, Allegro Milano.
The Greatest Discovery: Mike Batt Orchestra, Tony Butala, Bernie Taupin, The Lettermen, Rob Denys.

Hakuna Matata: Lebo M. and Jimmy Cliff.
Hard Luck Story: Kiki Dee.
Healing Hands: Tesca Company.
Hero on Parade: Albert Hammond, Frank Noel, Donatella Rettore, Connie Vanderbos.
Hey Lord, You Made the Night Too Long: Long John Baldry.

Honky Cat: King's Road, Country Gazette, 101 Strings, Benny and the Jets, Claude Denjean, Canadian Brass, Westminster String, Holly Strings Quartet, The Diamonds, Doc Watson, Prima Vera, Sonnie Carr.
House of Cards: Linda Kendricks, Ian and Sylvia, Allegro Milano, London Concert Orchestra, The Spectrum.

I Can't Go on Living Without You: Cilla Black, Polly Brown, Stewart A. Brown, Dave Sealey, Lulu.
I Don't Care: Lulu.
I Get a Little Bit Lonely: The Ghoasters.
I Guess That's Why They Call It the Blues: Johnny Lee, Royal Philharmonic Orchestra, Paul Nauriat, Allegro Milano, The Spectrum.
I Loved a Man: Bonnie Tyler.
I Need You to Turn To: Mike Batt Orchestra, Euson, Paul Windsor Orchestra, Geoffrey Love Orchestra, Larry Barbara, Elly Zuidenoyn, Ron Randstechner, Django and Bonnie.
I Think I'm Gonna Kill Myself: John Denver.
Idol: Flying Steaks.
I'm Still Standing: David Cassidy, Cover Band, Ritchie Dennis.
Indian Sunset: Mary Travers.
Island Girl: 101 Strings, London Starlight Orchestra, Bobby Crush, London Concert Orchestra.
It's Me That You Need: Equipe 84.
I've Been Loving You: Polly Brown, Jack Bendient, Chessmen, Guys and Dolls, Wednesday, Edwin Bee.

Jamaica Jerk Off: Pioneers.

Lady Samantha: Mike Batt Orchestra, Three Dog Night, Orange Bicycle, Westminster String, Holly String.
The Last Good Man in My Life: Kiki Dee.
The Last Song: James Galway.
Let Me Be Your Car: Rod Stewart.
Levon: Mary McCreary, Jon Bon Jovi.
Little Jeannie: Sound Sensation, Mario Cavallero, International Disco, Bobby Crush, James Galway, Allegro Milano.
Lonely Heart: Sylvia Griffin.
Lonnie and Josie: Kiki Dee.

Madman Across the Water: Bruce Hornsby.
The Man Who Loved to Dance: Kiki Dee.
Mellow: Jimmy Stewart.
Mona Lisas and Mad Hatters: Gotham, Branford Marsalis, Richard Frost, Indigo Girls, Flying Steaks.

Never Gonna Fall in Love Again: Tom Robinson.
Nice and Slow: Lulu.
Nikita: Twilight Orchestra, Sound Sensation, London Starlight Orchestra, Erasmo Carlos, Tesca Company, Royal Philharmonic Orchestra, Cover Band, Edson Vieira, Trini Lopez.

Nobody Wins: Twilight Orchestra, Tesca Company.

The One: Allegro Milano.
One More Arrow: Ana Belen.
One Time, Sometime or Never: Spencer Davis.

Part-Time Love: Tesca Company, Bobby Crush, Twilight Orchestra, Paul Mauriat.
Philadelphia Freedom: 101 Strings, Hugo Montenegro, Geoffrey Love Orchestra, MFSB, Hall and Oates, London Starlight Orchestra, Ester Phillips, Tina Turner, The Spectrum, London Concert Orchestra
Planes: Colin Blunstone.

Remember: Donatella Rettore, Frank Sinatra (unreleased).
Return to Paradise: Twilight Orchestra, Tesca Company.
Rock Me When He's Gone: Long John Baldry.
Rocket Man: 101 Strings, Hugo Montenegro, Paul Windsor Orchestra, Kings Road, Geoffrey Love Orchestra, Danny O'Brian, Django and Bonnie, M. Morton, Kate Bush, Twilight Orchestra, Terry Baxter, Fastbacks, Bobby Crush, Westminster String, Holly Strings Quartet, The Diamonds, Tesca Company of Singers, John Morrell, Royal Philharmonic Orchestra, In Flames, Sonnie Carr, John Keating, The Spectrum, London Concert Orchestra, Allegro Milano, Elton Dunkley, Neil Diamond (unreleased).
Roll On: Garth Hewitt.
Roy Rogers: Theu Boermans.
The Rumour: Olivia Newton-John.

Sacrifice: Twilight Orchestra, Sinead O'Connor, Richard Clayderman, London Starlight Orchestra, Ultramix, Tesca Company, Brenda Cochrane.
Sad Songs: London Starlight, Francis Moore Orchestra, Royal Philharmonic, James Last, Allegro Milano.
Saturday Night's Alright (for Fighting): James Last, King's Road, Flotsam & Jetsam, Savage Brothers, The Who, London Starlight Orchestra, Sonnie Carr, Sound Effects, The Spectrum, Pierced Arrow.
Season of the Rain: Nite People (also known as The Banana Bunch), Rich Fever, Nomadi.
Seasons: Heart.
71-75 New Oxford Street: Mr. Bloe.
Shoot Down the Moon: Rob Dneys.
Sing Me No Sad Songs: Guy Darrell.
Sixty Years On: I. Nomady, Hayden Wood, Silver Metre.
Skyline Pigeon: Westminster String Quartet, Holly String Quartet, Bob Fields, Fusion Band, Guy Darrell, Paul Windsor Orchestra, Geoffrey Love Orchestra, Mike Batt Orchestra, J. J. King, Deep Feeling, Roger Cook.
Smile That Smile: Neil Basham.
Snookeroo: Ringo Starr.
Someone Saved My Life Tonight: Paul Windsor Orchestra, Leo Sayer, Twilight Orchestra, Walter Jackson, Bobby Crush, Tesca Company.
Son of Your Father: Spooky Tooth.
Song for Guy: Twilight Orchestra, London Philharmonic Orchestra, Paul Mauriat, Robert Jones, Acker Bilk, London Starlight Orchestra, Mary Cruz Soriano, Fausto Papetti, Michael

Gordon Orchestra, Europe International, Bobby Crush, Royal Philharmonic Orchestra, Munich Symphonic Sound Orchestra, Allegro Milano.

Sorry Seems to Be the Hardest Word: Suzy Bogguss with Chet Atkins, Denise Nolan, Paul Windsor Orchestra, Mary Burns, Dottie West, Dee Dee Bridgewater, Mina, Elaine Page, Twilight Orchestra, Joe Cocker, Shirley Bassey, London Starlight, Bill Henderson, Eddy Star Orchestra, Connie Vanderbos, Tesca Company, Kim and Marty Wilde, Skip Ewing, Ray Coniff, Walter Jackson, Collin England, The Spectrum, Mary Belsam.

Step into Christmas: Wedding Present.

Stone's Throw from Hurtin': Wynona Judd.

Strangers: Randy Meisner and Ann Wilson.

Supercool: Kiki Dee.

Sweet Painted Lady: Michel Delpech.

Sweetheart on Parade: Judy Collins.

Take Me to the Pilot: Westminster String Quartet, Holly String Quartet, Orange Bicycle, Benny and the Jets, Hugo Montenegro, Geoffrey Love Orchestra, Enoch Light, Mike Batt Orchestra, Jose Feliciano, Joy Unlimited Orchestra, Latimore, Birds of a Feather, Soulosophy, Ben E. King, The Chanter Sisters, Brenda Lee, The Mormon Tabernacle Choir, Odetta, Percy Faith, Ena Sharples.

Taking the Sun from My Eyes: Plastic Penny, Ayshea.

Talking Old Soldiers: Bruno Winzell.

Tell Me When the Whistle Blows: Brian and Brenda Russell.

Thank You for All of Your Lovin': Dukes Noblemen.

The Tide Will Turn for Rebecca: Edward Woodward.

This Time: Donatella Rettore.

Ticking: Theu Boermans.

Tiny Dancer: Benny and the Jets, Lani Hall, Vicky Leandros.

Tonight: George Michael.

Turn to Me: Plastic Penny, Guy Darrel.

Warthog Rhapsody: *The Lion King* cast.

We All Fall in Love Sometimes: Paul Windsor Orchestra.

When the First Tear Shows: Brian Keith.

Where to Now, St. Peter?: Mike Batt Orchestra, Sergio Mendes, Lani Hall.

You Gotta Love Someone: Cover Band.

Your Song: Mia Martini, Al Jarreau (twice), Billy Paul, Michel Delpech, Paul Windsor Orchestra, Benny and the Jets, Hugo Montegnero, Geoffrey Love Orchestra, Johnny Lee, Lena Horne, Oliver Swofford, Sound of '70s Orchestra, Stars Unlimited Orchestra, Studio London Orchestra, Mike Batt Orchestra, Maynard Ferguson, Three Dog Night, Bobby Goldsboro, Rod Stewart, Twilight Orchestra, Roger Whittaker, Andy Williams, Cissy Houston, Zamfir, Lisle, Rod Peters, Joe Kenyon, London Starlight Orchestra, Roger Williams, Piet Souer, Bobby Crush, Cilla Black, Westminster String Quartet, Holly String Quartet, Anita Kerr Singers, New Seekers, Francis Goya, Tesca Company, Royal Philharmonic Orchestra, Harry VanDorf, Sonnie Carr, Jack Jones, Allegro Milano, The Spectrum, Sacha Distel, Buddy Greco, The Osmonds, Gerry Marsdan.

You're So Static: Benny and the Jets.

The following artists and groups, most mentioned above, have recorded tribute albums to Elton John: 101 Strings, Mike Batt Orchestra, Benny and the Jets, Black Tulip (tribute to Elton and David Bowie), Sonnie Carr, Bobby Crush, Ritchie Dennis, The Diamonds, Peter Eagles, Enoch Light and the Light Brigade, Alexandra Gemeau, Holly Strings Quartet, King's Road, London Starlight Orchestra, Geoff Love Orchestra, Hugo Montenegro and His Orchestra, The New Sensations, Rocking Man, The Royal Philharmonic Orchestra, Sound Sensation, Sounds of the '70s Orchestra, Stars Unlimited Orchestra, Tesca Company, Twilight Orchestra, Westminster String Orchestra, Paul Windsor Orchestra.

Appendix II

Songs Elton John Has Performed in Concert

Ain't No Mountain High Enough: 1975.
All Across the Havens: 1968.
All Quiet on the Western Front: 1982.
All the Girls Love Alice: 1973, 1980, 1982, 1989, 1992.
All the Nasties: 1971.
Amoreena: 1970-71.
Amy: 1972.
Angel: 1974.
At the Hop: 1970.

Baby You're a Rich Man: 1984.
Back in the U.S.S.R.: 1979.
Bad Side of the Moon: 1970-71.
Ball and Chain: 1982.
Ballad of a Well-Known Gun: 1970-71.
The Ballad of Danny Bailey (1909-34): 1973, 1988.
Be-Bop-a-Lula: 1979.
Believe: 1994-95.
Bennie and the Jets: 1973-80, 1980, 1982, 1984-86, 1989-90, 1992-95.
Better Off Dead: 1975-77, 1979, 1982, 1984-86, 1993-95.
Big Dipper: 1978.
The Bitch Is Back: 1974-76, 1982, 1984-86, 1988-90, 1992-95.
Bite Your Lip (Get up and Dance): 1977, 1980.
Bitter Fingers: 1975-76.
Blowing in the Wind: 1988.
Blue Avenue: 1990, 1992.
Blue Eyes: 1982, 1984-86, 1989-90, 1992.
Blueberry Hill: 1995.
Bohemian Rhapsody: 1992.
Boogie Woogie Bugle Boy: 1979.
Border Song: 1970-72, 1974-77, 1991-92.

Breaking Down the Barriers: 1981.
Brown Sugar: 1989-90.
Burn Down the Mission: 1970-71, 1974, 1985-86, 1988-90, 1992.

C.C. Rider: 1989.
Cage the Songbird: 1977.
Can I Get a Witness: 1985-86.
Can I Put You On?: 1970-72.
Can You Feel the Love Tonight?: 1994-95.
Candle in the Wind: 1973-79, 1984-90, 1992-95.
Captain Fantastic and the Brown Dirt Cowboy: 1975, 1976, 1982, 1992-93.
Carla/Etude: 1986.
Chameleon: 1975.
Charlie Brown Theme Song: 1984.
Chattanooga Choo Choo: 1984, 1986.
Chloe: 1982.
Circle of Life: 1994-95.
Close Encounters Theme: 1984, 1986.
Club at the End of the Street: 1989.
Cold as Christmas: 1986.
Come Down in Time: 1971, 1989-90, 1992-93, 1995.
Country Comfort: 1970-72, 1974-75.
Crazy Water: 1977, 1979, 1993-94.
Crimes of Passion: 1986.
Crocodile Rock: 1972-74, 1977, 1979, 1982, 1984, 1993-95.
Cry to Heaven: 1985-86, 1990.
Crystal: 1984.
Curtains: 1975-76, 1993.

Dan Dare: 1975-77.
Daniel: 1972-74, 1976-77, 1979, 1982, 1984, 1986, 1988-90, 1992-95.
Dear John: 1982.
Dixie Lily: 1975, 1984, 1995.
Don't Be Cruel: 1979.
Don't Go Breaking My Heart: 1976-77, 1984-85.
Don't Let the Sun Go Down on Me: 1974-77, 1979, 1984, 1986, 1989-95.

Ego: 1978-80.
Elderberry Wine: 1973.
Elton's Song: 1979, 1982, 1990.
Empty Garden (Hey, Hey Johnny): 1982, 1988, 1992-93.
Empty Sky: 1975, 1976.

Falling in Love Again: 1972.
Feeling Alright: 1986.
First Episode at Hienton: 1971.
Friends: 1971, 1977.
Funeral for a Friend/Love Lies Bleeding: 1973-77, 1979 (without Love Lies Bleeding),

1980, 1982, 1984, 1988-90, 1992-95.
Fur Elise: 1986.

Georgia: 1978.
Get Back: 1970-71, 1979, 1988.
Getting to Know You: 1976.
The Girl Can't Help It: 1970, 1995.
The Girl from Ipanema: 1991.
Give Peace a Chance: 1970.
God Save the King: 1985.
Good Golly, Miss Molly: 1980.
Goodbye: 1971, 1972, 1977.
Goodbye Marlon Brando: 1988.
Goodbye Yellow Brick Road: 1973-77, 1979-80, 1982, 1984.
(Gotta Get a) Meal Ticket: 1975-76, 1982.
Great Balls of Fire: 1980, 1994-95.
The Greatest Discovery: 1971, 1976-77, 1986, 1992-94.
Grey Seal: 1974.
Grimsby: 1974-75.
Grow Some Funk of Your Own: 1976.

Happy Birthday: 1985 (and probably many other years, too).
A Hard Day's Night: 1994-95.
Harmony: 1975, 1980, 1989.
Have Mercy on the Criminal: 1973-75, 1980, 1986, 1988-89, 1995.
Healing Hands: 1989-90.
Heartache All Over the World: 1986.
He'll Have to Go: 1979, 1988, 1992.
Hercules: 1972-76, 1984.
High-Flying Bird: 1973-74, 1992.
Higher: 1970-71.
Higher Ground: 1974.
Highlander: 1985.
Holiday Inn: 1971-72, 1974-76.
Honesty: 1994-95.
Honey Roll: 1970-71.
Honky Cat: 1972, 1973, 1974, 1975, 1985, 1995.
Honky Tonk Women: 1970-71, 1973, 1986.
Hound Dog: 1979, 1982, 1988.
House: 1995.

I Don't Wanna Go on with You Like That: 1988-89, 1990, 1992-95.
I Feel Like a Bullet (in the Gun of Robert Ford): 1977, 1979.
I Feel Pretty: 1994.
I Got the Whole World in My Hands: 1978.
I Guess That's Why They Call It the Blues: 1984-90, 1992-95.
I Heard It Through the Grapevine: 1977-79, 1988-89.
I Love Paris in the Springtime: 1979.

I Need You to Turn To: 1970-72, 1974-76, 1986, 1988-89, 1993-94.
I Put a Spell on You: 1992.
I Saw Her Standing There: 1974-75, 1979-80, 1984.
I Think I'm Gonna Kill Myself: 1972, 1976-77, 1979, 1993-94.
Idol: 1976-79, 1993-95.
Il Es Amores: 1979.
I'm Going to Be a Teenage Idol: 1984.
I'm Still Standing: 1984-90, 1992-95.
Imagine: 1980, 1992.
In the Mood: 1982, 1984.
Indian Sunset: 1970, 1993-95.
Island Girl: 1975-77, 1989.
It's a Lovely Day Today: 1994-95.
It's All over Now: 1989.
It's Your Thing: 1989.
I've Got a Lonely Bunch of Coconuts: 1970.
I've Seen That Movie Too: 1973.

Japanese Hands: 1988.
Jingle Bells: 1984.
Johnny B. Goode: 1986.
Jumpin' Jack Flash: 1986, 1992-93.
Just Like Belgium: 1982.
Just Loving You: 1988.
Just the Way You Are: 1986.

The King Must Die: 1970-72, 1973, 1986, 1988, 1989.
Kiss the Bride: 1984-86, 1989.

La Donna e Mobile: 1994.
Lady Samantha: 1969.
The Last Song: 1992-95.
Let It Be: 1975.
The Letter: 1972.
Levon: 1971-72, 1975-76, 1984, 1986, 1989, 1992-95.
Lies: 1995.
Li'l 'Frigerator: 1984.
Little Jeannie: 1980, 1984.
Live Like Horses: 1994-95.
Lost Soul: 1992.
Love Is Worth Waiting For: 1988.
Love Song: 1971-72, 1974, 1976, 1986, 1992.
Lucille: 1989, 1994-95.
Lucy in the Sky with Diamonds: 1974, 1988-89.

Mad Dogs and Englishmen: 1992
Made for Me: 1990.
Made in England: 1995.

Madman Across the Water: 1971-74, 1986.
Madness: 1978.
Mama Can't Buy You Love: 1979.
Mammy: 1982.
Match of the Day: 1985.
Me and My Shadow: 1984.
Mellow: 1972.
Mercedes Benz: 1971.
Midnight Hour: 1970.
Mockingbird: 1975.
Mona Lisas and Mad Hatters: 1972, 1988-90, 1992-95.
Mona Lisas and Mad Hatters Part Two: 1988-90, 1992.
Mr. Tamborine Man: 1973.
My Baby's Left Me: 1970-71.
My Father's Gun: 1970-71.
My Life: 1994-95.
My Sweet Angel: 1974.
My Sweet Lord: 1986.
My Way: 1979.

New York, New York: 1986.
New York State of Mind: 1994-95.
Nikita: 1985-86, 1988.
Nobody Wins: 1981-82.
The North: 1992-94.

Oh, Boy: 1980.
Oh, Suzanna: 1974.
The One: 1992-95.
One Horse Town: 1985-86.
One More Arrow: 1984.

Pain: 1995.
Paris: 1986.
Part-Time Love: 1978-79.
Passengers: 1985.
Philadelphia Freedom: 1975-77, 1980, 1984, 1986, 1988-90, 1992-95.
Piano Man: 1994-95.
Pinball Wizard: 1975-76, 1979, 1982, 1989, 1992-95.
Princess: 1981.
Pub Piano Song: 1976, 1988.

Razor Face: 1971, 1974.
Restless: 1984-86.
Rock Me When He's Gone: 1971-72.
Rocket Man: 1972-80, 1982, 1984-86, 1988-90, 1992-95.
Rotten Peaches: 1971.
Roy Rogers: 1977, 1979-80.

Rudolph the Red-Nosed Reindeer: 1973.
Run Away Child, Running Wild: 1989.
Runaway Train: 1992.

Sacrifice: 1989-90, 1991-95.
Sad Songs (Say So Much): 1984-86, 1988-90, 1992-93.
Salvation: 1972.
Sartorial Eloquence (Don't You Wanna Play This Game): 1980.
Saturday Night's Alright (for Fighting): 1973-77, 1979-80, 1982, 1984-90, 1992-95.
Shake: 1971.
Shape of My Heart: 1994.
Shine on Through: 1977-78.
Shoot Down the Moon: 1985.
Shooting Star: 1978-79.
Shotgun: 1970.
The Show Must Go On: 1992-93.
Simple Life: 1992-95.
Singing in the Rain: 1971-72, 1974.
Sixty Years On: 1970-72, 1976, 1979, 1986, 1988-90, 1992-94.
Skater's Waltz: 1971-73.
Skyline Pigeon: 1968, 1971, 1974, 1976, 1979, 1990, 1993-94.
Sleeping with the Past: 1989.
Slow Rivers: 1986.
Smile: 1994.
Solar Prestige a Gammon: 1977.
Someday Will Come: 1992.
Someone Saved My Life Tonight: 1975-76, 1980, 1982, 1985-86, 1994-95.
Someone to Watch over Me: 1994.
Song for Guy: 1978-79, 1981-82, 1984-86, 1989, 1992, 1994.
Song for You: 1985-86.
Sorry Seems to Be the Hardest Word: 1976-78, 1980, 1984, 1986, 1988-90, 1992-95.
Sound of Music medley: 1994.
Stand by Me: 1987.
Step into Christmas: 1973.
Stone's Throw from Hurtin': 1989.
Strangers in the Night: 1986, 1990.
Street Kids: 1975.
Streets of Philadelphia: 1995.
The Stripper: 1985.
Strolling Through the Park: 1977, 1979.
Stronger Love: 1987.
Superstition: 1972-74.
Suzie (Dramas): 1972.
Sweet Little Rock 'n' Roller: 1974.
Sweet Painted Lady: 1976-77.
Sweet Rock and Roll Music: 1974.

Take Me to the Pilot: 1970-72, 1974-75, 1977, 1979, 1986, 1992-95.

Talking Old Soldiers: 1971, 1993-95.
Tchiakoysky's First Piano Concerto: 1979.
Teacher I Need You: 1973, 1982.
Tear It Up: 1989.
Tell Me When the Whistle Blows: 1975-76.
Thank You (Falettinme Be Mice Elf Agin): 1989.
That's Entertainment: 1986.
That's What Friends Are For: 1988, 1992.
This Old Heart of Mine: 1972.
This Song Has No Title: 1973.
This Town: 1985-86.
Ticking: 1974, 1977, 1982, 1992, 1994.
Tiny Dancer: 1971-72, 1980, 1984, 1986, 1988-92.
Tonight: 1976-77, 1979, 1985-86, 1993-94.
Too Low for Zero: 1984, 1989.
Too Young: 1985.
Tower of Babel: 1975.
Town of Plenty: 1988.
Twist and Shout: 1979, 1982, 1984, 1989.

Waltzing Matilda: 1971, 1986-87.
We All Fall in Love Sometimes: 1975-76, 1993.
When a Woman Doesn't Want You: 1992.
Where Have All the Good Times Gone?: 1982.
Where to Now, St. Peter?: 1977, 1982, 1993-94.
Whispers: 1989.
White Christmas: 1973-74.
White Lady, White Powder: 1980.
Whitewash County: 1992.
Who Wears These Shoes?: 1984.
Whole Lotta Shakin' Going On: 1971, 1973, 1979, 1982, 1984, 1988.
Will You Still Love Me Tomorrow?: 1987, 1992.
A Woman's Needs: 1993.
A Word in Spanish: 1988.
Working in a Coal Mine: 1994.
Wrap Her Up: 1985.
Writing: 1975-76.

The Yellow Rose of Texas: 1971.
You Are the Sunshine of My Life: 1974.
You Gotta Love Someone: 1991.
You May Be Right: 1994-95.
Your Song: 1970-95.
You're in My Heart: 1991.
You're Never Gonna Get It: 1992-93.
You're So Static: 1974.

Selected Bibliography

Allman, Kevin. "Bernie and the Jets." *The Adovcate*, Nov. 17, 1992.

Bashe, Philip. "Captain's a Fantastic Feast." *Circus*, June 1974.

Bender, W. "Handstands and Fluent Fashion." *Time*, Dec. 14, 1970.

Bernie Taupin: The One Who Writes the Words for Elton John. New York: Alfred A. Knopf: 1976.

Bivona, Joe, and Gerald Newman. *Elton John*. New York: Signet, 1976.

Black, Susan. *Elton John: In His Own Words*. London: Omnibus Press, 1993.

Burstein, Patricia, and Susan Crimp. *The Many Lives of Elton John*. New York: Birch Lane, 1992.

Charlesworth, Chris. *Elton John*. London: Bobcat Books, 1986.

Charlesworth, Chris. "The Second Coming of Elton John." *Melody Maker*, April 7, 1973.

Clarke, Donald, ed. *Penguin Encyclopedia of Popular Music*. New York: Viking, 1989.

Cohn, Nik. "I'm a Mess But I'm Having Fun." *New York Times*, Nov. 22, 1971.

"Davey Johnstone History." *Melody Maker*, March 18, 1973.

Demorest, Steve. "Rockets over the Rainbow with Goodbye Yellow Brick Road." *Circus*, December 1973.

DeVoss, D. "Elton John: Rock's Captain Fantastic." *Time*, July 7, 1975.

DiStefano, John. *The Complete Elton John Discography*. New Baltimore, MI: East End Lights, 1993.

Doershuk, Bob. "Elton John: Poetry with a Beat." *Keyboard Musician*, February 1981.

Doggett, Peter. "Elton John: One of the Most Successful Rock Artists of All Time." *Record Collector*, February 1986.

Elton John and Bernie Taupin: The Complete Lyrics. New York: Hyperion, 1994.

Edwards, Henry. "Interview with Elton John." *New York Times*, Aug. 8, 1976.

Felton, David. "Elton John." *Rolling Stone*, June 10, 1971.

Finch, Alan. *Elton John: Only the Piano Player*. London: Omnibus, 1983.

Fong-Torres, Ben. "Elton: The Four-Eyed Bitch Is Back." *Rolling Stone*, Nov. 21, 1974.

Gambaccini, Paul. *A Conversation With Elton John and Bernie Taupin*. New York: Flash Books, 1975.

Gambaccini, Paul, Jonathan Rice, and Tim Rice. *British Hit Albums*, Vol. V. London: Guinness, 1992.

Gambaccini, Paul, Jonathan Rice, and Tim Rice. *British Hit Singles*, 8th Ed. London: Guinness, 1991.

Goodall, Nigel. *Elton John: A Visual Documentary*. London: Omnibus Press, 1993.

Hauptfuhrer, F. "The New Elton John." *People*, Jan. 6, 1978.

Hilburn, Robert. "Elton's Exorcism." *Los Angeles Times*, Aug. 23, 1992.

Hilburn, Robert. "John and Taupin's Playback Session." *Los Angeles Times*, Aug. 13, 1989.

Hilburn, Robert, and Connie Pappas. *Elton John: Five Years of Fun*. Los Angeles: Boutwell, 1975.

Jahn, Mike. "Elton John Reveals Rich Song Talents." *New York Times*, Nov. 22, 1970.

Jahn, Mike. "Solo or with Group, Elton John Thrills Carnegie Audience." *New York Times*, June 12, 1971.

Jasper, Tony, and Dick Tatham. *Elton John*. New York: Octopus, 1976.

Lazell, Barry. *Rock Movers & Shakers*. New York: Billboard, 1989.

Norman, Philip. *Elton John*. New York: Harmony Books, 1991.

Norman, Philip. "The Rebirth of Elton John," *Rolling Stone*, March 19, 1992.

Nutter, David, and Bernie Taupin. *It's a Little Bit Funny*. New York: Penguin Books, 1977.

Peebles, Andy. *The Elton John Tapes*. New York: St. Martin's Press, 1981.

Robinson, Lisa. "Elton John Tells All to Our Lisa." *Chicago Sun Times*, July 18, 1976.

Robinson, Lisa. "I'm the Male Betty Boop." *Hit Parader*, January 1978.

"Rock Family Affair." *Life*, Sept. 24, 1971.

Rohter, Larry. "Elton John: The Music Machine." *Washington Post*, July 1, 1976.

Rohter, Larry. "Elton John: Why Fans Are Hooked on His Act." *Washington Post*, June 29, 1976.

Roland, Paul. *Elton John*. London: Proteus Books, 1984.

Salewicz, Chris. "Elton John Without the Glitz." *Musician*, March 1987.

Salewicz, Chris. "The Rise and Fall of Reg Dwight." *Q*, December 1986.

Sandall, Robert. "The Other Half of Elton John." *Evening Standard*, June 25, 1992.

Shaw, Greg. *Elton John: A Biography in Words and Pictures*. New York: Sire Books, 1976.

Sholin, David. "Elton John: Candle in the Wind." *Playing Keyboard*, April-May 1988.

Stein, Cathi. *Elton John: Rock's Piano Pounding Man*. New York: Popular Library, 1975.

Taupin, Bernie. *A Cradle of Haloes: Sketches of a Childhood*. London: Aurum Press, 1988.

"The Elton John Story," parts I-III. *Zig Zag Magazine*, July 1972.

"The Elton John Story," parts IV-V. *Zig Zag Magazine*, August 1972.

"The House That James Built." *Billboard*, Sept. 18, 1971.

"The Last Days of Ryan White." *People*, April 23, 1990.

Toberman, Barry. *Elton John: A Biography*. London: Weidenfeld and Nicolson, 1988.

Towne, Terry. "Elton John." *Jazz & Pop*, January 1971.

Townsend, Martin. "I Took a Lot of Drugs and I Drank a Lot..." *Vox*, August 1992.

Two Rooms: Elton John and Bernie Taupin in Their Own Words. London: Boxtree, 1991.

Von Lustbader, Eric. "He's Only Just Begun." *Contemporary Musician*, September 1974.

Whitburn, Joel. *The Billboard Book of Top 40 Albums*. New York: Billboard, 1991.

Whitburn, Joel. *The Billboard Book of Top 40 Hits*. New York: Billboard, 1989.

The authors also relied heavily on hundreds of items that appeared in *Billboard*, *Cash Box*, *Circus*, *Cream*, *East End Lights*, *Hit Parader*, *Melody Maker*, *Rolling Stone*, and *Variety* magazines, as well as in newspapers and on radio and television.

Index

About the Authors

CLAUDE BERNARDIN is a nationally honored watercolorist and a parochial school-teacher. He is well known in rock-fan circles as one of the premier Elton John historians.

TOM STANTON is publisher of the Elton John fan magazine, *East End Lights* and is a nationally honored journalist. He is the co-owner and editor of five suburban Detroit weekly newspapers. He hosts the international Elton Expo.